The Poetics of the Mind's Eye

The Poetics of the Mind's Eye

Literature and the Psychology of Imagination

Christopher Collins

UNIVERSITY OF PENNSYLVANIA   Philadelphia

Publication of this work has been supported in part by a grant from the Abraham and Rebecca Stein Faculty Publications Fund of New York University, Department of English.

Permission to reprint published materials is gratefully acknowledged. These sources are listed at the end of the Preface.

Copyright © 1991 by Christopher Collins
All rights reserved
Printed in the United States of America

Library of Congress Cataloging-in-Publication Data
Collins, Christopher.
  The poetics of the mind's eye: literature and the psychology of imagination / Christopher Collins.
    p. cm.
  Includes bibliographical references (p.   ) and index.
  ISBN 0-8122-3133-3
  1. Imagination in literature. 2. Imagery (Psychology) in literature.
3. Visualization in literature. 4. Criticism. I. Title.
PN56.I45C58 1991
801'.92—dc20   91-20561
                                                              CIP

For my children,
Jennifer and Jesse

Contents

Preface ix

1. Verbal Visuality 1
Oral Mimesis
Oral Diegesis
Literacy
The New Universe of Imaginal Discourse
Image as Trope

2. Science on the Nature of Imagination 21
Exorcising the Phantoms of the Night
The Microcosmology of Associationism
Literary Theory Versus Psychology
The Threat from the Depths
The Return of the Ostracized

3. The Poetics of Play: Reopening Jakobson's "Closing Statement" 47
Psychological Sets and the Poetic Message
Addresser, Addressee, and Message
Monologic Context
Dialogic Contact
Analogic Code

4. Tactics and Timing 67
Hypotaxis
Parataxis
The Structure of Kairotic Play
Cognitive Modes
Affect and Cognition

5. Simulations of Perception 89
Disguised Rituals of the Eye
Saccadic Movement on the Pictorial Plane

Depth Perception and Vergence
The Imagery of Perceived Motion
Translating Percepts into Language

6. Transformations of Memory — 119
Stored Imagery
Retrospected Experience and Asserted Convention
Retrospective Imaging
Nominative Images and the Transformation
   of Experience
The Transformations of Convention

7. Introspection and the Visionary Imagination — 142
Metaphor as Introspective Transfer
Reading as Introspection
"Notice What This Poem Is Not Doing"
Visionary Imaging
Recalling the Dead

Notes	169
Bibliography	175
Index	185

Preface

The ways in which the mind processes verbal cues to form visual images is the central concern of this study. But, before we can undertake this study of imaginative procedures, we must first examine the act of reading as itself an imaginative procedure. Some of the preliminary remarks that follow may, to some, seem polemical. This is not my intention. I wish only to propose a clearly modeled theoretical grounding for an inquiry into the moves of the mind's eye.

It would be helpful if the terms used in the human sciences had some of the stability of terms used in the natural sciences. It is several millennia too late to lament the fact that they do not—that, for example, the words, "poetics" and "hermeneutics" have over time come to represent partly overlapping activities of theorizing and of practice, of tacit understanding and of overt explanation. Anyone who now wishes to distinguish these two must, after consulting historical and contemporary usage, assume the obligation of drawing his or her own definitional boundaries upon this disputed map.

The definitions of poetics and hermeneutics that follow will not correspond to every reader's usage of these terms. To some, my definition of poetics may seem at first glance rather nebulous: the purpose of subsequent chapters will be to offer a systematic cognitive theory of the poetics of visualization. To some, my definition of hermeneutics, namely the traditional practice of textual explanation, will seem overly restrictive. The relation of this practice to the theoretical work of philosophers such as Dilthey, Heidegger, Gadamer, Ricoeur, and Habermas I will leave to others to assess.

Broadly viewed, the study of literature employs two alternative methodologies, the poetic and the hermeneutic, and does so on the basis of their different orientations to the text. Poetics regards the text as an *instrument,* a scripted means by which the reader performs a particular action; hermeneutics, on the other hand, regards the text as an *object* that must be scrutinized in order to be translated via another code into the critical text. Poetics includes all the methods of examining those complex conventions and procedures by which the author synthesizes through composition and the reader synthesizes through performance the various elements of the text. Hermeneutics includes all the methods by which the reader analyzes the text into its elements and construes their meanings. As is the case with many another discipline, poetic and hermeneutic theory are after-the-fact elaborations of method. As students and teachers of literature, we have learned to practice both skills but tend, consciously or not, to favor one method of engagement (poetic or hermeneutic), justifying this preference usually by borrowing a theory from some methodologically cognate discipline.

Though we are trained to approach a text from either of these two vantage points, it is no secret which of these has the more visible halo of respectability. We have only to examine the terms we use when we currently speak of literary study. "Criticism," "critical theory," and "literary theory"—such terms, left undefined, obscure the methodological bases of these enterprises. "Criticism," whether evaluative or explicative, generally implies the hermeneutical approach—the objectification, though not necessarily the reification, of texts. "Critical *theory*," accordingly, is the attempt to ground hermeneutic activity in a particular set of principles. "Literary theory," the vaguest of all these terms, is applied loosely both to hermeneutics and to poetics, but, since the overwhelming majority of articles and monographs that currently call what they do "literary theory" propose or justify or critique the principles by which decoded texts may be recoded, this term has come to mean "hermeneutical theory."

There are many historical reasons for the present dominance of hermeneutics (including the "negative hermeneutics" of deconstruction) and for its virtual subsuming of the discipline of poetics. These would include the tradition of Greco-Roman rhetorical pedagogy, which has always used literary texts as analyzable models, and that of Judeo-Christian exegesis, which has treated biblical texts as coded messages. Another, perhaps not unrelated, factor has been the absence of a clear functional distinction between *poetic reading* and *hermeneutical reading*. Of course it would be a help if these two adjectival terms were properly differentiated, but the greater problems lies in the ambiguity of that common term "reading," an ambiguity that we might usefully begin to examine by choosing as our angle of inquiry that technically more denotative term "interpretation." How do we and how should we interpret "interpret?" The preliminary questions I will raise here are, as they say, "matters of semantics," but every collective enterprise since Babel has had to ask itself from time to time if it knew what it really meant by the words it used. The two terms that we need to interrogate are first "interpretation" and then "reader." The fundamental question I will pose is this: where within *interpretation* is the *reader* situated?

Though etymologists dispute the origins of the Latin word *interpres*, all agree that it designated some sort of go-between. As a specifically linguistic go-between, the interpreter listens to the speech of one party, then turns and translates it for the benefit of another party. Serving the function of a relay, the interpreter's first task is to make sense out of the message as originally coded, that is, decode it into meaning; his or her second task is to select equivalent signifiers from a code available to the audience, that is, recode it. This second task cannot be a verbatim iteration, because in this case the message must be translated into another symbolic system, a process that requires a critically judicious kind of bilingualism. An interpreter may defer the second task or may omit it altogether, but any interpreter who chooses to do the second task must obviously first perform the first task.

If most of us regard the work of the interpreter as a unidirectional action, it is perhaps because we view this as a transaction between a knowledgeable insider and a mystified outsider, the needy beneficiary of this translation. If we fully identify with the interpreter, however, we situate ourselves at the midpoint of a line and, Janus-like, view this function as properly bidirectional.

The two principal dictionary definitions of "interpret" make this clear: (1) to construe meaning, as in "I interpreted his reply as favorable," and (2) to translate or explicate, as in "She interpreted the parable for her grandchildren." It belongs to an interesting family of verbs that denote the transfer of information across codes. The verb "tell," for example, can be shown to have two informational phases, as in "I could tell it would rain, so I told my son to bring his raincoat." That very crucial word "read," though its principal meaning now is to peruse written material, still retains traces of its bidirectional origins, as in "The sheriff read the mood of the crowd, then read them the Riot Act." In its preliterate Germanic forms "to read" meant both to make a guess, for example, as to the significance of a sign or riddle, and to offer advice. Presumably, only those able to "read" the indications of things could give reliable counsel.

In Peircean semiotic terms, the first interpretive act may be a construal either of indexical signs (e.g., my example above, "I could tell it would rain..."), of iconic signs ("I could tell it was a depiction of Venus and Vulcan, so I told them the myth"), or of symbolic signs in which one speaker using one conventional code tells the interpreter, who then tells others using another conventional code ("The gendarme told me where we would find lodgings and I told this to my companions"). Though the first phase of the relay may be a decoding of any kind of sign, the second always requires a symbolic system, which in most instances, and in all instances as far as we are herein concerned, takes the form of language.

"Interpretation," like similar terms of information-transfer, is relational in character and denotes particular phases in an operation (cf. the Latin word *altus*, which could mean either "high" or "deep," because it designated opposed extremes on a vertical axis). In order to distinguish them as operations and yet stress the useful biform unity of the interpretive activity, I will use the terms *poetic interpretation* and *hermeneutical interpretation*. By poetic interpretation I mean the direct receptive synthesis and interior performance of the text, and by hermeneutical interpretation I mean its explicative analysis and translation into a code of critical discourse. Poetic interpretation is "interpretation" in the same sense in which we speak of a pianist's interpretation of a Mozart concerto or an actor's interpretation of Lear—a performed realization, not a translation. (I might add that, if "hermeneutical interpretation" sounds to us like a pleonasm, it is only so because the activity we commonly recognize as "hermeneutics" has preempted the word "interpretation," as it has also indeed attempted to preempt the word "reading.")

If we grant to "interpretation" its legitimate scope of meaning as a bidirectional activity, we can begin to consider its function in relation to its ostensible object, the text, and to its ostensible subject, the reader. To do so, we will first need to reflect upon the peculiar nature of this verbal entity, the text. After that, we will distinguish three relations to the text: (1) that of the initial reader, (2) that of the poetic interpreter, or synthesizing rereader, and (3) that of the hermeneutical interpreter, or analyzing rereader.

Like every stored cultural artifact, a literary text exists to be reused. But each time we reuse this bounded linear entity we discover we are adding to an extended linear entity—our own personal series of construals of this script, each similar, no doubt, but each somewhat different. As we begin the poem once again, we bring to it all this previous experience of it. But, if we have learned to keep our previous decodings in the background, our habitual assumptions will be less insistent than the words we once again confront, and our renewed alertness to this utterance will usually lead us to construe this script each time in a slightly different manner. Minor though these differences may be, the general conclusions we come to by the end of our present reading may qualitatively alter our overall reception of this text. Wolfgang Iser has spoken of this cyclic process as "illusion-building" (*Implied Reader* 287–88), a process by which the reader fills in gaps and, responding to the suggestive cues provided, creates the illusion of a coherence that exists only for the duration of this interior performance. This reconstructive process, he has said, is possible only because literary texts insist on undermining their own coherence and on compelling readers to break their former illusions.

Readers who insist on a single correct construal of a text or believe that such an ultimate decoding is possible are bedeviled by what some have referred to as the "hermeneutical circle," the *circulus vitiosus* in which our conclusions about a text are used to establish the meanings of the premises upon which we have based these very conclusions. Such a circle is vicious when it ends where it began and when one recommences the process, armed both with an unshakable confidence in one's prior final conclusions and with an amnesia of how one derived them.

Alternative to the circle model of rereading might be the spiral, a cycle that maintains the linearity and unity of each performance-loop, but by adding the extra dimension of depth assigns each reading its own "space" and its own variant character. Each time we read a text and expose ourselves to the turning arc of this spiral, the words, even of a very familiar poem, come toward us with a renewed aura of strangeness and once again we acknowledge that this is, after all, not *our* utterance, but someone else's. At this point we find ourselves yielding to one of two impulses: to step back from it or to let ourselves be drawn into its illusional center. Recoiling from this vortex is the impulse of hermeneutic interpretation; yielding to its centripetal tow is the impulse of poetic interpretation.

The accompanying diagram schematizes these options. The reader is always physically situated facing the written text, indicated in the diagram as the contact-point (or c-point). If the perceiver of graphemes is also encountering the text for the first time, the reader's attention is obliged to remain here and keep a narrow focus on the words in their syntactical setting. The perplexed divagations of this c-reader Stanley Fish traced in his 1970 essay "Literature in the Reader: Affective Stylistics"; the hunger of this reader for foreshadowing Barbara Herrnstein Smith justified in *Poetic Closure* (119–120). Studies of readerly innocence such as these provide valuable insights into literary cognition, for even when we return to a now familiar text we try to simulate to some extent the adventure of a first reading. However, if by "text" we mean a verbal artifact that is deliberately stored in order to be reread (as distinct from conversation or writing not customarily preserved for later perusal), then the initial experience of the c-reader (the occasion at which reading is strictly defined as c-reading) cannot be considered normative. If a literary text is composed to be stored (in memory, writing, or some other retrieval system) and reread, then it is

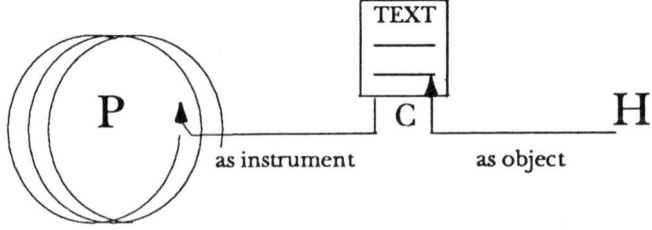

the *re*reader's experience that must provide the norms and data from which literary theory develops its principles. The rereader may indeed imitate the perplexity and surprise of the initial reader but is unable, and should not try, to blot out all prior knowledge of this text.

When in the past literary theorists have made a distinction similar to mine between poetic and hermeneutical interpretation, there has been a tendency to identify poetic interpretation with c-reading, and to identify this c-reading with its initial phase. The New Critics distinguished the individual reading from the Poem Itself, the performance from the "concrete universal," the subjective response from the textual object (Wellek and Warren 146–48; Wimsatt, *Verbal Icon* 21–39, 69–83). In his *Validity in Interpretation* E. D. Hirsch designated them the aesthetic and the critical moments, Michael Riffaterre termed them the heuristic and the retroactive readings (*Semiotics of Poetry* 5), and David Bleich called them "symbolization" and "resymbolization" (*Subjective Criticism*, 39, 96). Despite their many other differences of approach, these interpretation theorists have agreed on at least one point—that the hermeneutical phase alone is worth the attention of the literary specialist, the poetic (which for them means the "initial," "prereflective," or "partial" reading) being flawed, untrustworthy, and, moreover, unexaminable. Having identified poetic synthesis with the narrow, laborious construal of the c-reader, they quickly dismiss it and warn their readers to do the same, lest it contaminate the rigorous clarity of a hermeneutical analysis. This misrepresentation unduly constricts interpretive activity and, I submit, by undervaluing poetics impoverishes hermeneutics.

The lines in the diagram that extend at 180 degrees from the c-point represent the two alternative projections of the reader-as-interpreter, who not only has the advantage of choosing, but *must* choose, either the poetic-interpretive vantage point (P) or the hermeneutical-interpretive vantage point (H). The reader who chooses point P cognizes the words that during this reading pass through the c-point. These graphic signs unfold a linear artifact that because of the reader's prior encounters with it is information unconstrained by the ordinary rules of linear time: this reader remembers the immediate textual past, that is, what was read a minute or so ago, but is endowed also with the extraordinary ability to remember the future, for example, how a text will end. For example, as rereaders of Keats's "Ode to a Nightingale," we know even in the first stanza that the bird's song will modulate from "happiness" and "full-throated ease" to a "plaintive anthem" at the end. As a result we sense this final forlornness brooding within each earlier moment of hectic joy. We "know" a reread poem just as we know a familiar ritual. This knowledge does not exclude the prior benefits of hermeneutical scrutiny, but is not *itself* a hermeneutical activity. This privileged knowledge permits us to be meditatively present within, as it were, the interiors of such performances and to construe their component elements as copresent signifiers.

A prior experience with a text, both poetic and hermeneutical, is the precondition for poetic interpretation. Therefore poetics is the theorizing that undertakes to account for this repeatable experience. What sort of poetics would be derived from a study of texts that after an initial encounter no reader ever chose to reexperience? A poetics of ineffectiveness, if ever it existed—a proper hypnopoetics, so to speak— would at any rate be impossible to systematize without reference to texts that readers in a given community have found to be worth rereading. The traditional agenda of poetics since Aristotle has obviously been to study the effective elements within performing arts. The very first sentence of his *Poetics* announces his intention to consider the various kinds of poetry and the *dynamis,* or potentiality, of each. By this he apparently meant that which can pass from potency to act by means of performance. When I speak of "effective elements" in specific reference to literature I mean factors such as themes, images, and phonological patterns that produce effects within readers. By "performing arts" I mean media of social play that take the form of scripted reenactments and that, in literature, require the reader both to perform and to witness the performance. The P-position in my diagram represents the center at which the reader-as-poetic-interpreter undertakes this performance by skillfully engaging the effective elements of the script. The *poiesis,* or "making-up," like the interpretation we ascribe to the actor of a stage play, is the function of this reader, who, with nothing but graphic signs to perceive, must interpret by imagination alone the roles of actor(s) and of spectator.

Now, when we set out to locate the reader-as-hermeneutical-interpreter (H), we take our leave of this intra-cyclic center. Relative to the readerly poiesis of the text, the vantage point of the hermeneutical interpreter is deliberately decentered. A critical text, that is, an essay commenting in some way upon a literary text, that this hermeneutical withdrawal makes possible may be organized upon one of two principles. In a formalist hermeneutic, for example, that of mid-century Anglo-American New Criticism and most structuralist analyses, this new point will implicitly become a new center, a more or less stable hub for a closed loop of critical activity. The justifications for such an assumption are several. The first is common to every narrowly programmed hermeneutic: the very fact of its detachment from point P convinces its practitioners of its enlightened objectivity and its perspicuous insight into the essential workings of the text. Other justifications include the supposed rigor of its exegetical method and the supposed stability of its ideological grounding. In the 1960s and 1970s all three of these justifications were questioned. Its most systematic critique, Derridian hermeneutic, found the vicious circularity of this formalism all too apparent and argued that every new center must itself be decentered. In what is often played out as an agon of self-reflexion and self-interrogation, the typical poststructuralist stages a potentially infinite series of combative stands and tactical retreats.

Geoffrey Hartman in 1976 recommended this new method as a "negative hermeneutic." In that same year his colleague, Hillis Miller, viewed its consequences as a happy prospect: the older hermeneutical method had been able to regard itself as centered only because it assumed reading to be the discovery of what was somehow *there* in the text; it was based on "the notion of the self-enclosed literary work and . . . the idea that any work has a fixed, identifiable meaning." Now, however, opinions had changed. Interestingly, Miller implies that hermeneutical interpreters have derived some methodological inspiration from poetic interpretation or, to put it another way, that from introspecting their direct experience of reading texts they have learned to doubt the validity of their own and all others' interpretive conclusions:

> The literary work is seen in various ways as open and unpredictably productive. The reading of a poem is part of the poem. This reading is productive in its turn. It produces multiple interpretations, further language about the poem's language, in an interminable activity without necessary closure. (Davis, ed., 418)

Miller's model is clearly not a self-enclosed hermeneutically vitiating circle but rather an ongoing spiral. By "reading" he seems to have meant the same process that I have called poetic interpretation. But the practical question remained: What do we professional hermeneuts do with this radically unstable entity? His answer was: We produce things. What things? Hermeneutical responses. And not one or two competing interpretations of a text but an infinite number.

If, as I have suggested, the prototypical experience upon which this deconstructive hermeneutic is based is poetic interpretation—the direct internal performance of the text—then one might ask why it is that those who have rejected the old positive hermeneutics have not made more of an effort to observe the "reading of the poem [that] is part of the poem." Miller implies one answer when he says that the reading constitutes only a *part* of the poem. This follows from the traditional hermeneutical premise according to which the poem is an ideal entity that exceeds the scope of any and every conceivable reading performance. Certainly Miller assumes here that no mere act of reading is complete: if it were, hermeneuts would need to look for another line of work. The "part" injected into this entity by reading, itself the product of spontaneous interpretive choice, deliberate misreading, invincible ignorance, or simple inadvertence, produces the interpretations that constitute the interminable activity of the decentered hermeneut. Every poetic interpreter likewise knows that every encounter with the text is a partial realization of its inherent factors. This is not, however, a problem to this interpreter, for without this incompleteness, which is always a necessary result of selective attention, selective in part among mutually exclusive constructions, there would be little incentive to repeat the reading performance of this text on another occasion. From the vantage point of the poetic interpreter the reading is not part of the poem: it *is the poem*—the *poēma,* the made, or rather the perpetually remade, thing.

Having sharply contrasted these two interpreters, let me add this disclaimer: by defining interpretation as a bidirectional concept and distinguishing poetic from hermeneutical interpretation I am not setting up these two as competing methods of reading. They are diametrical opposites, yes, but they are also terminal points in a single line. Whether or not the hermeneut spins out of one point H to establish another one at yet a further remove from point P this 180-degree opposition of polar complements remains. The polemic that has raged most loudly over the last quarter century has not been between poetic and hermeneutical stances, nor should it have been. It has been fought between competing hermeneutics, that is, between formalist and deconstructive theories of decoding literary signs.

The poetic interpreter (who, I might add, may be a person who on another occasion practices a hermeneutical discipline) is not in the least concerned with analysis, whether that analysis serves the impressionistic hermeneutic that Roland Barthes called the *plaisir du texte* with its browsings and its unpredictable moments of *jouissance* or serves the activity of those whom Barthes characterized as fools of all kinds, who decree foreclosure of the text and of its pleasure, either by cultural conformism or by intransigent rationalism (suspecting a "mystique" of literature) or by political moralism or by criticism of the signifier or by stupid pragmatism or by snide vacuity or by destruction of the discourse, loss of verbal desire. (*Pleasure of the Text* 15)

Poetic interpretation is a function defined by a discipline, a *technē*, that differs from these and any other hermeneutical stances. If deconstructionists like Miller and Barthes, not to mention Jacques Derrida, have injected into hermeneutic theory and practice some of the problematic excitement of poetic interpretation, they are not alone. We should note that some latter-day formalists like Murray Krieger in *Theory of Criticism* (1976) and Denis Donoghue in *Ferocious Alphabets* (1981), have also recognized the role of the subject in the construal of the poetic object.

Donoghue in contrasting his "epireader" to his "graphireader" has set imagined voice against perceived writing as competing values in reading. These readers do not, however, differ from one another on issues of poetic performance versus hermeneutical translation: both are hermeneuts. The question at issue for them is: What for the decoder is the relevant content of a text? One would center on the imagined presence of the author's consciousness articulated in a unique voice; the other, who associates this latter focus with a theocratic tradition of vocal coercion, would expose the text as a set of freestanding signs to the reader's hermeneutical domination. As described by Donoghue, the epireader is essentially a formalist, but one who wishes to keep faith with the poetic pole of interpretation. The graphireader is the deconstructionist who regards the hermeneutical adversary, the epireader, as a sentimentalist attempting to salvage a reactionary logocentric world view by engineering a few superficial reforms.

If, over the recent past, the hermeneuts have borrowed some of the methods of linguistics and analytic philosophy, the poeticians have drawn upon those of psychology and phenomenology. Hermeneuts have also borrowed, as we have seen, some debating points from the poetic-interpretive experience, but only poeticians, and of them only a few, have essayed a careful examination of the poiesis of reading: Roman Ingarden, Louise Rosenblatt, Wolfgang Iser, Georges Poulet, and the early Stanley Fish come perhaps most readily to mind.

Gradually, however, this focus on poetic interpretation on the part of those who profess a reader-response perspective has faded, as reader-response itself becomes, in the minds of most at least, a subfield of hermeneutics. Again I think the problem is partly semantical. The term "reader-response" conceals in itself a mischievous ambiguity. Having the Janus-like bidirectionality of "interpretation" and those other words of information-transfer, "response" can mean either an internal and unspoken realization or an openly expressed reaction. When it comes to mean the latter, as, for example, in the writings of Norman Holland and Hans Robert Jauss, it refers to hermeneutical interpretation. For Wolfgang Iser, however, it usually means the former. In his preface to the English translation of *Der Akt des Lesens: Theorie aesthetischer Wirkung,* Iser expresses his misgivings about translating *Wirkung* as "response":

> The German word "Wirkung" comprises both effect and response, without the psychological connotations of the English word "response." "Effect" is at times too weak a term to convey what is meant by "Wirkung," and "response" is a little confusing. Confronted by Scylla and Charybdis I have finally opted for "response." (*Act of Reading* n. ix)

As we see, he values the clearer bidirectionality of the German word and fears that the English word has become so identified with behaviorist stimulus-response as to imply an exclusively overt reaction.

The professional bias in favor of hermeneutical interpretation is so pronounced that many reader-response advocates have come to define "response" strictly in terms of verbalized "feedback," accounting for such responses in sociolectic terms (institutionally determined expression of opinion), idiolectic terms (verbal-associative rereading, or "misreading," of the text), or psychoanalytical terms (a debriefing of the affects and fantasies experienced when reading the text). At any rate, a large number of these readers profess that old article of belief—that texts accrue *real* meaning only retroactively. In Susan Suleiman and Inge Crosman's *Reader in the Text* Robert Crosman defines the reader's role as that of a critical interpreter:

> The text . . . supplies me with words, ideas, images, sounds, rhythms, but I make the poem's meaning by a process of translation. That is what reading is, in fact: translation. (124)

And Crosman leaves no doubt what he means by "translation": taking a text, adding to it, "subtracting from it, rearranging it, changing it from verse to prose and so on," in short, substituting a personalized paraphrase for the original. This revisionary activity that Crosman advocates, whatever its merits as a mental exercise, is not the performance of the text but rather the creation of a critical text, which, but for its unashamed impressionism, offers us little more than a new New Critical agenda.

Jane Tompkins's edited anthology of essays *Reader-Response Criticism: From Formalism to Post-Structuralism* (1980), while of unquestionable value, obscured the issue by its very title. What is there to *criticize* in reader response? Readers' responses? If so, we have a pedagogical project like that of I. A. Richards in *Practical Criticism*. The dialectic of many of these essays does indeed critique theoretical positions, but "criticism" in a literary context does not imply a theoretical debate. "Criticism" in this context connotes a judging either of artistic merits (a criticism of specific literary texts) or of hermeneutic interpretation (a criticism of assigned significance). The greater part of these essays have as little to do with hermeneutical practice as does Aristotle in his *Poetics*. Just as Aristotle was not concerned with examining the meanings of *Oedipus Tyrannus* but focused rather on the *dynamis* of tragedy as a verbal performance, most of the essayists in this anthology refer to texts to illustrate the complex processes by which readers realize writing. These processes have hermeneutical implications, but these are secondary to their poetic relevance, a fact that Tompkins's subtitle obscures by inserting reader-response theory into recent intra-hermeneutic polemic.

Tompkins's own final essay, "The Reader in History," is partly a justification of her choice of titles. In it a poetics of reading, which equates language with action, is naturally opposed by a hermeneutics of reading, which equates it with signification (203):

What is most striking about reader-response criticism and its close relative, deconstructive criticism, is their failure to break out of the mold into which critical writing was cast by the formalist identification of criticism with explication. Interpretation reigns supreme both in teaching and in publication just as it did when New Criticism was in its heyday in the 1940s and 1950s. . . . Professors and students alike practice criticism as usual; only the vocabulary with which they perform their analyses has altered. (225)

We are left wondering what the value of such a terminological alteration might be.

Having acknowledged her debt to Suleiman and Crosman and to Tompkins, Elizabeth Freund in her study *The Return of the Reader: Reader-Response Criticism* briskly tolls the death-knell for a "lectocentric criticism" that now (in 1987) has "a past rather than a future" (10). The return of the reader appears to be a return from a passing infatuation with reading to the respectable business-as-usual of assigning meaning to texts. If, as I have argued, "criticism" implies a hermeneutical objectification of texts, "reader-response *criticism*" could hardly fail to resemble "criticism as usual." As a logical consequence, Freund's accounts of erstwhile "reader-response critics" read like case histories of marvelous conversions followed by prudent recantations. One after another they came to agree with Stanley Fish that, whatever critics do, "it will only be [hermeneutical] interpretation in another guise because, like it or not, interpretation is the only game in town" (*Is There a Text* 355).

As I have so briefly summarized them, the principal literary debates over the past quarter-century have focused on the H-point of the bidirectional line of interpretation. Disputants have drawn upon certain features of the poetic-interpretive experience to discomfit their opponents but not to shed light on this experience or even to suggest that the performative interpretation of a text is the professed end for which writers, if we may believe them, compose their works. As I have insisted, poetic interpretation is an activity radically different from any and all hermeneutical stances toward texts—from deconstruction that spins the text in hermeneutical circles to produce an infinite series of new significations glimpsed from positions of greater and greater remoteness and from the older dogmatism that tolerates but one spin of the wheel. In the poetic mode the reader is not outside the hermeneutical circle or self-transforming spiral, pumping the treadle, but at the very center of this cyclic performance.

If I have pleaded a case for the poetic pole of the interpretive process, it is not because I would wish, or could conceive of, the institution of literature without hermeneutics and without the debates its practice engenders. Not all readings, from any interpretive standpoint, are satisfactorily skillful, and so this corrective mode has a part to play in the careful stop-and-go perusal of an unfamiliar, or indeed any revisionable, text. Our early acquaintance with a text usually involves trial-and-error attempts to achieve satisfactory constructions: whenever we step back from the text and try to verify our conclusions, we engage in hermeneutical interpretation, albeit of an informal and rudimentary sort. Like the rehearsals that precede the actual playing of a difficult piece of music, acts of hermeneutical interpretation usually precede our first complete poetic reading. On the other hand, the formal work of hermeneutical interpretation, that is, the translation of the read text into an analytic essay, cannot simply proceed by dint of analysis. It can begin only after a synthesis, in the form of a skillful poetic interpretation, has been performed. These two poles are, then, mutually supportive. Without one, the other is impossible, as impossible as a stick with a single end.

As an essay in poetics, this book is concerned with the *dynamis* of texts, a potency that only readers have the causative power to convert into *energeia*, or act. But "readers" are not only particular readers, individuals with their own life experiences, habits of thought, and ideological allegiances: a poetics must take into account such specific differences, but must do so by grounding its theorizing on more general premises. A poetics must be willing to hypothesize that human subjectivity is not wholly anarchic and, moreover, that a reader engaged in construing a text—in poetic interpretation—is constrained to an appreciable degree by internal, cognitive mechanisms that are in turn prompted by cues established by the text. In short, it must assume in the reader a complex *dynamis* that is reciprocally activated by his or her engagement with the text.

If then a poetic theory achieves a degree of general applicability to readers and texts, it will undoubtedly be of use to hermeneutical readers. If a text may be said to mean what it does, the activity of poetic interpretation, as one may reflect upon it, will illuminate *what*, as well as *how*, that text signifies. But this hermeneutical spin-off, valuable as it may be, ought not to be the primary concern of any essay in poetics. In the following pages, therefore, I will refer to texts *only insofar as they illustrate the processes they induce in readers*. The occasional analyses I use for purposes of demonstration will inevitably have hermeneutic aspects, critical judgments that must themselves be judged on their own merits.

This is a book of *poetic* theory specifically concerned with the processes by which language mediates mental images. As a poetics of the *mind's eye*, it is an examination of the relation of mind to eye: in other words, of mental imagination to visual perception. As the phrase the "mind's eye" suggests, my study has led me to believe that the reader of words does indeed replicate some of the procedures of the perceiver of visual objects. As my subtitle indicates, my interest in the phenomena of imaging has drawn me to the border between psychology and literature where the history of interdisciplinary commerce is interlarded with cautionary tales, a sampling of which I summarize in Chapter 2.

A convergence of interests on the part of psychologists and literary theorists has always seemed to be a chance occurrence. Psychologists have never been professionally interested in poetic texts unless these could demonstrate psychophysical mechanisms, reveal the symbolization of unconscious drives, be used to quantify "aesthetic preferences," or similarly serve as "data." And literary theorists, for their part, have never been particularly concerned with psychical health or mental behavior.

True, several marriages of convenience have been celebrated over the past two hundred years, but, since in their objects, objectives, and methodologies these two disciplines are quite different, these marriages have been brief and, to be at all fruitful, have always required the midwifery of some other discipline. As a literature-to-psychology crossover, the process has worked somewhat like this: one conceives an interest in a particular topic, but one's concept is as yet only an unformed inkling, its dimensions as yet undefined. Since it seems to coincide with topics of concern to psychology, one hopes to find somewhere a psychological explanation for it, but discovers that, while psychologists have acknowledged this phenomenon and placed it in relation to other functions, they have dealt with it only in passing or from an angle unsuitable to one's objectives. To place it with any degree of clarity within a psychological context one first has to distinguish it conceptually from other similar phenomena. At this point of impasse one makes another interdisciplinary leap and seizes upon a concept from a cognate discipline that, *mutatis mutandis,* can serve as a model by which relevant literary and psychological data can be correlated, further inferences drawn, and fresh hypotheses constructed and tested. As maieutic devices, models drawn from Marxism, neurophysiology, structural linguistics, and semiotics have been of great service in this interdisciplinary effort.

The model that I will use to bring these two disciplines into partial and momentary conjunction is play theory, specifically that proposed by Gregory Bateson in "A Theory of Play and Fantasy," first published in 1954. Central to Bateson's theory is the notion of the "play frame," a conventional understanding that all that is said and done within what is designated as a "play" will have meanings that are quite different from, even contradictory to, their non-play meanings and that this understanding is conveyed by a metacommunicative act. By "metacommunication" he simply means a signal that to participants in a communication declares the rules under which ensuing signals will be processed.

To treat play as the fundamental behavioral mode of literary reception is simply to reconsider seriously and apply with rigor the notion that Samuel Taylor Coleridge proposed in *Biographia Literaria* when he declared as the precondition of reading is "that willing suspension of disbelief for the moment [that] constitutes poetic faith" (*Biographia,* vol. 2, p. 6). Poetic play is no less than a voluntary decision to suspend the customary norms by which we assess our reality. When we disentangle Coleridge's double negative, we can interpret "suspension of disbelief" as "invitation to believe": play therefore is initiated as an "as if" activity, a game of "pretend," surrounded by a "play frame," a clear signal that the signals to be communicated within this spatiotemporal frame will not mean what they mean outside the frame.

This suspension of disbelief is similar to the religious confession of faith and the scientific hypothesis, but with these important differences: play is premised upon its own untruth, its purely conventional fictiveness, and its temporariness. This latter trait is quite important for, as a secession from the ordinary world of consensual reality, its excursion into its own ad hoc consensual reality would be madness if it were not bounded by a beginning and an end.

The conscious character of Bateson's "metacommunication" and Coleridge's "suspension of disbelief" makes a cognitive, rather than a psychoanalytical, approach appropriate to the poetic performance. Every depth psychology of literature must approach texts as demonstrations of particular latent processes and cast a bright, objectifying light on their verbal surfaces in order to see through these veils and observe their latent contents. While this is not the specific project of this essay, there is nothing here in this book, subtitled a "psychology of imagination," that disputes the value of a psychoanalysis of verbal images. Freudian or Lacanian interpreters have compelling arguments to make concerning the motives and means of fantasy: from their point of view this present study may be helpful in revealing the surface and subsurface play of illusion, the web of imaginal indirections poems use to body forth their otherwise hidden meanings. In this respect, here again, poetics can be a valuable resource for hermeneutics.

The application of any play theory to poetry becomes complicated when we ask: Who are the participants in this play behavior? The communicative medium of poetry—whether it is dramatically enacted, recited from memory, or recorded in graphic symbols—seems to alter the nature of the metacommunicative transaction or at the very least complicates the way we think of it. Such terms as "author," "text," "reader," and "referent" certainly become problematic as soon as we try to apply them cross-culturally or from one mode of literary production to another within the same culture.

My first two chapters attempt to come to terms with these problems by introducing and confronting certain issues of definition and method. The study of verbally evoked images is really only several centuries old, but the authority of classical, biblical, and medieval texts had already established the terms of discourse prior to the seventeenth century and did so, as I will propose, to the detriment of this field of study. In Chapter 1, "Verbal Visuality," I argue that prior to the development of print literacy the notion of imagery was entangled with oral presence and perceptual visuality. If we define literary imagination as the formation of percept-like concepts in response to written cues, we must acknowledge that these older studies did not directly address this phenomenon. Moreover, they had other agendas, for example, to defend or disparage divinatory practices, to interpret prophetic writings, or to attack fantasy, erotic or political.

In Chapter 2, "Science on the Nature of Imagination," I continue this broad historical overview. Here we find post-Renaissance science attempting to deal with what it regarded as a middenstead of images—private mental images, theories about images, and theories fabricated out of images. Since mental images more often reflect the mind and its subjective needs than things-as-they-are, natural science regarded them with the same contempt that King James's translators of the Bible used when they regularly associated "images" with "false idols" and invariably used the word "imagination" as synonymous with idle, wicked thinking. When the anglicized Psalmist asks, "Why do the heathen rage, and the people imagine a vain thing," the seventeenth-century diagnostician replies that imagination is the recourse of the unenlightened. As far as Bacon was concerned, the imaginings he called "idols of the mind" were worth classifying only if such attention led thoughtful people to detect and abjure them. Though the British Empiricists devoted considerable attention to the mental images they called "ideas," their main mission was to regulate them and account for human error and delusion as dysfunctions of imagination.

Some of the specifically literary questions the eighteenth century posed were: Does the imagination that poets display accord with the "laws of the association of ideas"? If so, does that make a poem more "natural" and more "human," that is, "better"? Do the "pleasures of imagination" constitute a harmless good in themselves or should they always serve a didactic purpose? Or is the imagination a noble and ennobling faculty that releases the mind from its earthly trammels to soar on the wings of such feelings that it alone can rouse?

In various ways nineteenth- and twentieth-century psychology continued the work of seventeenth- and eighteenth-century empirical philosophers particularly in trying to establish the relation of "somatic" to "psychic," and of unconscious to conscious, processes. While literary theorists often expressed uneasiness and sometimes hostility toward this research into the sacred penetralia of feelings and imagination, they stayed abreast of these developments and took what insights they could from psychologists if only to define themselves in opposition to them.

Coleridge was one literary theorist who early on saw the value and the immense difficulty of this interdisciplinary endeavor. David Hartley's adaptation of the Empiricists' "laws of the association of ideas" seemed to promise to naturalize the poet's work and preserve it from the artificialities of conventional rhetorical structure. But Coleridge's experience of the poetic imagination inevitably persuaded him that, whatever it was, it was a power beyond the scope of positivist psychology. "Fancy," he came to believe, may be dependent on the "laws of association" (*Biographia Literaria* XIII) but no determinism could ever account for the behavior of "Imagination."

In Chapter 3, the "Poetics of Play: Reopening Jakobson's 'Closing Statement,'" I examine Roman Jakobson's influential essay, "Linguistics and Poetics," in terms of play, a premise that Jakobson imperfectly concealed within his project to subsume poetics within linguistics. By alluding to a preliminary invitation, which every poetic text tacitly conveys, to the reader to participate in fiction under the terms that "what I say is true and is not true," Jakobson seems to restate Coleridge's dictum on the "willing suspension of disbelief" based upon a metacommunicative understanding on the part of all participants. This initial commitment to paradox, it has seemed to me, is the primary act of readerly imagination that makes possible all subsequent acts, including the verbally cued acts of visualization that we usually refer to as "poetic images."

My theory of poetic play I develop further in Chapter 4, "Tactics and Timing." Here I take up an idea introduced in Chapter 3, that of "cognitive modes," six spatiotemporal "zones" of being into which the objects of consciousness are necessarily projected: three "outer" and three "inner" modes corresponding to past, present, and future. Though this is an analogy of limited applicability, we might think of these as sectors of a playing field: the concepts and images of a poem would in the reading performance of that text be deployed and made to interact now in one, now in another of these modal zones.

The last three chapters of the book explore the implications for imagery of four of these cognitive modes: perception, the two memory modes, and introspection.

Since mental imagery, as has been widely recognized, is a mimesis of perception, it is only reasonable to begin this exploration of cognitive modes with a study of visual perception. (In subsequent chapters I will discuss the extent to which the recollection of the past, retrospection, and the imaging of the purely imaginary, introspection, both imitate particular perceptual routines.) Accordingly, in Chapter 5, "Simulations of Perception," I present a somewhat technical summary of eye movements and then apply this to the poetry of William Carlos Williams.

Chapter 6, "Transformations of Memory," considers the process of encoding, storing, and retrieving two kinds of information, personal experience and general knowledge (or convention). While current theories of memory organization and function are various and new hypotheses continue to be proposed, the one I have found particularly helpful is that of the Canadian psychologist Endel Tulving. Whether or not his theory adequately accounts for all memory-related phenomena, his distinction helps clarify certain basic issues in literary imagery and genres. My terms, experience and convention, correspond roughly to Tulving's episodic and semantic systems of memory as these concepts may be adapted to poetics. "Experience" is a satisfactory term to label perception and retrospection (of perception) insofar as their objects are personally encountered at a particular time and place and become the stuff of narrative and description. "Convention" as a term for general knowledge, including opinions and beliefs, is, without redefinition, not wholly satisfactory. Much of this knowledge is indeed received from others, culturally absorbed, implicit in natural language, and accepted as consensual reality, but not all general knowledge is conventional in that cultural sense of the word. Some elements, it seems to me, derive from the genetically determined structure of the central nervous system, while others are generalizations derived inductively from personal experience. "Convention," as I use this term, is therefore broadened to mean axiomatic principles arrived at and agreed upon within the individual memory as well as within the collective memory, or culture, of the community.

The importance of the collective reservoir of memory to the individual reader's poetic imaging is incalculable. As we know, language is a conventional sign system and as such is stored in what I have called conventional memory. When we read a poetic text, even one that purports to narrate or describe personal experiences, we construct this experiential display out of conventional materials. In my final chapter, "Introspection and the Visionary Imagination," I discuss this primary act of imaginative play, namely, reading, as one of the functions of the introspective mode. As the accessing of the conventional code of language, reading is a looking within for meaning, a process that I refer to as the "primary introspective stage." In poetic play, as contrasted with critical analysis, we look *through* language to construe meaning and by so doing we look through the introspective mode and its conventional schemata to contemplate narrated experience.

Metaphor, a trope that all researchers into poetic imagination have felt is somehow central to this topic, I here identify as the irruption of the introspective mode into the contextures of other modes. The introspective mode, so intimately connected with verbal semiosis and, consequently, with propositional thought, is always on the verge of asserting its privilege to intervene and to preempt the play of other modes. When it does so, it breaks through this surface with motives of its own, like the ghost of Hamlet's father calling from below. When it manifests itself in the metaphor-image, or vehicle, it reveals a subtext of spectral schemata beneath the realistic surface play of narration and description.

That which is ghostly about metaphor is best revealed in texts that thematize the introspective moment. Texts that portray dreams, reveries, hallucinations, and other visionary events might be considered metaphor-vehicles writ large. Reading them, we can observe the liminal point at which schemata become images and archetypes become personae. This study of the poetics of the mind's eye concludes here with a brief glimpse over this threshold and into the underworld of the mind.

I wish to express my gratitude to Paul Vitz and Michael Heller of New York University and Ellen Esrock of Rensselaer Polytechnic Institute for their early and generous interest in this project; to Michael Brown of Northeastern University for his faith in the worth of cross-disciplinary endeavors like this one; to Alan Nyysola of the Shawangunkkill Conference for valuable suggestions on visual memory; to Albert Cook of Brown University for his careful and discriminative reading of the manuscript; to Charles Boer of the University of Connecticut, whose insights helped inform the final revision; and to Jerome Singerman of the University of Pennsylvania Press, who saw this book through its various changes with patience and skill.

An earlier version of Chapter 5 appeared as "The Moving Eye in Williams' Earlier Poetry," in *William Carlos Williams: Man and Poet*, ed. Carroll F. Terrell (Orono, Me.: National Poetry Foundation, 1983), pp. 261–285. Copyright © 1983 National Poetry Foundation. Reprinted by permission.

An earlier version of Chapter 7 appeared as "Groundless Figures: Reader Response to Verbal Imagery," *The Critic*, 51, no. 1 (Fall 1988): 11–29. Copyright © 1988 College English Association. Reprinted by permission.

Permission is acknowledged to reprint published materials from the following sources:

W. B. Yeats, "The Magi" and Note to "The Dolls," from *Collected Poems of W. B. Yeats* (New York: Macmillan, 1956). Copyright © 1956 Macmillan, Inc. Reprinted by permission.

William Carlos Williams, "The Source," "The Red Wheelbarrow," "Nantucket," "Poem," "Flowers by the Sea," "Between Walls," "Spring Strains" (lines 5–8, 25–28), "Spring and All" (lines 1–15) (New York: New Directions, 1938). Copyright © 1938, renewed, New Directions, Inc. Reprinted by permission.

William Stafford, "Notice What This Poem Is Not Doing," from *Things That Happen When There Aren't Any People* (Brockport, N.Y.: BOA Editions, 1980). Copyright © 1980 by William Stafford. Reprinted by permission of BOA Editions, Ltd.

Albert Cook trans., *Homer: The Odyssey* (New York: W. W. Norton, 1967), Book XI, lines 34–43, 48–52, 82–98. Translation copyright © 1967 Albert Cook. Reprinted by permission.

Chapter 1
Verbal Visuality

"Image," as it is generally defined, is a representation of something else. But when we apply this broad definition to verbally mediated experience, we quickly decide we must become more precise. A photograph is a visual representation—at least our culture recognizes it as such—but an image one "has" while reading a book seems to be a quite different kind of likeness. It is a "having," a momentary event that one experiences as a solitary reader. But then what about the word-accompanied images that are momentary *and* public, the staged likeness of a medieval court or a nineteenth-century garden party, constructed by set designers and collectively portrayed by actors? And doesn't the individual actor assume the likeness of another? Isn't this kind of image different from the image she generates by a speech in which she describes a scene from childhood? And isn't the metaphor she utters to embody some idea yet another kind of image-likeness?

The confusion that often besets discussions of imagery does not derive from the misapplication of this one term to unrelated referents. All the phenomena mentioned above are certainly related, but to use the single term "image" to apply to every instance of this multiform activity is to preclude its usefulness in more specific inquiry. Accordingly, I propose to use the term "visuality" for the broad class of experiences within which I will locate mental imagery prompted by written texts. But before I can narrow my focus to this, I must pare down this superordinate term.

First I will exclude purely visual artifacts. When I do refer to iconography, it will only be to sharpen the distinctions between it and verbally accompanied or verbally cued imagery. My subject matter may therefore be termed *verbal visuality*. Second, I will consider the verbal image as an entity produced with language but not usefully locatable *in* language. While it may be a legitimate concern for others to inquire into the way image-generating signs are encoded and codes are constituted, I will bracket these concerns and focus rather on the decoding process. Third, I will regard this process by which the verbal and the visual come together as a specifically conscious activity: while not wishing to deny the potential effects of repression and displacement on the formation of images by individual readers, I wish to draw attention to the specifically cognitive aspects of this process. The reasons for these decisions I will more fully set forth in the next two chapters. The task of this chapter, however, is to define the poetic image in terms of a typology of verbal visuality.

Oral Mimesis

Imitation through speech generally implies presence, which in turn implies a visual as well as an auditory reception of sense data. When we attend a dramatic performance, besides hearing the oral addressers, we see them and construe what Cicero called their "body language" (*sermo corporis*). The specific aspect of utterance that characterizes such mimesis is indeed this corporeal discourse, this representation of a persona's bodily presence, not merely his words.

Because of the nature of this presentation perceptual and verbal data both lay claim to visuality: what we see on stage and what actors' words evoke in our minds compete for visual attention. They are not merely concurrent; they are counteractive. Perceptual presence and imaginal absence, when they overlap, create a condition that psychologists term "interference." When these two compete, however, the outcome is almost always the same: the verbal imagery of speech, while it may momentarily blaze forth in descriptive clarity, will soon be overwhelmed by the depictive presence of the actors and their actions.

A similar interference occurs in all oral exchanges in which verbalized visual information is an important element. Consider the situation in which we stop our car to ask directions of a gas station attendant. We say we want to know how to get to "Route 17 North." As he tells us the directions (the number of traffic lights and particular landmarks), we turn our eyes away and unfocus them. "Conjugate lateral eye movement," the technical term for this maneuver, allows us to create a schematic mental image, or map, without visual interference from our informant or from any other potentially interferent visual object. He for his part understands this optical move of ours as exhibiting proper attention to his words. In another speech-act circumstance our behavior might be interpreted as shy or disrespectful or devious ("shifty-eyed"), but, if in the circumstance I just described we had stared unblinkingly at our informant, we would have seemed inattentive or uncomprehending.

As spectators at an oral mimetic event, however, we can afford to stare at an actor because we are not the primary addressee of his speech. We are less concerned with visualizing a persona's message than with viewing how other personae, by their overt responses, appear to have visualized it. As dramatis personae, these exist in an orally mediated world where the interiority of mental imagery is continually converted into the exteriority of gestural and verbal response. The world beyond the visible stage may be quite important to these characters, but they, not it, are most important to us. The *theatron* is first and foremost the viewing place, the *Schauplatz*, where those who come to witness the drama are spectators first and auditors second.

This interference factor accounts for the relative paucity of extended verbal description in drama. For a playwright to include such description would be in effect to ask the spectators to turn their gaze from the stage and to visualize a word-mediated image, to veil the speaker in invisibility, to render him or her a disembodied voice, and indeed to de-theatricalize drama.[1]

When, for example, we search Shakespeare for instances of extended description, we note that he resorts to it sparingly and that, when a block of description does occur, it is normally offered to another interested and responsive character or characters. It is meant to provoke a reaction. (If these addressees were not responsive, the only dramatic justification for including such a passage would be to portray their unresponsiveness as itself a specific kind of response to the speaker's inappropriate prolixity.) When we think of extended description, Enobarbus's account of Cleopatra (*Antony and Cleopatra* II.2) readily comes to mind. Though very much a vivid evocation of an absent scene, it is uttered in order to affect the present scene. Enobarbus recounts it to create an impression upon his onstage addressees of whom Agrippa plays the choregus with avid interjections ("O, rare for Antony! . . . Rare Egyptian! . . . Royal wench!"). Another celebrated moment in Shakespeare when the absent is made present in the minds of the onstage addressees occurs in *Hamlet* (IV.7) when Gertrude describes the death of Ophelia. Here again the account is offered to onstage addressees, Claudius and Laertes, whose acutely contrasting responses are immediately apparent.

These two descriptions are presented as examples of recollected imagery, products of the process that Kant in the *Critique of Judgment* termed "reproductive imagination." There are also examples to be found of what he called "productive imagination" that range from the one extreme of unbidden, hallucinatory imagery, for example, Macbeth's vision of the dagger (*Macbeth* II.1), to the other extreme of deliberate fabrication, for example, Edgar's description of the view from the cliffs of Dover (*King Lear* IV.6). Again, in Macbeth's case we do not try to enter into his vision of the mental object: *he* is our perceptual object and has himself become an unsheathed instrument of death. Edgar's benign lie accentuates his father's blindness and suicidal motive and draws us, undeceived by the imagery he is trying to evoke in his father's mind, to view the pathos of the perceived scene and its true location.

Thus in terms of the semiotics formulated by Charles Peirce actors are bearers of three kinds of signs, two of which are visual and one of which is auditory. They bear *iconic* signs insofar as each visually portrays a certain character of a certain nationality, rank, and so on. They bear *indexical* signs insofar as their presence, accoutrements, or behavior visually furnish information about other persons, objects, and conditions. These two kinds of signs ground their mimetic function in perceptual visuality, or showing. The third kind of signs, which Peirce called the *symbolic* and identified primarily with language, functions in drama as expressive speech, the information that personae tell us about what they feel, what they intend to do, and how they justify their behavior. The language of drama tells us what actions are on a person's mind, but seldom what *images* are *in* that mind. The reason for this reticence is, as I have been suggesting, dramaturgical, for perceptual and imaginal visuality are mutually interferent. In any one-on-one competition for attention a percept will always win out over a mental image. That is, in oral mimesis icons and indices occlude symbols whenever those symbolic signs attempt to convey visual information.

Oral Diegesis

The standard distinction between mimesis and diegesis is usually referred to as that between showing and telling, between iconic and indexical signs on the one hand and symbolic signs on the other, between drama and recitation. Even a superficial examination will reveal the approximate character of this contrast: actors are often called upon to tell and reciters to show. In drama, expository discourse, for example, presented in prologues and actor-narrated flashbacks, is often inserted early in a play, and, later on, messengers are often used to accelerate climactic action: these instances, though their imagery may be somewhat counteracted by perceptual presence, are nevertheless diegetic in function. Storytellers, for their part, have always altered their voices to impersonate different characters and have used gesture to indicate emotion and action.[2]

For our discussion of verbal visuality these two types of oral performance must be differentiated on a basis more precise than mere showing and telling. One might begin by observing that the mimetic artist pretends to be only one persona, while the diegetic artist pretends to be every person whose words he or she utters. The mimetic artist, the actor, is bounded by a *prosopon* (a face, a mask, a persona) and locatable in time and space among other impersonators. From the vantage point of the spectators, however, the stage with its several actors exposes an open space, a three-dimensional visual field that invites viewers to scan, fixate upon, and visually explore any number of separate details from addresser to addressees to costumes to scenic designs. The mimetic artist may be bounded, but the visual array in which the artist acts is open to a potentially unbounded set of spectatorial acts. This situation is reversed in the case of the diegetic monologist: here the unbounded protean narrator, who invites us to imagine he is now one character now another, now in one place and now hundreds of miles removed—this oral narrator, this single locus of speech is visually fixed in space. Since he must serially portray many personae and tellings-within-tellings, he is costumically (iconically) neutral and gesturally (indexically) restrained. We therefore can afford to look away from him or unfocus or even close our eyes as he evokes a series of persons, places, and things through the referentiality of his symbolic signs.[3] We are in a situation here that resembles that of the travelers earlier described who seek directions to Route 17 North. We do not need to fixate on our informant but to imagine what he says. On the other hand, this being an oral communication, perceptual visuality is always a factor, and may indeed be enhanced by gesture. Like the gas station attendant, when he uses his palm expressively in a bladed arc to tell us to veer left around the municipal parking lot, the diegetic artist has the option of calling us back with a gesture appropriate to a narrated character or event. Let us now consider several examples of oral diegesis as it affects visuality.

Though it was not unusual for contemporary playwrights to use diegetic devices to comment on their compositions, Shakespeare resorted to them only when background information was absolutely necessary. Prologues, choruses, and epilogues he apparently deemed quaint and awkward conventions. "The Most Lamentable Comedy and Most Cruel Death of Pyramus and Thisby" (*A Midsummer Night's Dream*, V.1) has a prologue as does "The Murder of Gonzago" (*Hamlet*, III.2). In both we also find a curious disjunction of pantomime ("dumb show"), presenting perceptual information only, and declamation, revealing character through the spoken expression of emotion, these declamations being more like concert arias than like dramatic dialogues. In both the effect is one of dissociating *actio* and *passio*. The Prologue, besides announcing the play and soliciting the indulgent attention of the "gentles," was supposed to provide the information needed to explain the speechless action and the actionless speeches. This diegetic function in his "Most Lamentable Comedy" Peter Quince performs with supererogatory thoroughness: "Gentles, perchance you wonder at this show; / But wonder on, till truth make all things plain" and so forth. But in *Hamlet* the entire plot of "The Murder of Gonzago" is summarized in the dumb show. Only then does the Prologue appear. Both Ophelia and Hamlet expect him to explain the pantomime (Hamlet: "We shall know by this fellow: the players cannot keep counsel; they'll tell all"). That this Prologue does not "tell all" seems to surprise him and so, when the players return to perform the spoken play, Hamlet himself tells all. "You are as good as a chorus, my lord," comments Ophelia.

Shakespeare had once before resorted to a chorus, in *Henry V*, where it served as Prologue to every act and as Epilogue. It plays such a prominent role in the performance that the mimesis of speech and pageantry (that here functions as a "dumb show") may be viewed as virtually embedded in diegesis. The Chorus not only presents itself as informational, supplying historical background and identifying personae that might be beyond the knowledge of some in the audience, but in its first speech it characterizes its theme as actually beyond the bounds of Shakespearean dramaturgy:

O for a Muse of fire, that would ascend
The brightest heaven of invention,
A kingdom for a stage, princes to act,
And monarchs to behold the swelling scene!

(I, ll. 1–4)

The diegetic interventions of this Chorus in producing a kind of pre-Brechtian epic drama, despite its most un-Brechtian of themes, demonstrates the combining of the oral-mimetic and oral-diegetic types and of the separate kinds of visuality proper to each. As the first act Chorus proceeds, it asks the audience to permit the actors to "work" on their (the audience's) "imaginary forces." This is somewhat technical language: according to the medieval "faculty psychology" imagination is the *vis imaginaria* (or *imaginativa*), the "imaginative force." What the Chorus is requesting is permission to affect the mind of its audience by stimulating a different visual faculty, that of the mind's eye. As the Prologue, it significantly closes by asking them "Gently to hear," for epic diegesis is primarily a telling, not a showing. When it appears for the last time, as an Epilogue, and refers to the less heroic descendants of Harry who "lost France and made his England bleed," it adds the clause "Which oft our stage has shown": follies and vices can be *shown* but the sublimely heroic, apparently, can only be *heard*.

Shakespeare's verbal cues to diegetic imaging are themselves worth examining. Note the Chorus's Prologue to Act III:

Thus with imagin'd wing our swift scene flies,
In motion of no less celerity
Than that of thought. *Suppose that you have seen*
The well-appointed King at Hampton pier
Embark his royalty; and his brave fleet
With silken streamers the young Phoebus fanning.
Play with your fancies; and in them behold
Upon the hempen tackle ship-boys climbing;
Hear the shrill whistle which doth order give
To sounds confused; *behold* the threaden sails,
Borne with th' invisible and creeping wind,
Draw the huge bottoms through the furrowed sea,
Breasting the lofty surge. *O, do but think*
You stand upon the rivage and behold
A city on th' inconstant billows dancing;
For so appears this fleet majestical,
Holding due course to Harfleur. *Follow, follow!*
Grapple your minds to sternage of this navy
And leave your England as dead midnight still,
Guarded with grandsires, babies, and old women,
Either past or not arriv'd to pith and puissance;
For who is he whose chin is but enrich'd
With one appearing hair that will not follow
These cull'd and choice-drawn cavaliers to France?
Work, work your thoughts, and therein *see* a siege;
Behold the ordnance on their carriages,
With fatal mouth gaping on girded Harfleur.
Suppose th' ambassador from the French comes back;
Tells Harry that the King doth offer him
Katharine his daughter, and with her to dowry
Some petty and unprofitable dukedoms.
The offer likes not; and the nimble gunner
With linstock now the devilish cannon touches,
                    [Alarum, and chambers go off.]
And down goes all before them. Still be kind,
And *eke out our performance with your mind.*
                                        [Exit.]
                                  (III, ll. 1–35)

Imperatives, such as those that I've emphasized above, are implicit in every genre of verbal poiesis. Every drama conceals the command "Suppose that this stage is such-and-such a place and this actor such-and-such a character," but since its conventional code includes such commands, drama has rarely needed to be so self-referential. Written fiction and poetry also conceal imperatives (imaginal rather than perceptual), imperatives of the same diegetic order as those in the above passage, but they seldom appear in writing, that is, in texts written to be read to oneself, because literary competence assumes them. Generally, it is only when the boundaries of verbal visuality types are breached, as in *Henry V,* that such commands are overtly stated.

My last example of oral diegesis is not actually the public performance of a telling, but a representation of it in writing. I include it here because it vividly exemplifies the oral-diegetic situation as it approaches its boundary with the literate situation.

In Joseph Conrad's *Heart of Darkness* an invisible, self-effacing narrator frames a narration delivered by the old seaman Marlow. In the very center of his "yarn" Marlow stops and realizes that at one point in his African quest for the enigmatical Mr. Kurtz he had only the evidence of others to go on, had even let himself be fictionalized by these narrators, and had come to exist in a thick atmosphere of lies and half-truths. And Kurtz?

"He was just a word for me. I did not see the man in the name any more than you do. Do you see him? Do you see the story? Do you see anything? It seems to me I am trying to tell a dream—making a vain attempt, because no relation of a dream can convey the dream sensation, that commingling of absurdity, surprise, and bewilderment in a tremor of struggling revolt, that notion of being captured by the incredible which is the very essence of dreams. . . ."

He was silent for awhile. (Conrad, 82)

The narrativized narrator is struck by the difficulty of his task, which in this case is understood as the conveyance of an experiential message, a message from his past to his present, a present that he now shares with his four old friends on board a cruising yawl riding at anchor in the Thames estuary. He continues:

"No, it is impossible; it is impossible to convey the life-sensation of any given epoch of one's existence—that which makes its truth, its meaning—its subtle and penetrating essence. It is impossible. We live, as we dream—alone. . . ."

He paused again as if reflecting, then added—

"Of course in this you fellows see more than I could then. You see me, whom you know. . . ."

It had become so pitch dark that we listeners could hardly see one another. For a long time already he, sitting apart, had been no more to us than a voice. There was not a word from anybody. The others might have been asleep, but I was awake. I listened, I listened on the watch for the sentence, the word, that would give me the clew to the faint uneasiness inspired by the narrative that seemed to shape itself without human lips in the heavy night-air of the river. (82–83)

The visual image of the diegetic messenger, his perceptual presence, now as the darkness advances, has begun to vanish into the message (cf. the radio broadcast of a monologue). He is an invisible voice and his narrative seems to "shape itself without human lips." This place of darkness and speech that Conrad describes is the very edge of orality, the point at which the teller disappears into the tale and, like Echo, diminishes into mere voice—a voice that, as Hillis Miller asserts, is "spoken by no one to no one" ("*Heart of Darkness* Revisited" 219). Beyond this point in our typology of verbal visuality lies only the silent, repeatable text.

Literacy

Discussions of orality and literacy inevitably take an historicist turn. It is therefore important that, while acknowledging the developmental aspects of our topic as it pertains to verbal visuality, we not reduce it to a simple succession of epochs. Mimetic and diegetic orality are equally ancient, and writing, for that matter, has been in use for millennia. Oral forms of artistic expression did not begin to wither away in the second millennium BC with the invention of alphabetic script or in the second millennium AD with the invention of movable type. We find cultural clashes associated with different modes of information storage and retrieval, but we also note remarkable evidence of ongoing synergy and assimilation.

For one thing, writing as a mnemonic aid facilitated the oral performance of plays and recitations and helped them spread from community to community. The oral compositions, for their part, provided writing with its earliest genres as well as its structures and themes. Literary epics, odes, pastorals, closet dramas, satires, philosophical dialogs—all these classical and neo-classical genres carried over into writing the unmistakable traces of both oral structure and oral performance. The formal and formulary structures of classicist poetry are clearly derived from oral mnemonics. The so-called impersonality of tone is similarly derived, because mnemonically stored poetry is modified by a collective process of performative recomposition that is more editorial than authorial. The classicist restraint in respect to imagery at first poses a problem: if verbal imagery is a mnemonic enhancement, and ample evidence, ancient and modern, affirms that it is, why did not the oral models of early classicism revel in imaginative play? Why, to be specific, does Homer, the very font of Western classicism, give us epithets instead of full descriptions of his heroes and heroines? What I have already proposed concerning visuality in oral performance would suggest that mental imaging is inhibited by the perceptual overload of the performance-situation and that, while it tolerates much more imagery than the mimetic, the diegetic performance places its own constraints upon descriptive referentiality. Rhapsodes, the "song-stitchers" of ancient Greece, having had to tailor their texts to the attention of their auditors, must have known that the imaginal representation of human action and speech "worked," while the description of appearances, removed from action, soon palled. Descriptions of men and women in action abound in Homer but static appearances, when they are described, are kept to a minimum. Even the famous shield of Achilles passage, though it is an ekphrasis, is a description of iconic representations portrayed *in action*.

Western writing in its Hellenistic cradle was nurtured in the diegetic conventions of public speech. For centuries the prestigious tradition of political and forensic oratory and, later, Christian preaching exerted a powerful constraint on the verbal visuality of this medium. Classicism may have aspired to a depersonalized, but not to a voiceless, ideal. The implied presence of a speaker remained, either as that of a single narrator of diegesis, of multiple dialogists of dramatic mimesis, or of a combination of the two in which a narrator frames a dialogic exchange. Aristotle in the *Rhetoric* spoke of this as the "agonistic" style, as distinguished from the "graphic," that is, written, style; to the extent that classical genres retain the agonistic style, even when they are written to be read, they reproduce the relatively low imaginal visuality of oral discourse.

There are two technical factors that also slowed the full literate revolution and with it the rise of the postclassical imagination. One pertained to the writing surface, the other to the writing itself.

For two millennia the writing surface in the eastern Mediterranean centers of literacy had been the long, continuous sheet of papyrus rolled on a spindle. When a roll was thirty feet long, as some were, it was very inconvenient to skip about in a text. Since it was easier to "scroll down" it, as we might say in computerese, the papyrus roll reenforced the speech-like sequentiality of writing. Not until parchment made paginated books (*codices*) possible were readers able to flip back and forth quickly from one passage to another. This may have influenced writers to compose collections of shorter works (odes, elegies, epyllia, and eclogues) and longer works encrusted with brilliant set pieces.

The other factor that inhibited the verbally cued mental imagery that one might have expected from this medium was the physical writing itself. Written texts were *hand*written and, while some publishers could produce copies that were orthographically quite uniform, even these displayed some scribal stylization. "Style," after all, originally meant penmanship. Handwriting seemed to require hand*reading*, if we may judge by the medieval depictions of readers who often place their hand upon a passage as though holding it in place or picking it out (*legere* in Latin and *lesen* in German mean both "to read" and to "pick out"). The chirographic text could function as a visible surrogate for the erstwhile visible speaker and, as percept, could, to some extent at least, occlude the mental image. There is, furthermore, I suspect, an inverse relationship between manuscript illumination and verbal imagery. For these reasons, it would follow that the literary imagination could not become fully emancipated until graphic symbols became clear and uniform, that is, with the technology of movable type, and when illustration was reduced to a minimum.

Print, literacy, and imagination do indeed seem related developments. Writing is visually mediated language, but it need not be visually obstructive. By decreasing the need for overt phonetic articulation (a kinesic back-up procedure of word recognition) uniform typography increased the speed of reading. This speed, which allowed a reader to organize mentally a detailed structure of referents, also enhanced the mental imagery that print could prompt.

The New Universe of Imaginal Discourse

With literacy came the possibility of storing information not simply more than, but different from, that possible in an oral or orally dominated culture. This new information was largely descriptive—how things looked and worked. But when description is defined as a writing *down*, a sort of taking of dictation from a visual array, it presumes an equivalence of language to percept. This presumption, however, ignores the fact that such equivalence is culturally determined and that the discourse of a community defines the environment with which that community is engaged.[4] Whether writing created the new descriptive insights it recorded or recorded existing or hitherto inchoate apperceptions of the world, it made possible an ever-expanding storage system for them. Every new act of description was simultaneously also an act of *in*scription, a writing *upon* a heretofore uncoded field of objects. The universe of literate discourse, once language could be entrusted with the task of prompting visualization, could expand to the limits of visual experience and beyond that to spheres of visionary conception.

In thematic terms this literate revolution heralded a new domestication of nature. As late paleolithic and neolithic peoples began to live with animals as herders, rather than as hunters, and as they began to plant vegetables, instead of foraging for them, a new sense of space came into being, the stabilized human community as a central point of reference, a hub, for the surrounding non-human, but humanly coded, landscape. The centralized intramural community was the domain of the oral chronicler, the bard of kings and heroes, the singer of praise songs and epics. The extramural poetry and proverbial wisdom of herders and tillers persisted—there is no doubt about this—but, unsupported by the resources available to the town and to its rulers, these compositions had much less chance for mnemonic survival and oral augmentation. Oral transmission of relatively fixed texts presupposes professional memorizers and performers and the social institutions that can support such a class. Scattered marginal settlements, I am suggesting, would find it difficult to maintain such a division of labor. Writing could preserve this hinterland discourse, but literacy was rarely vouchsafed the country folk. Pastoral and georgic compositions have therefore always been transcribed, edited, and indeed composed by city-dwellers. As Raymond Williams has pointed out, the country has received its textualized definition from the town. By so doing, literature expanded its universe of discourse and its verbal visuality.

Pastoral, as a uniquely literate genre, permitted readers to enter, through writing, the unlettered oral world of shepherds whose alternate (*amoebean*) verses were as agonistic as any orator's, but had as their underlying themes the facts of existence that talking about does little to change. Theocritus, Moschus, Bion, and later Vergil took these themes—the weariness of work, the pleasures of rest, the longing for love, and the sorrows of betrayal and bereavement—and placed them in a spatially expanded hinterland that literacy had now for the first time made imaginable. To look through the eyes of shepherds is to visualize mountains and beyond them more mountains and somewhere beyond them the blue level of the sea. This was not the close quarters of a king's palace, a corner of a battleground, a warrior's tent, or a lover's chamber. Like empire, the literate imagination was provoked by a distant horizon.

The prose romance *Daphnis and Chloe,* written toward the end of the second century AD and attributed to Longus, had inherited this tradition of sophisticated pastoralism. At the beginning of the fourth and final book appears a passage that epitomizes the new visuality that the "written style" (*lexis graphikē*) took delight in exhibiting. The scene described is a garden in the summer estate of a certain gentleman of Mytilene, the principal city of Lesbos. It was a princely park, two hundred by three hundred yards, and filled with all manner of ornamental and fruit trees.

This garden had been geometrically landscaped, the trees having been placed at precise intervals, but overhead allowed to weave and interweave their boughs and foliage: the whole impression was of a natural wildness springing up from careful art. There were also beds of different flowers, some wild and others planted. The cultivated ones included roses, hyacinths, and lilies; the wild ones were violets, narcissus, and pimpernels. In spring there were flowers, in summer shade, in autumn fruit, and for every moment some unique delight. (120)

Here was an aesthetic that maintained a continuum between the controlled and the wild, cultivating what Horace had called a *curiosa felicitas*—Horace, whose own world had stretched in a line from the palace of Augustus to his farmhouse in the Sabine Hills.

The literature of the Greco-Roman era, of which *Daphnis and Chloe* is an apt example, had introduced an imagery of spatial depth that coincided with an interest in pictorial perspective. Note now how Longus, continuing his description of the garden, directs the mind's eye of the reader outward and then draws it back.

Up there one had a fine view of the coastal plain with its separate herds of grazing animals and, beyond that, the sea and the ships that moved across it. This garden-park was so planned that what one viewed beyond it became part of what one enjoyed within it. (120)

Here in this glimpsed vista, commanded from above by a privileged viewer, the reader possesses a pictorialized world, a landscape of passive space not thrust toward us by human action or human speech, but conveyed by the silent written word alone. Human commerce is itself a mere detail in a seascape.

In Longus's written tale there is also a considerable amount of oral coding that is thematized. Not only do the unlettered characters amuse one another by telling myths but, according to Pan, who intervenes when Chloe is abducted, no less an author than Eros has composed the plot (the *mythos*) and cannot go on with the story without her. The transmission of this tale is also worth noting: the plot was engineered by a mythic personage, Eros, became a local folk tale, was pictorially coded as a mural in a shrine of the Nymphs in Lesbos, was viewed by Longus, was re-oralized by a local guide, and then finally recoded in writing. The relation of pictorial to oral media was intimate and the conversion from one to the other easy and "natural." But the final act of literate encoding, Longus's writing, took all that preliterate history of transmissions as a mere prelude or, less than that, a mere point of departure, an occasion to exercise the new literate imagination and to explore a newly inscribed universe.

It is interesting that the garden described in the fourth book that links the imaging reader to the pastoral slopes and the distant sea has at its precise center another shrine, another repository of oral lore. Dedicated to Dionysos, its walls are covered with depictions of his exploits and images of that other divinity of wilderness, Pan, whom allegorizing mythologists had come to regard as the Earth-Spirit, the "All." This central shrine is emblematic of the *ancien régime* of orality with its enclosed myths and icons, about which it governs a domesticated nature that writing now reveals, extends, and incorporates in an ideal continuum.

A "world view" seems to be a compilation of propositions that generate a more or less coherent image of humankind's place in the cosmos. My assumption has been that the manner in which such propositions are communicated has in the past determined the fundamental structure of these models. Every oral world view has had the severe limitations of particularism, since it is centered in a communal space no broader across than a speaker's voice could carry. This Center, governed by human agreement, is bonded by vocal presence and maintained generation after generation by oral mimesis and diegesis. Larger settlements would need to designate a special place of assembly, an *agora*, temple, church, and so on; in an amphictyony it would be located centrally. But, in lieu of a single omphalic hub, the center of the oral world existed wherever an authoritative voice was raised and accepted as such by any grouping of underlings. Beyond the oralized Center lay the Hinterland, a less populated fringe where agriculture and herding was carried on and where oral authority was less coercive. In the Hinterland lived a species of humanity that the Center regarded as autochthonous and aboriginal, lawless as Cyclopes, bestial—yet canny—as Centaurs and Satyrs. Their contact with the Center was to bring in their goods on market days and then shamble back to their hovels and lairs by nightfall. In the caste system that oral societies always elaborate only the central community that was ranged about its godlike ruler was truly human, while the toilers of the Hinterland were half assimilated to the soil and the herds. Beyond the Hinterland lay the barbarous Outland, where people babbled like birds or howled like dogs, where strange gods ruled and monsters awaited the reckless wayfarer.

Literacy shrank the perceived world in order to expand the imagined world. Orality had permitted a central communicative space that might be perceived as a hundred meters across, but literacy narrowed its perceptual space to one quarter meter—the distance between the page and the reader's eye. Yet as a means to prompt mental imagery, literacy made an immeasurably vaster world conceivable and eventually perceivable as well. Writing places the solitary reader at the center of the world that he or she imagines and, by imagination, seems to oversee. Since writing is virtually non-interferent with mental imaging, it becomes a means by which the oral multiverse can be imaginally cosmicized. Perhaps equally important, it becomes the means by which the literate imager, whose consciousness pervades this world, can become *micro*cosmicized. As reading becomes the privileged mode of information transfer, each reader assimilates *by analogy* the morphology of the older oral world, and the oral topology becomes the literate psychology: consciousness becomes the ruling Center; the body becomes the Hinterland, sometimes divided into animal and vegetative processes, emotive provinces always restive, if not rebellious; and the ineradicable darkness within—variously identified as Original Sin, the irrational, and the unconscious, becomes the new Outland of alien beings.

For one to step beyond the closed space created and preserved by orality and enter the space defined by writing was thus to enter an unrestricted worldscape, a Hinterland of emotive "children of Nature" and an Outland now humanly inscribed, albeit demonized by racism. The outer darkness now was illumined, having been drawn into a dualism with human consciousness as object to subject and matter to mind. All things perceptible were declared intelligible, if not to the mind of mortals, then to the mind of God, and if not to the mind of mortals *now*, then at some future time or through some special grace or gnosis. Writing, having increased information and accelerated its exchange, proved to be a medium by which a new professional elite could wield power. Since intelligence can mean potential dominion over the intelligible, writing generated a politicized image of the universe in which cosmic power was identified with omniscient intelligence.

As writing became the basis upon which universal states were built, written imagery became an available substitute for culturally significant perceptual representation. Sacred icons, buildings, landscapes, and rituals became portable when written and *by the same means new ones could be created*. Part of the process that Joseph Campbell called "creative mythology" was the work undertaken by literary artists. But "work" is a misleading noun: "play" is more accurate, since literate poiesis, strenuous as it can be, is premised on the "as-if" principles of play: "suppose we say that, when we read this, we imagine we are in place A in the presence of person B" or "suppose that, for this moment only, term C means term D." This verbal algebra, this play of hypothesis, could be best performed in a literate situation for two reasons: (1) the solitary reader could not be detected entertaining what from the oralist point of view might seem a dangerously free conjecture and (2) this novel formulation could be read and reread at any speed and could thus become an object of serious speculative play.

Image as Trope

Any system of rhetorical devices developed first for public speech would necessarily have to be altered somewhat to account for effects produced by writing. The disparity between oral and written media may help account for the notorious fuzziness with which such classical rhetoricians as Cicero and Quintilian classified "figures." "Figures of speech," such as anaphora, antithesis, and isocolon, are patterns woven indeed out of the linear syntax of *speech*, that is, out of oral discourse. "Figures of thought," such as metaphor, metonymy, synecdoche, and irony, while they are also important devices in oral discourse, are more foregrounded in writing than in speech. The first three on this list of figures of thought, moreover, are "figures" in a different sense from that of figures of speech: they bring to mind *imaginal* figures. The close relation between literacy and mental imagery had this predictable result for rhetoric and stylistics: whenever literate discourse became viably independent of the oral situation, figures of thought, or "tropes," would increase, while figures of speech would decrease.

I have already suggested as another cultural inducement to the rise of these tropes, particularly of metaphor, metonymy, and synecdoche, the typically literate project to define a relationship with an unknown Other. Writing, which had stored this surplus of information, was now obliged to find some taxonomic principle by which to sort it out. Analogical thinking had already posited that the world was a totality: now resemblance, derivation, and causality seemed useful principles by which this vast compendium of Otherness might be officially registered in the literate nomenclature and conceptually dominated. When, for example, a new species of animal or plant was discovered, it could be named by iconic analogy (metaphor) or by indexical contiguity or habitat (metonymy). "Hippopotamus" combines both: it was iconically likened to a horse and indexically associated with rivers. Synecdoche was resorted to in nomenclature when a particular part of the whole was deemed noteworthy, for example, "bloodroot" and "two-toed sloth." The second part of the latter name is metaphorical but, unlike the relation of "horse" to "hippopotamus," this association is that of an abstraction with a concrete referent.

After the hippopotamus was named, there remained of course the question of *why* the hippopotamus. Religion, philosophy, and natural science had their own particular starting points and methods, but the common quest to find meaning in Nature implied an effort to find evidence of purposefulness in the universe beyond the human community. This was a semiotic and hermeneutic quest, a quest to identify phenomena as signs and then to interpret them properly. There certainly were abundant data in natural happenings that could indicate the character and intentions of powerful forces at work over long stretches of time. Besides these indexical signs that could be seen everywhere, evidence of divine wrath or benevolence, there were signs that were not so much effects as representations—natural forms similar to those experienced in dreams, percepts that looked like, sounded like, or otherwise resembled other things and concepts—iconic signs charged with ulterior meanings. Finally there were symbolic signs (language). Animals could be managed by indices, people could be awed by iconic displays, but only one's associates were worth exchanging speech with. Scriptural religions preserved what they asseverated were oral communications from god(s) and, appealing to this most human of all semiotic means, projected Culture upon Nature.

In his commentary on the Book of Genesis (*De Genesi ad Litteram*, 12.23–27) Augustine presents an interesting illustration of these tendencies. Here he uses Scripture to distinguish kinds of *visiones* (extraordinary manifestations of God to humans). He finds only three: "corporeal," "spiritual," and "intellectual." Corporeal *visiones* are sensory events—signs such as the skeptical required of Jesus—that are ordinarily subject to misinterpretation. The example Augustine chooses is from Exodus:

And Mount Sinai was altogether on a smoke, because the Lord descended upon it in a fire: and the smoke thereof ascended as the smoke in a furnace, and the whole mount quaked greatly. (Exodus 19:18, King James Version)

This example of theophany Augustine calls a *visio corporalis*, a sign that in Peircean semiotics corresponds to an index.

God communicates a spiritual *visio* in quite a different way. The images of dreams or of other altered states are privately received mental representations that are assumed to carry coded significance. At the first stage of interpretation a recipient must treat this imagined entity as an iconic sign and decide what it resembles. Only subsequently can he or she place this apparition in context and question its import. The examples Augustine presents are the entire Book of Revelation and the first verse of Isaiah, chapter 6: "In the year king Uzziah died I saw also the Lord sitting upon a throne, high and lifted up, and his train filled the temple." An iconic sign like this may or may not be "from God." The prevailing view of the mind, moreover, was that the human *spirit* was a substance in which the fallible senses exchanged information with the potentially pure *intellect*. It was, in effect, the locus of metaphor. As spirit, it could be illuminated by the Holy Spirit, but it could also be deceived by those myriad disembodied but carnally minded spirits swarming in the air, intent on deluding the unvigilant.

The fifth century of the Church was evidently no time to encourage private spiritualism; instead, Augustine recommended a spiritualism of scriptural interpretation, though only when a literal reading could not be reconciled with the mandates of charity.[5]

Though the spiritual *visio* is higher than the corporeal, the intellectual *visio* is supreme. The example Augustine chooses is from the twelfth chapter of the Book of Numbers. Miriam and Aaron have criticized Moses' marriage to an Ethiopian and God rebukes them verbally in the Tabernacle but in a corporeal *visio*, a pillar of cloud:

And he said, Hear now my words: If there be a prophet among you, I the Lord will make myself known unto him in a vision, and will speak to him in a dream [a spiritual *visio*]. My servant Moses is not so, who is faithful to my house. With him I speak mouth to mouth, even apparently [an intellectual *visio*]; and not in dark speeches; and the similitude of the Lord shall he behold. (Numbers 12:6–8)

As this passage indicates, the highest, least equivocal form of visuality is that least dependent on the visual. It is oral discourse and, in the imperative mood of legal statute, it is strictly categorical, as were Yahweh's first words to Adam in that first garden (Genesis 2:16). It is a *visio* only insofar as Yahweh allowed himself to appear in some perceptible form—whatever "mouth to mouth" or "face to face" might mean—while delivering oral speech. (For a more detailed discussion of oral presence, see my *Reading the Written Image*, chapters 1–3.)

Augustine's treatment of visual signs reveals some interesting characteristics of late classical literacy: (1) a hierarchical structure of consciousness in which each level has its own access to signs; (2) a similar ranking of signs according to their dignity as vehicles of God's meaning; (3) an attempt to use writing (Scripture and Scriptural interpretation) to reinstate the authority of oral presence; and (4) the outlines of a divine semiotics of tropes.

Oral poets had always used the elegantly extensible tropes of simile and the condensed tropes of epithet and kenning, but these, the condensed kind especially, tended to be formulaic and as such served to describe a world of stable forces in recurrent activity. Oral texts were produced, stored, and transmitted by persons who could trust that their *breosthord* matched the *wordhord* of their community, which in turn constituted a complete inventory of the universe. Writing, whenever it arrived in a traditional culture, honored oral poetry by graphically recoding its most prominent texts, an act of veneration that preserved them and at the same time ensured that their means of production would eventually become obsolete.

Writing was no longer dependent on such mnemonic devices as formulaic words and phrases. But the tropical innovation associated with writing may well have been fueled by factors other than a mere delight in newfangled conceits. It was, I would suggest, a means of organizing an embarrassment of riches revealed in and stored by writing. The impact of the unfamiliar upon a traditional oral culture tends to stretch its linguistic resources and, as soon as writing is a practical option, leads to intensified experimentation in tropology. Through this means an unfamiliar entity—plant, animal, tool, ethical value, psychological phenomenon, and so on—is drawn into the episteme by relation to a familiar term. Perhaps some common property is asserted that associates these two items despite their other differences: thereupon a metaphor (including simile and personification) is formulated. Or perhaps some object, such as a tool, accoutrement, garment, dwelling, or anything that bears the trace of having been touched or altered by some other entity is made to indicate that other entity: thus a metonymic image comes into being. (Metonymy, it should be noted, has come to include synecdoche, the use of a part or a sampling to stand for the totality from which it is excerpted.)

Tropical neologisms were required to name newly discovered natural phenomena and newly invented mechanical devices, but what about newly emergent *human* concepts and values? Did the mixed metaphors of Elizabethan dramatists and the metaphysical conceits of seventeenth-century poets correspond to preexistent ideas that until then had remained unspoken? Jacques Derrida in his "White Mythology" would say "no." In his critique of Pierre Fontanier, he characterizes the eighteenth-century rhetorician as believing that new concepts "could not have been tracked down, brought to daylight without the force of a twisting which goes *against usage,* without the infraction of a catachresis. This latter does not emerge from language, does not create new signs, does not enrich the code; and yet it transforms its functioning, producing, with the same material, new rules of exchange, new values" (257). Did catachresis reveal the "already-there" of a value or create it *ex nihilo*? Derrida appears to favor the latter. But between these extremes there lies the possibility that a new human value may have a preexistence in the form of fragmentary elements that a successful catachresis welds into a single concept.

The "light of reason" and the "two-toed sloth" may be quite different linguistic creatures, but they are specimens that writing captured with equal ease. It spurred the use of tropes and tropically formulated names because it could, far better than orality, store catachrestic images. But this surge of tropological invention that characterizes the

European renaissance of writing could not have been simply a response of writers to a leisured public enticed by vicarious views of a brave new world. The necessity that mothered this invention was, as I have suggested, the staggering mass of information that writing had itself amassed.

Chapter 2
Science on the Nature of Imagination

The visible world is obviously the ultimate source of verbal images. The significance assigned this world and the manner by which this world is believed to signify are therefore of utmost importance to any study of mental images and of the cultural products of verbal visuality. If the visible function of this world is believed to give glory to God, then its significance as a visual array may stand, as some reasoned, in iconic relation to a transcendent, absolute Being and realm: it reflects even in its smallest formal detail, albeit finitely, the attributes of power, duration, and magnitude of its maker. According to the iconism of the "Doctrine of Correspondences" specific plants and animals bore "signatures" that the astute could read. Even the seemingly random manner in which phenomena arranged themselves to the eye was meaningful to those with the grace to decipher it. As dreams were to Joseph and Daniel, so was nature to the spiritually minded poet—minutely metaphorical and wholly allegorical.

It was also possible for objects to perform indexical, as well as iconic, sign functions. As natural pointers supernaturally directed from nature to God, omens were indices of divine judgments and intentions and, as supernatural interventions into nature by the God of History, they had a more immediately predictive function than natural iconic representations. But there were other events, less cataclysmic, but nonetheless important to predict, that were also preceded by indexical signs. Fire, air, water, and earth, the "four elements," each had its ways of transforming substances and itself, ways that could be learned and controlled once their indexical signs were known. These signs accompanied the cause-and-effect behavior of contingent beings in "this world." In rhetorical terms, this renewed interest in the connectedness of natural phenomena led to an increased use of metonymy (including synecdoche).

Verbal poiesis, the art of making miniature worlds out of words, liberally played with all the possibilities of natural signs, their iconic and indexical relation to supersensual ideas and their wholly indexical relation to the purely sensual web of natural contingencies. Over the past five centuries literary study interpreted its function also in alternately mentalistic and physicalistic terms. In this chapter I will consider some of the influences of natural science on poetics, specifically on the poetics of imagery, and the responses of those who for various reasons denied the applicability of scientific method and scientific models.

The title of this chapter is deliberately peremptory in tone. It is meant to mimic the oracular confidence with which enthusiasts of the "New Philosophy" used to speak of their conclusions. It is sometimes surprising to recall that only a few decades now separate us from the age when persons could enforce an awed silence by beginning a sentence with "As Science teaches . . ." or "As Science has conclusively demonstrated. . . ."

Exorcising the Phantoms of the Night

During compline, the last of the seven canonical hours, ecclesiastics would pray to be preserved from, among other things, the *noctis phantasmata,* the phantoms of the night, the diabolical host that took on terrifying and seductive guises to tempt and torment believers. The belief that infiltrators from the nether realm assaulted Christians in their most defenseless state was unsettling to say the least.

Shakespeare's *A Midsummer Night's Dream* deftly dodged the serious issues of demonically induced mania and hallucination. It is set in mythologically ancient Greece; so, inconveniently Christian issues are not raised. In the place of Christian assurances of providential law and order, the stability of the State is underwritten by the patriarchal rationalism of King Theseus. After the bewildered lovers tell their tale of *noctis phantasmata,* Theseus issues that judicial conclusion that every study of poetic imagination seems obliged to quote. When Hippolyta says, "'Tis strange, my Theseus, that these lovers speak of," the king replies:

> More strange than true. I never may believe
> These antique fables, nor these fairy toys.
> Lovers and madmen have such seething brains,
> Such shaping fantasies, that apprehend
> More than cool reason ever comprehends.
> The lunatic, the lover and the poet,
> Are of imagination all compact.
> One sees more devils than all hell can hold;

That is the madman. The lover, all as frantic,
Sees Helen's beauty in a brow of Egypt.
The poet's eye in a fine frenzy rolling,
Doth glance from heaven to earth, from earth to heaven;
And as imagination bodies forth
The forms of things unknown, the poet's pen
Turns them to shapes, and gives to airy nothing
A local habitation and a name.
Such tricks hath strong imagination
That, if it would but apprehend some joy,
It comprehends some bringer of that joy;
Or in the night, imagining some fear,
How easy is a bush suppos'd a bear!

(V. 1., ll. 2–22)

Theseus regards imagination as a chronic medical condition that can in some persons erupt into an acute "seething" of the brain. And yet . . . and yet the audience did see fairies and their transformations. Theseus was no less the stuff that midsummer nights' dreams are made on than Puck or Oberon or Mustardseed. Despite the laughter at the final play-within-the-play, a troubling sense of ambiguity lingers concerning the nature, or supernature, of imagination. Some bushes may really be bears after all. If so, may not some really be bugbears?

Shakespeare's psychic forest of fairies notwithstanding, the new cosmological model that Copernicus introduced and Newton completed left scant room for elementals. Nimble as they were, the creatures of faery seemed to need as foils the solidity of earth and the stolidity of earthlings. Now that an unmoored earth had joined the other planetary orbs in the play of celestial mechanics and astronomers, not conjurors, now braved the noxious air of midnight, the drama of cosmic good and evil seemed diminished in magnitude. That every planetary movement was lawful and had been so since the fourth day of Creation failed to console more traditional Christians. Giordano Bruno was the messenger who brought the bad news when at the close of the sixteenth century he reintroduced the ideas of atomism and of an infinite universe. Copernicanism and the new physics had for John Donne cast one funerary pall too many over a universe already spoilt by sin and mortality. In 1611, one year after Galileo, having sighted the first four moons of Jupiter and the phases of Venus, confirmed the heliocentric theory, Donne wrote how the

. . . new Philosophy calls all in doubt
The Element of fire is quite put out;

> The Sun is lost, and th'earth, and no man's wit
> Can well direct him where to look for it.
> And freely men confesse that this world's spent,
> When in the Planets, and the Firmament
> They seeke so many new; then see that this
> Is crumbled out again to his Atomies.
> 'Tis all in peeces, all cohaerence gone.
> ("An Anatomie of the World" 205–213)

Milton, whose only reference to contemporary events in *Paradise Lost* was to Galileo, does with his usual cosmological discretion include a region for the "Atomies" to collide: it is the realm of Chaos, the "anarch old," and it is situated between Hell and the spherical Ptolemaic Creation.

As we know, many in the political and ecclesiastical establishment joined the majority of the uninformed in condemning these new ideas. The trial and condemnation of Galileo effectively stifled scientific thought in Catholic Europe for nearly a century during which the Protestant North fostered a high level of cosmological and philosophical speculation, provided only that these inquiries did not disturb public morality or personal privilege or directly contradict the demonology that firmly remained a tenet of scriptural Christianity. In a state of such ambiguity, when orthodox religion confidently asserted the reality of diabolical nightstalkers, rationalistic tracts that served to demystify imagery would be welcome reading to many. Many would be willing to trade in the excitement of witch persecutions and the piety of spiritual visions for the simpler pleasures of a good night's sleep.

The rite of exorcism was performed by English philosophers. While Oliver Cromwell's army was cleansing the British Isles of the visual representations of mental images, Thomas Hobbes was purging the imagination itself. "*Imagination*," he declared, ". . . is nothing but *decaying sense*" (*Leviathan*, I, 2). A mental image is a sort of long-term afterimage, as we might call it now. He went on to add that, when its decay has made it fade, it becomes what we know as a "memory." For Locke, images were merely the necessary concomitant of ideas and for Hume these image-conveyed ideas were deftly connected by the laws of association, a system that David Hartley developed in greater detail. Just as the new physics cleared the universe of planetary angels, subterranean devils, and all the intermediary beings that swarmed over land and sea and air, the new epistemology by the mid-eighteenth century purged the microcosm of most of its imaginal sprites and familiars.

The Microcosmology of Associationism

The new theory of the mind was derived by analogy from the new physics. The "movements" of thoughts were like the behavior of bodies in space. The gravitational laws of attraction, when they were promulgated, were assumed to be appropriate models for the laws of mental association. The new open universe of uniform physical law that Isaac Newton had revealed presented itself as the paradigm of the human mind, similarly infinite, lawful, and intelligible. John Locke, a friend of Newton, referred to himself as an "under laborer" of the scientist. David Hume in the *Treatise of Human Nature* (1739–40) announced "an attempt to introduce the experimental [i.e., Newtonian] method of reasoning into moral subjects" and declared to have found within the universe of the mind a "kind of *attraction*" that corresponded to the law of gravity (I, 1.4). Philosophers throughout the eighteenth century strove to locate within the mind this principle of coherence that would restore to the suddenly demystified world of the Enlightenment the harmony of microcosm and macrocosm, that old iconic ideal.

But here a problem intervened. If the mind were truly microcosmic, it would be expected to display in its most exalted creations the laws of the Deity's Creation. Literary texts but rarely mirrored the calm, august power of the Newtonian cosmos and when poets consciously attempted to do so, the results were often only nobly dull. While it is true, as Thomas Kuhn points out (260), the full import of gravitation was not widely appreciated before the mid-eighteenth century, later texts continued to display an associational structure that produced in the mind of the reader a species of billiard-ball chain reactions, which however could be traced only in a unilinear sequence one idea at a time.

The classical work that inaugurated and continued to inspire this speculation was Aristotle's *De Memoria*, particularly the passage 451a–453b. Here the notion of a recollective sequence is introduced: it takes time to remember some things because we must pass through a series of related mental images to find the one we want. Perhaps influenced, himself, by the mnemonic techniques of Simonides (the "mental walk" past specifically designated *topoi*, 452a), Aristotle regards recollection (*anamnesis*) as the finding of a bidirectional sequence of associations, a sort of Ariadne's thread of ideas within the labyrinth of memory. Ideas assume their position in this sequence either by necessity (*anangkē*) or convention (*ethos*). The sequentiality of association and the evident effort sometimes involved in recollection led Aristotle to conclude that this process is a "kind of search" (453a) and that the mind is a quasi-spatial entity that accommodates ideas (452b).

Students of mnemonics have always understood the usefulness of association, particularly the association of unfamiliar, abstract concepts with familiar, concrete objects and locations. This mnemotechnic was a very deliberate practice. But what about the function of association in ordinary mental activity—in crotchets, prejudices, and *idées fixes*? In an age convinced that the sun of Reason had finally been restored to its cosmic center, but still acutely aware of the dangers of sectarian fanaticism, philosophers were at first more concerned with the eccentrically orbiting meteors and exhalations of the inner universe, than with its more logically concentered ideas.

Thomas Hobbes is an Aristotelian when he launches his discussion of imagination from this deductive principle:

> When a body is once in motion, it moveth, unless something else hinder it, eternally; and what soever hindereth it cannot in an instant, but in time and by degrees quite extinguish it; and as we see in the water, though the winds cease, the waves give not over rolling for a long time after, so it happeneth in that motion which is made in the internal parts of a man, then, when he sees, dreams, etc. (*Leviathan*, I, 2)

Inertial force, therefore, maintains the sensory image, and the density of the interaural medium presumably accounts for its gradual decay. When in the next chapter Hobbes takes up the question of thought in terms of "Consequence or Train of Imaginations," he reasons again from Aristotelian principles:

> ... all fancies are motions within us, relics of those made in the sense; and those motions that immediately succeeded one another in the sense continue also together after sense.

A "train of thoughts, or mental discourse," is either "unguided" or "regulated." Unguided mental discourse is typified by reverie. "And yet in this wild ranging of the mind, a man may ofttimes perceive the way of it and the dependence of one thought upon another." As for regulated thoughts, these are linked by the principle of causality: we imagine an effect and link it to a probable cause or we imagine a potential cause and link it to "all the possible effects that can by it be produced, that is to say, we imagine what we can do with it when we have it" (*Leviathan*, I, 3). This associational activity Hobbes identifies with "seeking or the faculty of invention."

Like all pioneering thinkers, Hobbes (and Bacon, too) provoked more questions than they answered. What is the nature of "mental discourse"? Is it linguistic or imaginal or both? What indeed were these thoughts, these fancies, these imaginations? What entities in the mind would correspond to the bodies that populate the infinite space of the outer universe? The next generation of English Empiricists called them "ideas" and regarded them as the irreducible units of thought. Since they believed with Aristotle and Aquinas that mental imagery accompanies all thinking, they called this unit an "idea," which signified shape or likeness. For Locke, such mental shapes accompany both sensation and reflection. In the former case they are simply imprinted on the sensory organ and constitute experience, the primary source of all knowledge. In the latter case they constitute a source of ideas everyone has wholly in oneself: "and though it be not sense, as having nothing to do with external objects, yet it is very like it, and might properly enough be called internal sense" (II, 4). But he quickly redefined this source as "reflection," no doubt because "internal sense" still implied a "sixth sense," a visionary capacity to perceive supernatural beings. Unlike Hobbes, who had defined imagination as "decaying sense," what we might call a long-term afterimage (*Leviathan*, I, 2), Locke recognized its functional importance and began an inquiry into the process by which ideas, that is, mental images, not only accompany thought but, in obedience to inherent laws of their own, actually direct it—that phenomenon that he and the eighteenth century called the "association of ideas."

Locke, who is usually given the credit for renewing the study of mental association, was particularly concerned with the paralogical aspects of this phenomenon. In chapter 33 of Book II of his *Essay Concerning Human Understanding*, entitled "Of the Association of Ideas," he asks what causes unreasonable thinking and prejudices. His answer is: faulty association of ideas formed by chance impressions or by custom, a distinction that echoes Aristotle. His image is of stray, logically unrelated ideas linking up and, "if they are more than two which are thus united, the whole gang, always inseparable, show themselves together" (sec. 5). This mischief, he goes on to say, is the work of the "animal spirits," a curiously medieval concept that derives from the Platonic "lower soul" and the Aristotelian "sensitive soul" and that in modern parlance might be termed the subconscious and the libido.

Poets and critics were quick to appreciate the significance of these developments in the new empirical philosophy. Mental representation was, after all, the very stuff from which poems were created and later recreated in the mind of the reader. As early as 1712 Joseph Addison was already attributing to the association of ideas some of the "pleasures of the imagination." His account, echoing the quaint neurophysiology that Locke also used, is a fine example of Aristotelian mental kinetics:

The set of ideas which we received from such a prospect or garden [that we have experienced in the past], having entered the mind at the same time, having a set of traces belonging to them in the brain, bordering very near upon one another. When therefore, any one of these ideas arises in the imagination [having been prompted by a verbal description of such a garden] and consequently dispatches a flow of animal spirits to its proper trace, these spirits in the violence of their motion, run not only into the trace to which they were more particularly directed, but into several of those that lie about it. By this means they awaken other ideas of the same set, which immediately determine a new dispatch of spirits that in the same manner open other neighboring traces, till at last the whole set of them is blown up and the whole prospect or garden flourishes in the imagination. (*Spectator* 417)

It is highly significant that Addison prefaced these remarks on verbally cued associative imaging by saying that this would be how "a Cartesian would account for" this phenomenon.

This would obviously not be the René Descartes of the systematic doubt or the incontrovertible *cogito*, but Descartes the natural philosopher. His "corpuscular theory," an adaptation of Democritean atomism used to explain the motion of bodies in the new Copernican universe, is summarized by Kuhn as follows:

He began by asking how a single corpuscle would move in the void. Then he asked how this free motion would be altered by collision with a second corpuscle. Since he believed that *all change in the corpuscular universe resulted from a succession of free corpuscular motions punctuated by intercorpuscular collisions,* Descartes expected to deduce the entire structure of the Copernican universe from the answers to a few questions like these. Though all of his deductions were intuitive and though most of them were mistaken, the cosmology that his imagination dictated to his reason proved immensely plausible. Descartes's vision dominated much of science for almost a century after its details were first published in his *Principles of Philosophy* [*Principia Philosophiae*] in 1644. (238; emphasis added)

Later critics took pleasure in demonstrating how texts themselves betrayed evidence of this chain reaction, a process that in literature was energized, more often than not, by the principle of resemblance. Shakespeare's dramatic speeches became favorite demonstration pieces. In an influential work, *An Essay on Genius* (1774), Alexander Gerard applied the principles of association to a passage from *The Tempest* and in 1794 Walter Whiter published *A Specimen of a Commentary on Shakespeare Derived from Mr. Locke's Doctrine of the Association of Ideas*. In his 1815 *Preface* William Wordsworth analyzed stanza 9 of "Resolution and Independence" to show how association determined his description of the old man through the principle of resemblance: to a huge stone, a sea beast, and a cloud.

Imagination, as the notion developed in the seventeenth and eighteenth centuries, was a function of the association of ideas and its fortunes were linked with that psychological phenomenon. When association was implicated in error and excess, the imagination was felt to be mere literary freakishness, the "seething brain" syndrome; when association was linked with mild reverie and humane sentiment, imagination became a pleasing ornament; and when association came to be identified with creativity and genius, imagination became the very Pegasus of the inspired mind. The fortunes of these two terms rode a rising arc similar to that which took the meaning of the word "liberty" from licentiousness to rightful human self-fulfillment.

The "laws" of association were various, but those proposed by David Hume in his *Enquiry Concerning Human Understanding* (1748) were built upon three principles that recur in most systems in one form or another:

To me, there appear to be only three principles of connexion among ideas, namely, *Resemblance, Contiguity* in time or place, and *Cause* or *Effect*.

That these principles serve to connect ideas will not, I believe, be much doubted. A picture naturally leads our thoughts to the original [Resemblance]: the mention of one apartment in a building naturally introduces an enquiry or discourse concerning the others [Contiguity]: and if we think of a wound we can scarcely forbear reflecting on the pain which follows it [Cause and Effect]. (sec. iii, 19)

Hume then allows that others may adduce other additional principles, "Contrast or Contrariety," for example. But this, he says, "may, perhaps, be considered a mixture of *Causation* and *Resemblance*. When two objects are contrary, the one destroys the other" (sec. iii).

The weakness of Hume's resemblance principle is apparent. For one thing, his example, unlike the other examples, is of an association of a percept (a picture) with a mental image. A picture brings to mind what it represents, but does the mental image of a person—for example, a verbally cued mental image—bring to mind another person who resembles her? And to demote contrast to the rank of a secondary principle ignores the fact that, to identify a mental image as resembling B, one has to differentiate it from A and C. The later associationists Dugald Stewart (1753–1828) and Thomas Brown (1778–1820) were to make contrariety one of their three principles. Stewart's and Brown's third principle, nearness in time and place, was meant as another critique of Hume's system. Hume's distinction between contiguity in time and place and causation was properly logical: simply because Chanticleer crows at dawn does not mean he causes the sun to rise. Yet the association of ideas is not immune to the *post hoc ergo propter hoc* fallacy and the universe of the mind was never so reasonable as Newton's cosmos.[1]

Associationism had by the mid-eighteenth century established an important psychological foundation for a modern poetics, but it had not completed its work. Psychology had not yet turned its attention to questions of affect and it would take another century before it began that examination. Literature, inspired by Locke and Newton, however, had its own empirical agenda and would not wait.

Literary Theory Versus Psychology

An element also associated with recollection, wrote Aristotle, is affect (*pathos*): since the original experience of sensation is one of passive reception, the recollection of the event is also accompanied by a similar state of mind (*De Memoria* 451a). Based on the theory that affects are extrinsic forces that "move" us "from" one state to another and that passions are conditions of passivity that we suffer, Aristotle's ascription of "pathos" to recollective sequences may have served to keep an otherwise "cool" cognitive process "warm" in the minds of later enquirers.

The latterday pursuit of the "laws of association" was also to involve questions of feeling. What indeed is the contribution of affect to the workings of reflection? Francis Bacon, who was also concerned with the rules of thought, viewed affect as a mischievous intruder. Since mental imagery is notoriously infected with emotion, he concluded that "not any science . . . doth properly or fitly pertain to the imagination" (*Of the Advancement of Knowledge* 2, xii, 1). The irregular linkages of ideas, which Bacon condemned as "idols of the mind," later philosophers and poets regarded as evidence of "genial" agents. Samuel Taylor Coleridge in his letter to Robert Southey (*Letters* 428, August 7, 1803) spells this out with great conviction:

Association depends in a much greater degree on the recurrence of resembling states of feeling than trains of ideas. . . . I almost think that ideas never recall ideas, any more than leaves in a forest create each other's motion. The breeze it is runs thro' them—it is the soul or state of feeling.[2]

Eventually, powerful feelings became the hallmark of true creative activity. Whereas a century before they had been identified with the religious excesses of bigotry, fanaticism, and private revelation ("enthusiasm"), they now were identified with an inner spiritual knowledge, a revival of Neo-Platonic nativism, christened Transcendentalism, and with a new outwardly directed sense of fellow-feeling, a revival of Christian charity, known as sympathy. This latter concept was based on the belief that the heart, having its reasons whereof the reason knows nothing, is able to intuit the feelings of others. Anticipating

Coleridge's notion of an association of feeling-states, Edmund Burke asserted that poetry operates on this affective level by a process of sympathy. It affects "rather by sympathy than imitation, to display rather the effect of things on the mind of the speaker, or of others, than to present a clear idea of the things themselves" (*On the Sublime and the Beautiful* V, 5, in Chapman 351). A belief in the power of words to prompt affective states had to be based on a belief in the access of the passionate mind to universal human feelings, a new democratic prophetic power that could endow the poetic imagination with a new authority to explore and give utterance to the inner nature of humankind.

By 1800 the imagination had undergone a thorough renovation. The Neo-Classical Age with its new science had demystified it and freed it of its burden of guilt. From the Restoration on, writers consciously indulged and extolled it. "Imaging," rejoiced Dryden, "is, in itself, the very height and life of Poetry." And had not Horace advised poets to mix the pleasurable with the useful, that is, the delightful image with the ethical instruction? Here then was a power to warm and sway the sympathy of others in the cause of moral betterment. Here indeed was an eminently licit pleasure, as Addison and Akenside enthusiastically declared.

The fashionableness of a concept, as we know, often accompanies its co-optation. The "pleasures of imagination" was a popular concept that by the mid-eighteenth century threatened to trivialize what seemed to be left of a process that seventeenth-century philosophers had already almost succeeded in rationalizing out of existence. But, as Horace also said, you can drive out Nature with a pitchfork but she always comes back. The exorcists' spell would once again fail. Mental imagery had not actually been diminished when philosophers proclaimed it nothing but decaying sense or entrained ideas or bagatelles, or when litterateurs praised its ornamental value. Like Samson, it had been exploited to serve lesser functions but, like Samson, its powers were returning. The eruption of poetic imagery in the late eighteenth century and early nineteenth century, intensified by a century of denial and benign optimism, preceded the development of modern psychology. This was no coincidence. The "shifts in sensibility" that we observe in literary history are actually seismic in scope and involve entire cultures. Mary Shelley's Frankenstein and Baudelaire's Paris were not solely their authors' obsessions. With or without literary suggestions, the positivist, imperial Western mind was becoming increasingly troubled by images it could no longer understand or pray to or ritually expel. The dream of Reason had begun once more to produce monsters.

Writers responded to the contemporary image-overflow by entrapping these shapes in words. A poet's imagination, when it is not constrained by repressive belief systems, can give a local habitation and a name to images, monstrous as they might seem, that lurk in the collective mind of his or her community. This is the poet's rightful work. For this reason, the links between poetry, poetic madness, and clinical madness have always been acknowledged. The "poetic license" had long been recognized as a special dispensation that allowed poets to lie, rave, talk to themselves, converse with birds and trees, profess to be famous personages from myth and history, relive their own past with hallucinatory vividness, call up the dead and harangue them, and assert that the world was filled with secret messages that none but they could decipher. Behaving like this without a license, they would be ostracized or locked up "for their own good." Even with this license, if their public did not value the message in their madness, they would receive no more encouragement than would village idiots. Licensed poets provide an inestimable public good and, if by entrapping these menacing and seductive images in words they do not banish them, they do accomplish the next best thing: they isolate them as epidemical obsessions and thereby provide us all a way to live with them without succumbing to psychological paralysis. Psychologists might have been inspired by the Romantics' candid self-revelations, but, even if they had never read Hölderlin or Nerval or Hoffmann or Poe, the emotional distress of the general population would no doubt have led them to pick up the question of imagery where the eighteenth-century Associationists had left it.

Modern psychology was conceived not as an exorcism but as a therapy. The treatment of imaginal disorders could not succeed by magic spells, though these were tried in therapies that were later labeled pseudo-scientific quackery. If magic could not work, neither could philosophy. People troubled by recurrent unbidden imagery could hardly be given a copy of Hobbes or Locke and sent home to cure themselves. Psychologists were obliged to take these images seriously, as seriously as did their patients.

The "lower," or "sensory" (in Greek, the *aesthetic*), soul had once again reasserted its prerogatives: the production of images and the storage of affect. Unregulated by the higher consciousness, or reason, this lower soul, or *sub*consciousness, would prove dangerous to the individual and the community. How imagery and affect were connected and how they might be adjusted to the expectations of the community were the primary research tasks that late nineteenth-century and early twentieth-century psychology set itself.

As one might have expected, this scientific project was to parallel, and sometimes cross, the path that twentieth-century literary theorists were to take in their efforts to comprehend the profusion of post-Romantic metaphor, symbol, and structural innovation. As one might also have expected, this parallel project was often suspected of territorial encroachment.

There was nothing really new, however, about this convergence of interests. A look backward into the history of Western poetics will show that when literary theoreticians have come to grips with that fundamental question, What is poetry and why is it read? they have usually done so in terms of the non-rational, non-verbal mind. Insofar as it differs from that attainable through logic or patient dialectic, the knowledge one experiences through poetry has most often been described as a recognition or revelation, an insight evoked out of some depth within the reader or a message relayed via the poet from some supramundane agent. The affects that poetry excites have been characterized as either subrational in origin, in which case poetry purges or sublimates them, or suprarational, in which case they accompany some powerful transmission of knowledge. Whether in a given instance the result is cognitive or affective or, as is usually the case, a combination of the two, its customary vehicle is the visual image that, though prompted by the verbal text, forms itself as a mute mental representation beyond the dominion of language.

The visual image in descriptive stasis and in narrative motion is therefore the central issue of poetics, especially of the poetics of read, as distinct from dramatized, scripts, for in the literate situation the reader must collaborate with the text in concretizing a world of shapes, colors, and movements. Since reading is thus the mental performance of the reader, it is inevitable that the concerns of psychology should coincide often with those of poetics.

Some of the most durable of literary terms have been essentially psychological terms: the catharsis of emotions, anagnorisis, mimesis, the mixing of delight with instruction, anagogy, rhetorical tropes and most of the techniques of persuasion; inspiration (a parapsychological concept), wit, conceit, the sublime, the pathetic, the beautiful; imagination and fancy, the overflow of powerful feelings recollected in tranquility; the stream of consciousness, centers of consciousness, narrative points of view, persona, impression, expression, idea, affect, aesthetics, psychical distance, temporal and spatial structures, tension, tone, symbol, and archetype.

Most of these terms entered the canon of literary usage when psychology was still a rather tame branch of philosophy. During this long period, roughly from Aristotle to Kant, the mind was viewed more as a receptive than as a constructive organ. In its natural state, that is, when it was not visited by celestial or infernal influences, the human consciousness was regarded as a plastic entity subject to the imprint of sense data. It had to be in-formed, much as soft wax receives the form of a signet ring. Information was accordingly a process of receiving impressions. This description by the eighteenth-century aesthetician and minor poet Henry Brooke fairly represents this view of the mind as passive reactor to stimuli:

> When objects on the exterior membrane press,
> Th' alarm runs inmost through each dark recess,
> Impulsive strikes the corresponding strings,
> And moves th' accord of sympathetic springs.
> (*Universal Beauty* IV, 41–44)

The unobservable workings of *la machine homme* were visualized as a set of pipes, valves, cables, and resonators. Fluids accumulated within elastic chambers until some triggering sensation dispatched them to the brain or other executive organ, which then ordered the skeletal muscles into action.

Of course, this sequence could be interrupted by the intellect, which, theoretically capable of reflection, could compare the present situation with others stored in memory and then decide that restraint or some other course of action was appropriate. But most minds were so exceedingly impressionable that, if one could master certain simple rhetorical devices, one could easily impose upon these minds by moving their affections. Once this was achieved, one could sway their wills and even their intellects. Rhetoric thus seemed to demonstrate this passive, mechanistic model of human consciousness, a model that had been generally accepted from Greco-Roman times to our present century. Needless to mention, it is still accepted by those in commerce and public life who are perfectly satisfied if they can fool only some of the people most of the time.

In accordance with this rhetorico-psychological model, the belief that has dominated stylistics down through the centuries has been that literature uses imagery to stimulate responses, that the affective pleasure produced by imagery makes the didactic content of literature palatable, and that a great variety of imaginal devices trigger a small number of uncomplicated affects.

Holding to such time-honored assumptions, many twentieth-century literary theorists have deliberately ignored the reader's affective experience. W. K. Wimsatt and Monroe Beardsley's famous pronouncement concerning the "affective fallacy" made official what had become implicit in academic criticism. The following excerpt from an essay by another New Critic, Martin Levich, lays bare the premise that underlies this view. Suppose, Levich says, we are confronted with the argument that the "structure [of a statement] becomes poetical when it determines an imaginative event located in the reader ... [and] that no other combination of words can evoke the same event." How should we reply to this? Levich's reply goes as follows:

> The argument rests on the fundamental misconception that one and only one cause can obtain a stipulated effect, and there is no substantial evidence from any empirical domain to sustain this dubious view. A marlinspike or a baseball bat vigorously laid about the head can arouse the same sum total of pain, water or an electric grill can evoke the identical sensation of heat, and more than one identifiable order of words could conceivably evoke the same imaginative event. ("Form and Content in Poetry" in Levich 73)

A number of points in Levich's statement are open to question, for example, his notion of "stipulated effects" and the supposed insignificance of word order, but what is most questionable is his equation of "imaginative event" with intensity of affect. This view of a reader's response is even more reductionist than that presented by Henry Brooke. Brooke's contraption model at least had "corresponding strings" and "sympathetic springs." Levich's model is an algetic toggle switch activated by physical abuse.

Susanne Langer had confronted this same premise some twenty years earlier when she took Rudolf Carnap to task: "Where Carnap [in *The Logical Syntax of Language*] speaks of 'cries like "Oh, oh," or, on a higher level, lyrical verses,' I can only see a complete failure to apprehend a fundamental distinction" (*New Key* 81). The symbolic structures of poems, she maintained, are "not those investigated by logicians, under the heading of 'language.'" The belief that poems may be so analyzed is based, she said, on the "two fundamental tenets of current epistemology, namely, "(1) that *language is the only means of articulating thought* and (2) that *everything which is not speakable thought, is feeling*" (81). It automatically follows, she says, from these erroneous premises that beyond language-bound thinking "we can have only blind feeling, which records nothing, but has to be discharged in action or self-expression, in deeds or cries or other impulsive demonstrations" (81–82).

Our language itself reflects this anti-affect bias when it uses the word "feeling" to denote such diverse events as a painful or pleasurable sensation and a complex mood or intimation. The "feelings" we experience when we read poetry are not likely to be of the former, but rather of the latter sort—a conscious suspension, often affectively toned, between various possibilities of belief, value, and action. On this point

William Empson wrote, "much of what appears to us as 'feeling' (as is obvious in the case of a complex metaphor) will in fact be quite an elaborate structure of related meanings" (57). "Feeling" would appear to be a catch-all term assigned by language to any datum of consciousness not linguistically encoded. When applied to poetry, it has come to mean the imagery and affect evoked by, but not objectively locatable in, the words of the text.

The hostility toward psychology on the part of many twentieth-century critics should not obscure the fact that literary theory has always been based on psychological models, both explicit and unacknowledged. The crude notion of literary experience that exploits the loose terminology of "feeling" to lump together a wide spectrum of endocrinological and cognitive processes only to dismiss them all as unexaminable side effects is a notion that itself warrants examination. If we define "psychologism" as an illegitimate application of psychological theory or evidence to support a particular point of view, here then is a psychologistic premise used to buttress a critical fundamentalism that has always regarded the written word as the ultimate protection from, rather than the proper invitation to, the formation of mental images and the generation of affect. Beneath the surface of this covert literary psychologism may lie an even more secret *para*psychologism—the irrational fear of mental images, the ancient belief in *noctis phantasmata*. (For a more extensive discussion of iconophobia see my *Reading the Written Image*.)

The Threat from the Depths

Only in the late nineteenth century, when experimental psychology began to question the older models of the mind, did this philological establishment begin to feel uneasy. When scientists like Wilhelm Wundt, Francis Galton, and E. B. Titchener took up and reexamined the entire field of mental imagery, this seemed to literary specialists something of an encroachment on their territory. Then when psychological philosophers like William James and Henri Bergson began to influence younger writers, many traditional critics became alarmed. Finally when Freud presented his theory of mind, which posited the existence of an unconscious theater of affect-charged imagery, a critical establishment felt itself truly menaced by the reemergence of those very elements that, it trusted, had been so long ago safely laid to rest.

Suddenly that trusted old family retainer, psychology, had turned in Calabanish ingratitude on its hereditary masters, philosophy and literary criticism, and seemed intent on expropriating large parcels of their estate. Though the first principles of all literary theories invariably implied psychological premises and models, it became clear in the early twentieth century that the critical establishment would greet any new model of the mind with territorial hostility.

This hostility often assumed a desperate tone as the old-style critics observed a new generation of poets, playwrights, and novelists lured by the charms of depth psychology and eager to slip into what seemed the incoherence of dream imagery and stream-of-consciousness. These developments, according to Irving Babbitt, were the malignant aftereffects of Romanticism, a judgment echoed by Paul Elmer More and the Neo-Humanists of the popular press. With the advent of the New Critics in the 1930s came a new establishment, which, it is true, tolerated the psychological experiments of the new writers but continued to draw the line when it came to critics and theorists. Even the culture-hero T. S. Eliot lost his immunity when John Crowe Ransom detected in his critical essays the contagion of I. A. Richards. These were the times when everybody, even Susanne Langer, seemed clamoring for a pound of I. A. Richards's "psychologistic" flesh.

Richards had proposed that we examine the art work as an internal event rather than an external object:

We are accustomed to say that a picture is beautiful, instead of saying that it causes an experience in us which is valuable in certain ways.

. . . .

Indeed language has succeeded until recently in hiding from us almost all the things we talk about. Whether we are discussing music, poetry, painting, sculpture, or architecture, we are forced to speak as though certain physical objects—vibrations of strings and of columns of air, marks printed on paper, fabrics of freestone, are what we are talking about. And yet the remarks we make as critics do not apply to such objects but to states of mind, to experiences. (20–22)

The very suggestion that a poem happens *here* and not *there* was intolerable to those who demanded "objective" interpretive and evaluative standards. In its "symbolic form," said Langer,

the poem "exists" objectively whenever it is presented to us, instead of coming into being only when somebody makes "certain integrated responses" [a reference to Richards] to what the poet is saying. We may glance at a page and say to ourselves almost immediately "Here is a good poem!" (*Feeling and Form* 211)

The conflict between those who asserted the poem's "existence" and those who preferred to examine its function as a set of cues to an internal performance was a conflict of emphases. Obviously the events that occur when one reads a text are significantly determined by those "marks printed on paper." No less obviously are they "states of mind." In terms of imagery, they are private, affectively toned, mental representations made in response to public, verbally coded instructions. The theoretical opinion that dominated mid-twentieth-century criticism held that such mental representations must not be examined and certainly not by the means provided by psychology.

This hostility to the new science of the mind has continued up until recent times to be something of a conditioned reflex among literary academicians. Any cross-disciplinary fraternalization with psychology would carry the stigma of treason—like being sighted on the wrong side just as the battle lines were forming for Armageddon. We do indeed detect the barely contained hysteria in the tone of René Wellek's and Austin Warren's declaration that "anarchy, scepticism, a complete confusion of values is the result of every psychological theory, as it must be unrelated either to the structure or the quality of a poem" (147). And we note the uncompromising conclusion of R. P. Blackmur: "Let us say then that psychology turns aesthetics into the mechanics of perception" ("A Burden for Critics" in Polletta, ed., 66–67).

On the other hand, where there is smoke we might do well to look for fire. Such animated responses could not have been entirely unprovoked. Since few psychologists are trained readers, their approach to literary works can on occasion seem simplistic, crude, and tendentious. Their attempts to extract desired information from a text can seem invasive and bullheaded. A psychologist may try to be reassuring when he says that "the fears of the literati are misplaced: literature's roles as art and as aesthetic experience are not the primary issues for psychologists, literature's role as data is" (Lindauer 171). But to the "literatus" this is likely to seem a chilling attitude, like cherishing the Muse for the extractable gold fillings in her teeth. Literature *is* art and aesthetic experience: to derive data from it under some other aspect is inevitably to recast it to fit some preconceived theory.[3]

I do not question the broad applicability of depth-psychological theory toward an understanding of culture and to the structures of power. Over the past quarter-century numerous writers have illuminated more and more of the complex interrelationships of politics and sexuality, already implicit in Freud's later writings, and linked these problems to issues of linguistic structure, signification, and text-production. What I have taken exception to above is an inductive approach to literary texts, artifacts that are always too large and equivocal to be reducible to experimental objects or fractured into usable data. What I have now to question is a psychoanalytical approach to individual texts, artifacts that in this case are always too small and unresponsive to be interrogated as analysands.

This latter hermeneutical method, never able to conceal its doctrinaire agenda, has resolutely located in literary texts exactly what it had come there to find. Based on clinical data, here was a fully articulated theory of human behavior that no amount of specifically literary experience could ever alter or augment. The only legitimate function that literature could serve was to reveal itself as a medical theater of compensatory fantasy and primary process thinking. In the light of Freudian theory, literature is the dream-work of the waking mind, its authors and readers driven by the same need as dreamers to release through seemingly benign symbols and in safe quantities the repressed energies of the id.

Why does a reader get pleasure from the writer's daydreams? Freud had asked in 1908. The reader does so, he suggested, because the writer uses two strategies:

The writer softens the egotistical character of the day-dream by changes and disguises [e.g., a persona, "many component egos," or the "spectator" hero], and he bribes us by the offer of a purely formal, that is aesthetic, pleasure in the presentation of his phantasies. ("The Poet and Day-Dreaming" in Nelson, ed., 54)

The id and, indirectly, the superego are the compound author of the literary text (as they are of the dream). The ego is the intrapsychic persona who construes a shadowy tenor that it cannot or dares not "act out," or even contemplate in conscious experience. The analyst corresponds to the hermeneutical interpreter who, having deciphered the textual code, recovers the obscure tenor for the enlightenment of the naive reader. The analysand is, of course, this reader.

Here then is a systematic hermeneutics that places the critic in the secure position of anticipating the explication: after all there are just so many psychodynamic principles possibly lurking beneath the surface of the textual code. The technique of psychoanalytic criticism provides a handy cipher that, when skillfully applied to a literary text, produces a fairly standard and *ex hypothesi* wholly convincing critical text. Viewed in such a reductionist perspective, literature becomes merely a body of illustrative and corroborative texts.[4]

The foregoing is not meant to be a criticism of psychoanalysis as a theory of the mind or as a therapy, but merely as an instrument of literary analysis that tends to neglect particular aspects of a text in its desire to formulate doctrinally consistent generalizations. Though such generalizations may be suggestive and may lead to further insights, the truly rigorous Freudian must regard them as inconclusive. After all, the unraveling of the motivation of persons and the latent meaning of symbolic codes is supposed to require many therapeutic sessions and much probing on the analyst's part. No work of literature in itself provides adequate data upon which to base a valid diagnosis of either author or character. Written discourse, as Plato long ago complained, cannot be interrogated. As applied to literature, Freudianism—and Jungianism, too—have been fascinating hermeneutical devices, but their results have been of questionable value. As Northrup Frye remarked:

> When . . . Alice in Wonderland [is] discussed in terms of her hypothetical toilet training, or Arnold's "Where ignorant armies clash by night" taken as a covert reference to the copulation of his parents, one is reminded of the exempla from natural history made by the medieval preachers. The bee carries earth on its feet to ballast itself when it flies, and thereby reminds us of the Incarnation, when God took up an earthly form. The example is ingenious and entertaining, and only unsatisfying if one happens to be interested in bees. ("The Critical Path" reprinted in Polletta, ed., 53)

The interpretive behavior of the psychoanalytical critic itself inspires fantasy. Imagine such a hermeneut explaining to his analyst his "analyst-fantasy": "In this recurrent fantasy I see myself as a world-renowned psychoanalyst. The richest and most beautiful texts come to me and recline on my couch. I listen to *their* fantasies and part their dream imagery layer by layer. It is always exceedingly overdetermined. Whether they are responsible for the condensed complexity of their cathexes, either consciously or unconsciously, I don't know—Does it matter? I know they are palimpsests because I myself am overdetermined and, like them, a veritable concordance of symbols and allusions inscribed with the same babel of cultural codes. They try to conceal their latent meanings by alluding to them obscurely and with little emphasis, but since I know how the mechanism of displacement works, I know that the apparently insignificant proves always to be the most significant. I know that when they say one thing, they instantly invoke the opposite meaning and, when they don't say what I expect them to say, their avoidance and denial are no less revealing. The unconsciousness of texts is very clever but not cleverer than I. They recline, their formal conventions lightly folded beneath them, their compensatory narratives neat as a pin—these demure surfaces concealing their hot and problematical subtexts. They turn their eyes appealingly to me but say nothing—no, they need say nothing: it is me they need to hear and it is I who now free-associate, loosing the semantic locks and scattering the hidden words-within-words everywhere. After this fantasy I always feel better."

Probably no critic in recent years has borne the psychoanalytic banner into battle more resolutely than Norman Holland. Psychoanalysis, he declared in 1968, is "the only psychology I know that can talk about an inner experience with as much detail and precision as a New Critic can talk about a text" (*Dynamics* xv). Five years later he proposed criteria for judging a psychoanalytic critic. We should ask:

Does he deal with what the text says or translate it immediately and reductively by means of a symbolic decoding? . . . Does he deal with *language*? For the great thing psychoanalysis brings to the study of literature—something no other psychology offers—is a way to understand a writer's—and a reader's—choice of words. (*Poems in Persons* 173)

Holland's comparison of his approach with that of New Criticism is quite apt. Despite their differences in method, both limit themselves to the critical interpretation of texts—the author's text and, especially for Holland, the reader's verbalized response as a derived text. His version of reader-response criticism has amounted to a criticism of the comments of selected readers, an interrogation of the "choice of words" they use when, responding to the author's text, they produce their derived text. If we accept the view that readers participate in the daydreaming of authors, the verbalized reader-responses that Holland submits to analysis would represent their *manifest* dream as modified and potentially distorted by *secondary elaboration*. The analyst/critic must then decode this confabulated text in order to reconstruct the *latent* dream and ascertain its meanings.

Though his approach purposes to uncover the "inner experience" of literature, Holland's method of offering an after-the-fact interpretation (the analyst/critic's) of what is already an after-the-fact interpretation (the analysand/reader's) takes it even further from a poetics of the mind than any New Critic would have ventured out of distrust of "inner experience." In his ability to insulate inner experience with a buffer of discourse, Holland does indeed outdo Brooks and Wimsatt. Clearly, psychologies (e.g., psychoanalysis) that are methodologically committed to verbal evidence have strengths and weaknesses similar to those of literary theories that reify the text. In its heyday New Criticism tried to characterize itself as antithetical to the psychoanalytic approach. From a present vantage point these two hermeneutical stances seem almost to converge. Few back in the 1960s would have believed that by 1980 Holland's psychoanalytic theory of poetry, once castigated as a full blown "psychologism," could be seriously characterized by one critic as a "vulgarized and sentimentalized version of New Criticism."[5]

In 1988, Holland published *The Brain of Robert Frost: A Cognitive Approach to Literature*. In it he once again asks why readers (and writers) arrive at different interpretations of texts (and of the world). It does, however, take an innovative and interdisciplinary tack. (It is, by the way, only nominally about Frost's brain, but rather about the individualized brain of each one of us.) Applying cybernetic and artificial intelligence models to some of the problems of hermeneutic interpretation, he proposes as "different levels of reading literature" the following hierarchy, beginning with the executive level: "one's personal identity; canons chosen from the culture's repertoire because they suit one's identity; codes learned willy-nilly from the culture regardless of identity; physical and physiological limits imposed by one's body and the real world, again, regardless of identity" (*The Brain* 110).

Holland goes on to explain that, when a reader peruses a text, the lowest level of cognitive activity is that of perceiving the black marks on the page. The level that governs perception is that of the arbitrary codes of language. The level above these codes is that of canons, the belief systems and interpretive strategies "about which normal members of a culture differ" (110). The highest level is the identity, which is the uniquely personal arrangement of the individual brain. In computer analogy, the lowest level would correspond to the electrical input and VDT screen; the code would be the operating system hard-wired into the computer; the canons would be a variety of compatible software programs; and the identity would be a customized program permanently installed that is able to control the performance of other programs.

Without claiming for this model anything more than heuristic value, Holland has attempted to set his brand of reader response on a foundation provided by contemporary neuroscience. In effect, he has deftly bundled ideology, semiotics, and physiology into feedback loops subordinate to the psychoanalyzable ego. The psychodynamics that Freud had found churning in the turbid depths of the psyche and that half a century of literary critics had decried as a frightful irrelevance is now, after this palace coup, installed on the throne. The stubby nerve endings may still be where they were, still tasked like loyal peons with the stuff of sensation, but the codes and canons that over the years had come to dominate literary discourse are now reduced to the rank of rusticated nobles and supple courtiers. Holland has, in short, found a way to put structuralists, deconstructionists, undeconstructed New Critics, Lacanians, and neo-historicists in their place—a place of his own choosing. Perhaps metaphors like "house arrest" or "internal exile" are too strong to describe this place, but then again perhaps they do convey some flavor of his intentions.

Curiously lacking in this "cognitive approach to literature," however, is any mention of the cognitive processes that most cognitive psychologists assume to underlie the act of reading: memory and imaging also operate through feedback mechanisms in the brain, and have by now become valid objects of scientific attention. No matter how our quirky circuits were customized in the cradle, our modes of storing and re-imaging experience are now considered to be sufficiently universal to warrant scientific inquiry. Holland's avoidance of these processes, which he apparently relegates to the lowest servomechanical level of his cybernetic model, allows him to describe the personal identity as though it were the sole function of the neocortex—as though the frontal lobe could do without the 80 percent of the "new brain" that deals with sensation, representation, and response. The identity may indeed be the factor that accounts for personality differences, but everything else within the neocortex, not to mention the lower regions of the brain and the entire central nervous system, accounts for the vast common ground of human consciousness upon which these relatively minor but desperately cherished differences appear. While Holland's refurbished identity theory may help explain why readers sometimes passionately disagree in the act of hermeneutic interpretation, it offers little if any help in exploring the processes of poetic interpretation, that is, the processes by which literary texts present themselves to the "identity."

Despite the claims of Holland or of any other psychoanalytic critic to have located Oedipus and Hamlet among the dendrodendritic synapses, theirs is a language-bound hermeneutic, a verbal analysis of verbal responses to verbal artifacts, and can never hope to account for the *non*-verbal sources, processes, and effects of literary language. What had seemed at the beginning of this century a radical approach to literature, one that promised to uncover the hidden springs of creativity and imagination, has proven to be just another discourse on discourse.

The Return of the Ostracized

The phrase "the return of the ostracized" will be familiar to students of the psychology of mental imaging. It was used by Robert Holt in 1964 to announce the reinstatement of the image as a legitimate object of scientific investigation. In his article Holt reviewed several decades of experimental work in the psychology of learning and perception, work that implied, without theoretically acknowledging, the reality of imaging as an important function of the brain. By the early 1960s, countless phenomena had been accumulating that could not be dealt with adequately: theories of imaging had to be formulated and, he urged, the time was now propitious.

Imagery had not, however, been alone in exile: all phenomena that relied on introspective reports had been banned since, as Roger Brown put it, "In 1913 John Watson mercifully closed the bloodshot inner eye of American psychology [and w]ith great relief the profession trained its exteroceptors on the laboratory animal" (Brown 93). John Broadus Watson had that year announced that "The time has come when psychology must discard all reference to consciousness. . . . Its sole task is the prediction and control of behavior; and introspection can play no part in its method" ("Psychology as the Behaviorist Sees It" in the *Psychological Review, 20,* 158–177). Imagery (and those who regarded it as a valid object of scientific study) was ostracized because it was a phenomenon of consciousness. Actually the Behaviorist movement strove to banish the entire concept of "mind," and any attempt to account for a behavioral phenomenon in terms other than those of stimulus-and-response was branded "mentalistic." The fact that the Freudian unconscious mind was also proscribed did not, however, retard the growing influence of the "depth psychologies."

Roger Brown may have predated this general shift by a decade or so, but certainly by 1928 Watson's Behaviorism had won the day and Structuralism, the introspectionist movement in psychology founded in Germany by Wundt and established in America by Titchener, was buried in scorn. "The behaviorist," Watson confidently declared,

having made a clean sweep of all the rubbish called consciousness comes back to you: "Prove to me," he says, "that you have auditory images, visual images, or any other kinds of disembodied processes. So far I have only your unverified and unsupported word that you have them." Science must have objective evidence to base its theories upon. (*Ways* 75)

There is more than a suggestion here that Watson was intent on laying that troubled spirit that Gilbert Ryle had called the "ghost in the machine." Apropos of those images that go bump in the night, Bertram Lewin tells this anecdote:

I once heard the late John B. Watson, the behaviorist, tell in homey Southern language of his childhood fear of ghosts. He still could not be paid, he said, to go into a graveyard at night, even if he had in his pocket the left hind foot of a rabbit shot at midnight during the dark of the moon. (25)

A belief in disembodied spirits is not inconsistent with a disbelief in "disembodied processes": if images are not *here* in the mind, they may well be *there,* hovering in the night. This conclusion is logically consistent but not very reassuring.

Though the impact of Freud on twentieth-century literary practice was considerable, so was the considerable hostility it aroused in the critical establishment. Behaviorism was an unlikely ally, but this hardnosed, no-nonsense, unlibidinous psychology must have recommended itself to the literary foes of psychoanalysis. The rise of New Criticism was coincident with the rise of Behaviorism and, despite their mutual aversion, the two movements were in some respects strikingly similar. Both struggled for American academic ascendancy in their respective disciplines at a time when Freudian metapsychology was expanding its horizons. Both upheld the ideal of objectivity; both consigned imagery to the limbo of epiphenomena. Behaviorists built their system upon the rubble of introspectionism; New Critics built theirs on the rubble of impressionism. Both engaged in the objectively distanced explication of behavior: one, that of rats in a maze, the other, that of words on a page. And both, despite their substantial achievements, were in irreversible decline by the early 1960s.

About the same time that Holt was urging his colleagues to focus again upon mental imagery, word came to America that there were literary theorists, most of them associated with the University of Geneva, who openly spoke of the consciousness embodied in a text, an alien consciousness that could somehow take possession of the reader. In 1968, one year after Ulric Neisser's *Cognitive Psychology* established the credentials of the post-behaviorist psychology of consciousness, Sarah Lawall published her *Critics of Consciousness*, a study of Georges Poulet and his colleagues. Though her treatment of them is fair and even sympathetic, in her preface she steps about gingerly, like Scheherazade bargaining for her head:

The British or American reader will find it hard to reconcile his own views with those expressed by the critics of consciousness. These critics do not read literature as we read it, and their analysis does not seem useful to our manner of reading. We are trained to look upon each work as an object to be studied and appreciated for itself. Moreover, we are trained in certain analytical methods that are objective, easy to use, and invariably productive. . . . The critics of consciousness . . . look at literature as an act, not an object. (vii)

The Genevans, of course, were not the first in this century to dehypostatize the poem. A small number of theorists had independently chosen to approach literature as an act rather than an artifact and had asked what the conscious mind actually does when it reads a text. Without denying the potent influence of the unconscious, they examined their own conscious processes in the light of psychological findings then available. Among the more notable were I. A. Richards (*The Principles of Literary Criticism*, 1924), L. S. Vygotsky (*The Psychology of Art*, ca. 1925) Max Eastman (*The Literary Mind*, 1932), and Jean-Paul Sartre (*The Psychology of Imagination*, 1948). They had their own theoretical and ideological allegiances, of course, but tried to avoid the doctrinaire blinders that cancel out whole areas of inquiry in advance. Frederick Crews, author of *The Pooh Perplex*, unhumorously wore these blinders when, a quarter-century ago, he declared:

Psychoanalysis is the only psychology to have seriously altered our way of reading literature. [There are no] possible literary implications of physiological psychology, of perception and cognition psychology, or of learning theory [or] Gestalt psychology. (74)

This last sentence I hope to prove wrong in this present study, but in Crews's defense, "cognition psychology" was just emerging twenty-five years ago, just beginning then to construct models that could correlate information drawn from (neuro)physiological psychology, perception theory, and learning theory. The "return of the ostracized," which for psychology meant the return of conscious processes, imaging included, to a place of primary concern, also meant for literary studies the return of the conscious processes of reading to the foreground it now occupies.

But before the reader emerged, the text reasserted its primacy once again. In the 1960s Anglo-American formalists found themselves uncomfortably allied with another science, that of linguistics. As Robert Scholes put it:

For many tender spirits who in their undergraduate days fled from the sciences into the humanities, the spectacle of linguistic science pursuing them into their refuge like Grendel's mother, jaws dripping with pieces of broken poems, is indeed a nightmare. (22)

We next consider this nightmare, to which I will propose a happy awakening.

Chapter 3
The Poetics of Play: Reopening Jakobson's "Closing Statement"

The two decades following World War II was a time when literary scholarship felt a renewed need to define its purpose. The war had raised so many questions concerning the value of the European tradition of humanism and humane letters that returning to explication as usual seemed to many a tedious, not to say irresponsible, undertaking. With progressivist historicism in disrepute, New Critical formalism and its aging paladins in disrepair, and Behaviorism and orthodox Freudianism in disfavor, the dissatisfied looked for new ground to stand and build upon.

At this point the concept of "structure" seemed to offer that new ground. At first sight, at least, Structuralism seemed to redeem the ideals of the pre-war past: its architectonic metaphors struck the hopeful, progressivist note of rebuilding, its explanatory purposes sounded as practical as formalism had tried to be, and its methods seemed as scientific as psychology had claimed to be.

At the center of this activity structural linguistics offered itself as the queen of the arts and human sciences. Its principle of difference (that words and other signs are meaningful only in differential relation to other words and signs) and its principle of structuration (that these relations, characterized by binary oppositions and axes, form symmetrical systems) seemed to offer a key to the data that anthropology, sociology, folklore, psychology, and literary studies had for so long struggled to organize and rationalize. Just as eighteenth-century Associationism had proposed to explain the concatenation of intrasubjective thought by recourse to a diachronic model, twentieth-century Structuralism asserted its ability to explain the concatenation of *inter*subjective thought by recourse to a synchronic model.

Shortly after the war, American New Critics had begun to be aware of the work of the Russian formalists and the Prague structuralists and, especially through the efforts of René Wellek and Austin Warren, began shoring up their critical positions with selected blocks of European theory. They were not concerned with the structure of intersubjective ideas—their fidelity to the "poem itself" forebade that—but they were intrigued by the possibility of demonstrating the spatiality of poems, that is, the poem as a construct of synchronously interactive parts. Joseph Frank's "Spatial Form in Modern Literature," first published in a series of three issues of the *Sewanee Review* in 1945, had marked the culmination of much modernist speculation concerning the "Image" and the poem-as-image and helped stimulate attempts to retrofit Anglo-American New Criticism with European structuralist insights, particularly at the level of sound-texture, metrics, and semantics—and always in respect to the poem as verbal hypostasis.

In 1958 the "Conference on Style" held at Indiana University presented twenty-six speakers and panelists. They included such New Critical stalwarts as W. K. Wimsatt, René Wellek, Monroe Beardsley, and I. A. Richards (though by then it had become difficult to categorize him); psychologists with a special interest in language like George Miller; younger literary theorists like Seymour Chatman and John Hollander; linguists like Roger Brown, Sol Saporta, Dell Hymes, and, preeminent in age and reputation, Roman Jakobson.

It was at this conference that Jakobson defined poetics as "an integral part of linguistics" (350). Preliminary to specifying which part was occupied by poetics, he listed the six factors that constitute every speech event: message, addresser, addressee, context, contact, and code. A poem, he said, differs from other speech events because of its peculiar "set toward the message," that is, by a conventional predisposition on the part of the reader to regard the textual message as the primary, foregrounded factor, or, in the parlance of Russian Formalism, the *dominant*. The convention by which we detach the text from all the pragmatic circumstances normally attached to human social communication seemed to him to provide the poetic text with a linguistically analyzable structure and poetics with a clear identity firmly grounded in linguistic science. Back in 1960 here was some solace for the beleaguered New Critics. Jakobson's formalist concerns with the microstructure of poems seemed congenial to those who sought objective stylistic evidence for the separateness of its language, and Wimsatt in his essay "Battering the Object" viewed this as additional support for his theory of the self-referential text.

The past two decades, however, have not been altogether kind to Jakobson's reputation as a poetic theorist. The confident quest for linguistic universals has faltered. Literary interpretation based on the minute scrutiny of the linguistic features of a text, for example, Jakobson's and Claude Lévi-Strauss's analysis of Baudelaire's "Les Chats," has itself proved a reduction to the absurd. The definitive character of so many of Jakobson's pronouncements made it generally easy for his critics to point out instances where he had either misstated or overstated his case.

A rereading of the "Closing Statement: Linguistics and Poetics," delivered as one of the concluding papers at the Conference and published in 1960, does, however, reveal a somewhat less conclusive Jakobson, one who has left ample openings in his theorizing for further inquiry. The openings this linguist has left in his "Statement" are not, I would argue, linguistic at all. They are gaps he did not fill because to fill them would be to imperil the self-standing autonomy of his linguistic model of poetics. The nature of these gaps suggests the strategic exclusion of another discipline, one with which he was also profoundly concerned, *psychology*.

Psychological Sets and the Poetic Message

During the first half of this century Eastern European theorists, unlike their Western European and Anglo-American colleagues, did not as a group feel compelled to sequester literary theory from psychology and the social sciences. Western critics, though they had given one another license, sometimes grudgingly, to speculate on the unconscious motives of writers and fictional characters, had, until recent years at least, persuaded themselves and their readers to ignore all the mental processes, conscious as well as unconscious, that enter into the act of reading. Any consideration of the processes of memory, feeling, perception, and imagination (as the simulation of various perceptual states) the New Critical establishment had labeled "psychologistic," as though to recruit such cross-disciplinary assistance might undermine the critical method of the literary specialist and undercut his authority.

A like shyness does not seem to have afflicted the introspective Slavs. Their appropriation of early twentieth-century thought in philosophy and social science was broad and omnivorous. Attention, sensation, and the complex interactive relations of speech and thought—the Russian Formalists never deemed these illegitimate concerns and, by Anglo-American standards at least, Poles like Roman Ingarden and Czechs like Jan Mukařovský might also be considered "psychologizers." Even the historicist Mikhail Bakhtin opposed psychoanalysis on grounds that were partly psychological. Despite its considerable links with Eastern European thought, the American formalism of the New Critics, profoundly distrustful of the unconstrained reader, naturally tended to edit out the psychological premises of these Slavic theorists.

The version imported by René Wellek and Austin Warren in 1949 had been sanitized of those psychological premises upon which so much of this theorizing was based. As though to make sure their *Theory of Literature* could pass through U.S. Customs without a hitch, they diligently discarded such concepts as the figure/ground structure of Gestalt psychology, the phenomenon of "inner speech" as it pertains to thought, and other areas where psychophysiology touches upon speech and reading.[1] Wellek in the *Theory* was uncompromising in his opposition to any intrusion of psychology into criticism and poetics:

> The psychology of the reader, however interesting in itself or useful for pedagogical purposes, will always remain outside the object of literary study—the concrete work of art—and is unable to deal with the question of the structure and value of the work of art. (147)

It was not extraordinary, given this climate, for Jakobson's audience of literary critics to discount or ignore the psychological assumptions that underlay his "Closing Statement." When René Wellek, representing literary critics in his own "Closing Statement," remarked, true to form, that "From the point of view of the literary critic, the psychological papers were of least immediate interest" (409), he was not referring to Jakobson but to the professional psychologists.

These psychologists, for their part, also failed to comment on Jakobson's psychological premises, perhaps because to them these observations seemed too unastonishingly obvious. George Miller, the eminent American psychologist of verbal cognition, who followed Jakobson with his "Closing Statement" (from the point of view of psychology), chose rather to express his bewilderment at the array of unfamiliar terms and methods with which he had been confronted. The major question in his mind was, Which discipline provides the methodological grounding for the others? Though he appreciated Jakobson's assertion that poetics was a "subbranch" of linguistics, he himself regarded linguistics as a subbranch of psychology ("psychology includes linguistics includes criticism," 388). Noting that the speakers, more often than not, had been "talking past each other over the same domain in exactly opposite directions," he remarked that most of them assumed a reversed order of inclusiveness. What is unfortunate is that Miller apparently did not pick up on the psychological implications in Jakobson's statement, implications that the linguist had also, albeit covertly, posited psychology as the ground of linguistics.

The basic psychological assumption in Jakobson's "Statement" is that readers are able not only to recognize but to subordinate all other linguistic factors to one *dominant* factor at a time and that subsidiary attention could be proportionately distributed, a concept that had been

                    CONTEXT
                    (referential)

ADDRESSER   MESSAGE   ADDRESSEE
(emotive)   (poetic)   (conative)
....

                    CONTACT
                    (phatic)

                    CODE
                    (metalingual)

formulated by experimental psychology and supported by the Gestaltists. The accompanying diagram presents Jakobson's six factors (and functions) (355, 357). The reader of poetry, as distinct from other kinds of writing, is expected to regard the message, the peculiarly stylized poetic text, as the dominant factor and to have therefore a particular "set (*Einstellung*) toward the message" (356). While his literary colleagues might have called this attitude toward the text a "conventional norm," it is interesting that Jakobson chose to use a term ("set") drawn directly from psychology.

In most speech situations, he went on to say, the primary focus is on the context, or reference, but even in such cases this focus is not exclusively fixated, for the "accessory participation of the other functions ... must be taken into account by the observant linguist" (353). If this is true of the context when it is dominant, might it not also be true when the message is dominant? If so, what effect would the "accessory participation" of any of the other five have upon the poem? Jakobson briefly sketched several instances of this. The epic, he said, is characterized by the secondary foregrounding of the referential context, the lyric either by that of the emotive addresser or by that of the conative addressee. That is to say, these two genres, like all poetic genres, draw our attention primarily to the artfully patterned text, but secondarily to another factor: the epic foregrounds the persons and actions it represents, whereas the lyric foregrounds either the feelings of the addresser or the efforts of the addresser to receive a desired response from an addressee to a plea or exhortation (357). But why should the poem of any genre have only two functioning factors as its determinants? If a poem imitates a complete communicative act, subsidiary sets to all six factors would presumably be evoked.

Jakobson later complicates his argument when, after twelve pages in which he delves with delighted precision into phonemic and metrical patterns, he acknowledges with a nod to Empson the *ambiguous character of the poetic message*. From a normally unambiguous man, this comes as something of a surprise:

> Ambiguity is an intrinsic, inalienable character of any self-focused message, briefly a corollary feature of poetry. . . . Not only the message itself but also its addresser and addressee become ambiguous. Besides the author and the reader, there is the "I" of the lyrical hero or of the fictitious storyteller and the "you" or "thou" of the alleged addressee of dramatic monologues, supplications, and epistles. . . . Virtually any poetic message is a quasi-quoted discourse with all those peculiar, intricate problems which "speech within speech" offers to the linguist.
> The supremacy of poetic function over referential function does not obliterate the reference but makes it ambiguous. The double-sensed message finds correspondence in a split addresser, in a split addressee, and besides in a split reference, as it is cogently exposed in the preambles to fairy tales of various peoples, for instance, in the usual exordium of the Majorca storytellers: "Aixo era y no era" (It was and it was not). (370–371)

Jakobson does not designate this "splitting" as a differentiation, a state produced by a *differentia specifica,* the term he used some twenty pages earlier. "Aixo era y no era" is not quite the same as "fictionality": it does not simply mean that something is acknowledged to be untrue and need not be literally believed. It means that something *is* true and *not* true simultaneously. Denying absolute negativity, it affirms the possibility that contraries can coexist in matters of propositional truth. In speaking of "ambiguity" and the "double-sensed message," Jakobson is not speaking in terms of descriptive or structural linguistics but in terms of what we have come to call reader-response. This ambiguity, this doubleness, of "Aixo era y no era," this as-if play of poiesis can only be situated in the mind of a reader in the act of performing a text and not in the text itself.

The potentially "double-sensed" character of subsidiary factors requires of the reader a capacity to approach each of these factors with a double set, that is, with two ordinarily conflicting procedures of construal. This splitting of subsidiary factors, he says, ambiguates the message, which constitutes the *dominant.* But is it not reasonable to suppose that they derive their doubleness from the prior doubling of the dominant and that these various subsidiary splits proceed from the literary convention that requires not one but *two different sets toward the message*? If we are correct in assuming this, what might be the principle that governs this split? If we might infer from the three splits that he does explicitly mention, I would propose that the two sets toward the poetic message are the two kinds of interpretive stances that in the preface I termed the "poetic" and the "hermeneutical." Assuming the poetic set, the reader treats the text as an instrument of play, a notated script to be performed. Assuming the hermeneutical set, the reader treats the text as an object of analytic work, a problematical document to be interrogated. Jakobson calls the function of a poem's message "poetic," but his endeavor to subsume poetics under linguistics suggests that he attaches greater value to what could be termed the *hermeneutic* set toward the message. His "poetic message" conceals its doubleness so well because he presents it to us as an objectified and minutely labeled specimen for linguistic analysis.

It is perhaps in order to protect his linguisticized poetics from the risk of a widened psychological "opening" that he cuts short his tentative excursus on ambiguity and splitting. The doubling he attributes to the poetic addresser, the addressee, the context, and the message itself he chooses not to attribute to the remaining two linguistic factors, the contact and the code.

It is curious that he neglected to fill in this gap in his argument, which he stops with a sort of logical aposiopesis. No sooner does he state the Majorcan storyteller's paradox than he shifts focus from the doubleness of factors within a poem to the fact that poems not only repeat themselves through a system of internal equivalences, but are themselves, as verbal artifacts, repeated events. Here, midway through this paragraph on ambiguity, he ambiguates his topic. What has "this capacity for reiteration whether immediate or delayed, this reification of a poetic message and its constituents," have to do with ambiguity? Reiteration produces, he says, the reification of the poetic message: does it also ambiguate it? Is there a conflict between the linear time of a single reading and the cyclic time of a reading that is treated as a *re*reading? If so, there is another paradox implied in this oddly composed paragraph: the message is and is not a temporal speech event. Herein perhaps lies the double-sensed character of Jakobson's dominant. The poetic message is a played speech event because, unlike ordinary spontaneous statements, it is by its very nature a *re*played speech event. The radical doubleness of this *parole*—an utterance that we pretend is unidirectional when we assume the poetic set toward the message and a verbal artifact that we know is repeatable when we assume the hermeneutical set—this destabilizing doubleness lies at the very heart of poetic play. In terms of the Majorcan paradox: this message is a speech event and this message is not a speech event (but a written text).

After I discuss the further implications of splitting the message and the first three of its "accessory" factors, I will suggest ways in which the last two, contact and code, are also split and bundled into the message—how the message is itself split and is nothing more or less than the framed field within which the other five split factors play their game.

Addresser, Addressee, and Message

To understand the nature of the message as a function of a kind of communication requires that we understand the poles that Jakobson terms the "addresser" and the "addressee." Let us consider four ways in which to interpret this communication relay: as

1. an author-reader transaction,
2. a text-reader transaction,
3. a reader's identification with an author (or text),
4. a simulation of a transaction between personae.

The author-reader transactional model is weakened by the mutual absence of the two parties. Though I cannot unlearn my biographical knowledge of the addresser-as-author, its interpretive relevance to most poems is marginal enough to be negligible. And even though I may decide that Keats's sonnet "When I Have Fears" represents the author and not some conventional literary persona, I hardly suppose I am the addressee of this authorial message.

If, having examined and discarded the first model, we accept the second model, the text (= message) becomes the stand-in for the author, who, like Blake's Enion, hovers henceforth "on the margin of non-entity." The text is all we have. And we?—we are the addressee, or, more properly, the stand-in for the addressee. But no sooner is this second dyad formed than the question arises, Who shall be master—more specifically, which of these two will determine the critical interpretation of the poem? For those who equate "poem" with "text" the answer is simple: to unfold the meanings of the poem, all one has to do is unfold the given structure of the text. This was the approach Jakobson, with Lévi-Strauss, used two years later (in 1962) in the analysis of Baudelaire's "Les Chats" and for which he was notably taken to task by Michael Riffaterre in 1966 and by Jonathan Culler in 1975.

"How are we to pass from [linguistic] description to [literary] judgment—that is, from a study of the text to a study of its effect upon the reader?" asked Riffaterre (Tompkins, ed., 27), a loaded question that a New Critic would have found subversive and a Structuralist would have found irrelevant. That such questions could be asked and seriously answered in the sixties indicates that the reader, that is to say the professional hermeneut, was soon to be back in control and the text with its supposititious "structure" was going to have to bend itself to his will, suffer itself to be "browsed" by the *plaisir*-seeking reader, and made the occasion of his *jouissance*. This reader, this stand-in for the addressee, was like one who strolls past a placard on the street and tries to make out its meaning, an initial interpretation that most critics regard as flawed by the effects of one's struggle to construe this unfamiliar text. According to Riffaterre those elements that over successive readings are foregrounded *to the reader* will eventually emerge to organize the poem's meanings and are probably similarly salient to other readerly passers-by over time (cf. the "Superreader" concept in his essay on Jakobson).

But Riffaterre's vindication of readers' rights over the tyranny of the text and of its linguistic highpriest was not in retrospect the astonishing coup it seemed to be at the time. What Riffaterre said needed to be said, of course, for whenever an eminent philologue presents himself as a straw man, he cries out to be toppled. But Jakobson's 1960 "Closing Statement" hinted at an approach far less reductive than what he subsequently demonstrated in his ill-fated Baudelaire essay.

Let us now look more closely at his "addresser."

The function Jakobson assigned to the addresser he called the "emotive." Those who find no precise way to speak of poetic affect, and perhaps no precise way exists, sometimes prefer to characterize it in extreme terms. "Emotion" is itself one of these terms, since it implies a somatic disposition toward immediate action (see above, pp. 34–36). Literature is often about actions driven by lust, rage, and grief, but we are rarely aroused to such endocrinological spasms by the words we read and, when for any reason we are so moved, we are forced to discontinue our reading. By "emotive function" Jakobson surely means an affective state on the part of the fictive addresser that is shared in some attenuated way by the reader. How, we must ask, are these complex states signified and evoked in the reader? Certainly not by simply naming an emotion as though it were of the same referential order as a thing or a concept. Even when the speaker explicitly professes an emotion, we do not accept that at face value.

We believe the essentially psychological value woven into the message by the ever present voice of the addresser simply because we have suspended our disbelief in respect to addresser as well as to context. When we do allow ourselves to *feel* while reading a poem in this believing way, is it not because we have allowed ourselves to pretend that the addresser also believes in the state of mind and feelings that motivates his or her words? In his *Ars Poetica* Horace was only acknowledging this ancient convention when he advised the young writer that *si vis me flere, dolendum est / Primum ipsi tibi*—"if you want me to weep, it's first up to you to grieve." Moreover, we are willing, are we not, to assume that the form of the poem expressively correlates with its content? Since, as Riffaterre and others have amply demonstrated, phonemic and grammatical details in a text are not equally salient, that is, poetically operative, and since we understand that prosodic and stylistic devices do not always and everywhere trigger particular effects, these elements produce their "emotive" effects only by virtue of our ludic, or play, belief in this wraithlike addresser whose ambiguous presence Jakobson referred to in his 1960 statement. This second model, when it is applied to poetic play, thus implies a pretense of credulity on the reader's part, an aspect of the poetic set toward the message, that, applied to the addresser, desires to find, and insists on locating, particular semantic content embodied in particular phonological and syntactic forms. The poetic set toward the addresser's message conditions the reader to sense an intimate correspondence between form and content. In this set the reader agrees to ignore the power of linguistic signifiers to infuse phonological elements with semiotic content and allows him- or herself to project this sign-function onto these sounds and intonational features. When this same reader, having shifted to the hermeneutic set, attempts to prove that a particular sound, rhythm, or sentence construction caused or enhanced a semantic interpretation, the stylistic analysis that results is often flawed by an inability to discriminate ludically projected correspondences, from conventional associations and, in rare instances, genuinely imitative forms. The paradox of the addresser becomes: the addresser is present (in this emotively charged context) and the addresser is absent (only the traces of signification remain to link form to content).

The belief in the addresser's text-mediated presence is considerably intensified in the third model. Here the identity of the author-as-addresser predominates and is unquestioned but the locus of this domination becomes the reader. When in 1969 Georges Poulet spoke of the author as a consciousness that in the act of reading takes possession of the reader, he proposed that the authorial addresser becomes the *de facto* addressee. While it may indeed be true that at some level of mentation the reader must mime the utterance in what Ferdinand de Saussure called the "circuit de la parole," Poulet's absorption of the addressee by the addresser denies a split within addresser and addressee (Jakobson), as well as a possible split between text and reader (Riffaterre). Wolfgang Iser's reply to Poulet seems to elucidate Jakobson's position while contradicting Riffaterre's:

Text and reader no longer confront each other as object and subject, but instead the "division" takes place within the reader himself. In thinking the thoughts of another, his own individuality temporarily recedes into the background, since it is supplanted by these alien thoughts, which now become the theme on which his attention is focussed. As we read, there occurs an artificial division of our personality. (Tompkins, ed., 67)

Iser concludes that there are "two levels—the alien 'me' and the real, virtual 'me.'" Now, what in the play-script of the text constitutes this "alien"? Both the fictive addresser (narrator, central consciousness, etc.) and the fictive addressee, "actually" present to the speaker or apostrophized—these two persona-types, addresser and addressee, are both "alien" to the "real, virtual" reader, who is in turn divided between a self that acts out these embedded dialogues (what Jakobson calls "speech within speech") and a residual self that tacitly understands that it is not distributed among these personae. Jakobson's Majorcan paradox, if we apply it to this split situation, would be: the alien "me" is the real me *and* is not the real "me." The double consciousness of play, a kind of Negative Capability, accepts these contradictions as complementarities.

The two-fold reader is, therefore, invited to pretend to identify with a two-fold "alien me," namely, a fictive addresser and a fictive addressee—perhaps a whole series of these. How can the suspension of disbelief accommodate this extravagant play of impersonation? One answer to this question is that, in the act of reading, these personae become the creatures that this reader recreates in response to the verbal cues of the text. The reader may empathize with addresser or addressee alternately or sympathize with both simultaneously. When as readers we identify with the addresser, we are aided in doing so by the fact that it is *our* voice that we use to impersonate the speaker, whose expressive abilities, except for his or her choice of words and syntax of course, are only those that we ourselves are able to supply from our own oral-interpretive repertoire. When, on the other hand, we identify with the addressee, we do so because we recognize a commonality of status with this persona in that we are not responsible for generating the utterances that we receive. We are actually, of course, at a considerably further remove from the addresser's meanings, but here poetic play, allowing us to impersonate the addressee, eliminates that distance. One of the implications of being able, additionally, to identify with the fictive addressee of a fictive addresser is that we must pretend to possess the knowledge of the context, the maintenance of the contact, and the fluency in the code that this addressee presumably possesses vis à vis the addresser. For example, in the framing narrative of the "Rime of the Ancient Mariner," when we put ourself in the place of, or beside, the Wedding Guest to hear the central narrative, we pretend an immediacy of perceptual contact with the Mariner that would not quite be ours were this a dramatic monologue. In a poem that does purport to be a monologue, for example, the traditional lyric poem, the reader participates in the emotive tone of the addresser, but even in this kind of poetic play the addresser is never totally alone but speaking for the benefit of an addressee within himself into whom the reader also insinuates herself as the conative object of the address. Since, when the speaker talks to himself, *we* are the self that speaks and the self that listens, Iser's "alien 'me,'" even as an ostensibly solitary and unitary addresser, is itself thus doubled.

The reader not only becomes the multi-voiced central consciousness of every reading by necessarily impersonating the speech of all fictive personae but while doing so assumes the same centrality assumed by every one of us, including fictive personae, a degree-zero here-and-nowness from which a past and future, an inner depth and an outer depth, project themselves into ever increasing remoteness. Whenever we enter language, we enter a zoned field of consciousness the demarcations of which permit us to determine the remoteness of our referents, a remoteness relative to one another and to the spatiotemporal center occupied by ourself, the reader. The accompanying diagram represents six language-mediated cognitive modes. They may vary somewhat from one linguistic-cultural community to another, but I propose this diagram as one that has general applicability.

Every statement we send or receive implies a turning of attention from the center where the speech act is made and the subsequent orientating of both sender and receiver toward some signified object of consciousness. In a face-to-face oral speech event the Inner and Outer Present is presumably present situationally to both parties and can be deictically signified. In the case of writing, however, objects of consciousness projected into these cognitive modes are all radically absent from the reader, who, even when asked to pretend to witness a present perception does so in the same spirit of as-if play assumed when he or she pretends to enter with the fictive addresser into the reliving of a past or the visualizing of a future.

These six modes, which closely resemble the so-called faculties of classical and medieval psychology, are specific ways in which any contextualized referent may be targeted as an object of thought. Insofar as thought is linguistically mediated through inner, that is, subvocal, speech, these modes bear relations to grammatical tense and mood, a fact that reminds us how easily linguistics and psychology have since the time of Aristotle borrowed from one another's paradigms. These six modes, broadly defined, are a priori categories among which I can choose but beyond which I can neither think nor speak: I cannot, that is, *not* choose one of these when I focus on a referent. They therefore constitute the *prima materia* of discourse antecedent to structuration, that is, to the differentiation of voices and the shifts in thematic focus. Our tendency not to "see" them when we read is because we "see" all else *through* them, and, like eyeglasses, these cognitive modes work best

RETROSPECTION	PERCEPTION	EXPECTATION
personal episodic memory of the Outer Past (past tense)	input of new information from the Outer Present (present tense)	assessment of course of events in the Outer Future (future tense)

toward the past ← here & now (outward ↑ / inward ↓) → toward the future

ASSERTION	INTROSPECTION	JUDGMENT
beliefs drawn from experience and from the beliefs of others; the Inner Past (tenseless)	preconsciously formulated realizations; intuition; the Inner Present (present tense)	assessment of personal consequences of events and actions; the Inner Future (future tense, conditional mood)

when we do not notice them. Yet, unobtrusive as they are, whenever a shift from one to another of them occurs, it marks a structural development in the poem, either a logical addition or a response to an actual or anticipated question or objection. Since our tendency as readers is to focus on this newly introduced information, we tend to register this transition not as a cognitive, but rather a thematic, shift.

And what of the "real 'me,'" this subjectivity that we intuitively claim to be? The "real 'me,'" who moments earlier may have picked up the book, opened to page 47, and begun reading and may at any moment be interrupted by an irrelevant thought or a ringing telephone, remains unobtrusively present also. It must remain as a virtual participant in the poietic act, for without this ordinary self in the background the extraordinary selves of the poem, who simultaneously *are* and *are not,* whose speech becomes the impersonated speech of the reader, and who come into being in a six-fold universe of the mind—these alien beings could not be imagined, but would have to be hallucinated. The poetic set toward the message never permits this to happen: the performer of the play-script is never deluded, but like Walt Whitman's self is "both in and out of the game." On the other hand, the hermeneutical set toward the message, because of its narrower focus on the objectified text, is often less circumspect, less willing to acknowledge the "double-sensed" character of literature and therefore vulnerable to the Ate that de Man spoke of as the blindness of critical insight. The poetic set keeps its sanity only because it never denies the "real self" even as it produces, directs, and performs its play.[2]

Monologic Context

By "context" Jakobson means the real-world situation to which the message refers. Accordingly, it comprises the objects that the mind's eye shapes and fixates upon. In most speech events it is on account of this external environment that the discourse is initiated. Context is usually therefore the *dominant* upon which both addresser and addressee focus their attention. But because a text, either oral or written, is stored and retrieved in the absence of its generating situation, it is decontextualized and, since its referents are cited by fictive personae, its context depends absolutely upon the fictive reality that the reader grants to these speakers. Within this fiction, even when dialogic structures (overt or covert) appear, the context is the common topic that all personae agree to refer to, even when they characterize it differently.[3] The decontextualized, therefore fictive, context is "monologic" because, as theme, its development is the common project both of fictive addresser and fictive addressee; it is context that is variously revealed through the transparent windows of the cognitive modes.

Context, or reference, appears primarily in the form of propositions, that is, statements to which we may attribute truth or falsity. If the playscript tells us to assume the "truth" of these propositions, that is, that the fictive addresser intends them to be played as true, then we deem such propositions "literal statements." If we decide that this addresser believes them to be false or other than literally true, we deem them "ironic." At any rate, on this question of veridicality we take our cue from our sense of this addresser's conative intentions toward the fictive or implied addressee. Referential assertions may be abstract and general, such as we find in gnomic poetry, or concrete and particular, such as we find in narrative. In both cases, though more often the latter, we associate imagery with context. These verbal invitations to pretend to sense the world, especially to visualize it, presuppose our acceptance of referential cues at face value. Fictive speakers are always able to produce reference simply by engaging others' attention by an act of unidirectional verbal pointing. The eye, or in this case the mind's eye, is directed by and from an addresser outward toward an object; the reader is expected to conceptualize or visualize this object and then to await further instructions.

The monologic, phonocentric character of the referential context is not attributable to a strong central "voice," that of a persona or of the impersonating reader, but rather to its single-minded function, which declares: "Don't look at me—look at where I'm pointing." This context may be subsequently questioned or contradicted by the speaker or by others, but in the serial unfolding of language every referential word has its unconditional right to be heard and the right, if it appears in a poem, to be believed first, even if it is questioned later.[4] Even when a contextual item is explicitly negated, it maintains a kind of imaginal being, albeit fleeting. When I read that the "sedge is withered from the lake / And no birds sing," I first imagine a bird singing; *then* I cancel out that image. I have to imagine first what it is I am asked to dis-imagine and, as for other topics that might be raised by an actual environmental context, these do not exist for me except as supplied to me by the message. I am bounded by the boundedness of the text and forced to affirm and deny contextual data in what is virtually a single instant. A century before Freud declared that the negative does not operate in dreams, William Blake in *Milton* had spoken of the dream-world of Beulah where "all contraries are equally true." Poetic imagery is neither true nor false, simply because it is both true and false.

Context is monologic in its inherent tendency to represent in its single, totalizing discourse the world as a universe, a referent of referents all "turned into one," all turned through language into a "universe of discourse," and to divert attention from its own inner contradictions, which it strives to resolve without relinquishing its expository function. It is not for monologic context to draw attention to its own failings or to thicken the texture of its own utterance—to deautomatize or defamiliarize, to bare its devices or in any way to draw attention to its *modus operandi*. The success of its single-minded discourse depends on the supposed transparency of its verbal means. Dialogic and analogic structures, on the other hand, tend to ripple this transparency and reconfigure its constructions. What Jakobson has called the message, when considered solely as a string of propositions, is composed wholly of referential context. But when we choose to focus on other levels of "-logic" organization, as we have already begun to do, other factors emerge and offer to define themselves.

Dialogic Contact

At first sight one might suppose contact to be a minimal factor in the reading of poems. Oral recitation aside, the channel of contact is merely the intervening space between the print and the eye and, as long as the cat does not decide to jump onto our lap while we are reading or our eyes do not droop in drowsiness, this channel stays open. It is not, in other words, a matter of an addresser monitoring the attentiveness of an addressee. If this linguistic function operates in written texts, it would have to take some other form and, subject to the splitting effects of play, would *ex hypothesi* manifest itself as "double-sensed."

How shall we begin to understand a specifically poetic "contact"? The Spanish phenomenologist Felix Martinez-Bonati suggested a solution when he pointed out that Jakobson's examples of "phatic contact" are not paralinguistic gestures or channel-checking but

> are *questions*, a class of discourse with a special appelative dimension—because the intended effect is a particular verbal conduct on the listener's part, namely an *answer*—and a special representative dimension, namely a representation of a state of affairs as problematical. (145–146)

In an oral situation, when a listener does answer, of course, she becomes a speaker and the erstwhile speaker becomes the listener: we have, in short, an overt dialogue. Jakobson's basic speech event model is an oral, not a literate, model. But it is an exceedingly peculiar oral model in that it virtually ignores dialogue and treats speech communication as though it were a one-way, unquestioned discourse like a sermon or a formal lecture. Yet once again Jakobson provides a hint of a psychological opening when he defines a contact as a "physical channel *and psychological connection* between the addresser and the addressee, enabling both of them to enter and stay in communication" (353, emphasis added). Riffaterre, in an attempt to adapt this concept to the literate situation, redefined psychological contact in terms of stylistics. Calling it "the control the message has over the reader's attention," he asserted that the reader's "response . . . testifies to the actuality of a contact" (Tompkins, ed., 37).

It is undoubtedly true that the reader is, or rather can choose to be, a respondent to the text and that the text implicitly whispers continually: "Did you follow that metaphor? Did you understand that allusion? Are you losing interest in me? Are you worthy of my depth and subtlety?" What is problematical according to this view is the text-as-object and the ability of the reader to retaliate to this questioning by questions of her own, that is, by assuming the hermeneutical set toward the message and interrogating the objectified text.

But, this text/reader contactual dialogue notwithstanding, is there no dialogue represented *in the text*, a contact that the reader *plays* in the performance of the poem? The insights of Mikhail Bakhtin help us answer this. Language, he argued, is social and, to the extent that thought is verbally mediated, it too is social. His aesthetics, like that of his contemporary Lev Vygotsky, was built directly upon the work of German and Soviet psychologists whose experimentation had led them to conclude that we subvocally articulate (1) the words we hear spoken to us, (2) the words we read "silently," and (3) the words we use when we think. In these situations the speech centers of the brain actually innervate our laryngeal and oral muscles to a slight but measurable extent. Incipient speech thus accompanies most, if not all, of our conscious activity. This means that while speaking, when we pause for a breath or to recollect our thoughts, we may subvocally continue to "talk"—to talk to ourselves.[5]

This pause, which may be a second or two or only a fraction of a second long, is a critical moment in any conversation. It is the moment when we question, tacitly or explicitly, our contact with our addressee, when we ask ourselves if we are really making sense and if we need to take a different tack in order to inform or persuade our partner more successfully. It is the point at which we, as addresser, try to incorporate the addressee by anticipating this person's possible objections. This same pause is also the crucial moment for our interlocutor, who is now released from the obligation to mime our words subvocally and can think out and utter a response—a question, a comment, or an objection that may be taken as a friendly contribution to the development of the joint discourse or as a competitive attempt to divert its course. For us this pause in the dialogic agon is indeed a "moment of truth": if our antecedent discourse has been completely persuasive it will have exhausted the need, if not the possibility, of further development; but if it has revealed its own inner contradictions or the continuing problematicity of its topic, it only provokes a dialogic rejoinder.

Since verbally mediated thought replicates *mutatis mutandis* the structures of dialogic speech, when we engage in this "solitary," cogitative process, we not only talk to ourself, but ourself answers *in the persona of someone else*. This fictive "other," whom I will call the "conversant," is an interior addressee whose attention we must continually solicit, for this interior conversant is an entity that can become uncomprehending, unconvinced, or simply bored. When we bore this stand-in for the world of speakers beyond our subjective self, when we arouse no response whatsoever to our thinking, it is as though we have been talking to ourself, only to discover that ourself has not been listening. At this point thought has stopped. We have been drawn apart (*distracted*) from our inner communion. We are at an impasse. A deadly closure has supervened. Thereupon, if we wish to avoid a solitude that is this absolute, we strive to move the interior discourse forward with fresh data and observations.

Now, insofar as a literary text imitates the structure of thought, it will incorporate pauses that will either be filled or empty. If filled, they may take the form of a rhetorical question (e.g., "Why am I concerned with the origin of this condition?"), which may or may not be answered, or a proleptic remark (e.g., "Some will say I am overstating my case"). If empty, this pause will be marked only by a shift in the thematic development, the kind of shift we note when listening to only one side of a friend's conversation with someone else on the telephone. As though overhearing one side of a dialogue, when we encounter an empty pause and a shift in an ostensibly single-voiced poetic text, we infer the contribution of the addresser's unheard interior "conversant." This pause may be marked in the typography of the text by indentation, a dropped line (as in the verse paragraphing of blank verse), or by some other means. It may be marked, however, only by a shift in semantic material with or without a transitional conjunction, adverb, or phrase.

It is the dynamic of dialogic contact that thus determines the shifts from one cognitive mode to another, each internally organized in an associative sequence, and from one linguistic function to another (Jakobson's six factors and functions). Logical association, the so-called "laws of the association of ideas," which we briefly examined in the last chapter, includes such relationships as cause-effect, before-after temporal seriality, figure-ground contiguity, part-whole, resemblance, and contrariety. Each of these principles can generate an associative sequence, that is, a particular kind of thematic development, and, once announced, each associative "train of thought" progresses programmatically toward completion; it either achieves this, thereby exhausting its topical potential, or is detoured by another associative consideration or, more disruptively, by a function-shift. This latter shift occurs when the (or in an overt dialog *a*) speaker decides to shift focus from, say, the referential context to the emotive addresser ("Why does this topic get you [or me] so excited?"), or to the conative addressee ("Why are you telling *me* this? [or, why am I telling *you* this?]"), and so forth. When such interruptions, overt or implied, redirect the discourse and become thematized themselves, they radically alter the focus of this dialogic exchange.

Analogic Code

Jakobson says of the foregrounding of code in speech that this occurs when the meaning of a word is questioned and the speaker's attention is directed toward the code being used. Such a query is metalingual in that it uses language to discourse on language. The process, he says, is one of "glossing," of substituting one word for another on the basis of equivalence.

He was well aware how very close "metalingual function" might seem to his "poetic function," of which he said: "The poetic function projects the principle of equivalence from the axis of selection into the axis of combination." By this, the most celebrated passage in his "Closing Statement," Jakobson drew attention to the linguistic features, phonological, syntactic, and semantic, that appear to repeat themselves in equivalent forms in most kinds of poetry, that is, the similar sounds, stresses, grammatical constructions, and themes that are often used in verse to compose patterns normally avoided in prose. Lest anyone assume that this is a kind of metalingual glossing, he hastened to add that: "Poetry and metalanguage . . . are in diametric opposition to each other: in metalanguage the sequence is used to build an equation, whereas in poetry the equation is used to build a sequence" (358).

But can this opposition be any greater than that which characterizes the split functions he speaks of thirteen pages later (371), especially that between "It was and it was not"? Diametric oppositions are after all the result of two related entities moving in symmetrically split directions. (They are by no means unconnected: as I noted in my preface, every 180-degree difference does after all describe a straight line.) Of course, poetic equivalences and the redundant patterns they produce are distinguishable from lexical glossing and, insofar as they are not intended to draw analytical attention to themselves as code equivalences, they are indeed diametrically opposed to metalanguage. There is nothing especially unique about this diametric opposition: we have encountered such oppositions whenever we have reopened Jakobson's "Closing Statement," for, insofar as poetic performance is diametrically opposed, as a "set toward the message," to the work of hermeneutical analysis, poetics is itself diametrically opposed to linguistically grounded hermeneutic. This does not mean that the two are irrelevant to one another: like enantiomorphs and other bilateral symmetries, diametric oppositions are complementarities.

The *play* of metalanguage in a poem is certainly not a glossing of one word with another drawn from the extratextual code of a given language. (This would be the work of an editor's footnote.) It is therefore not prompted by an external deviation, a solecism that is introduced and then glossed. The metalingual play to which I refer is contained within the confines of the poem considered as itself constituting a kind of miniature, nonce language, a *parole* that we pretend is coextensive with its own *langue*. (See Posner 694.) We *know*, for example, that rhyming words are seldom synonyms—they are often "diametrically opposed" semantically—yet we are asked to play with the notion that phonetic similarity equals semantic synonymy. We associate the two items, while at the same time recognizing their dissociation. Wimsatt's essay "A Relation of Reason to Rhyme," which Jakobson alludes to (388), makes exactly this point. Rhyming words, he noted, "impose upon the logical pattern of expressed argument a kind of fixative counterpattern of alogical implication" (*Verbal Icon,* 153). This same play of equivalences Freud referred to as symbolic *displacement,* the process in dream-work in which affective significance is transferred from one object or person to another, the very process we find in that special kind of poetic glossing we know as metaphor.

Jakobson on page 358 sharply defined poetry and metalanguage as opposites, but on 370, just before he began to consider the ambiguity of poetry, he reversed himself and said: "In poetry not only the phonological sequence but in the same way any sequence of semantic units strives to build an equation." Going even further, he added: "Technically, anything sequent is a simile. In poetry where similarity is superinduced upon contiguity, any metonymy is slightly metaphorical and any metaphor has a metonymical tint." This remarkable admission makes sense only if he had somewhere in the back of his mind a double set toward the message—a standard linguistic set that recognizes metalingual glossing and a poetic set that recognizes a ludic glossing, namely, metalingual analogy.

I have termed the code of a poem "analogic" because its iterations are at best only roughly equivalent—not logical equations but quasi- or play-equations the analogic combination of which serves to highlight as much their differences as their similarities. Foot substitution in quantitative and accentual-syllabic verse, the counterpoint of syntax and meter at the line-unit level, and the requirement of metaphor that its two terms be ordinarily semantically distant: all these poetic conventions emphasize the importance of similarity-within-difference and difference-within-similarity, that is, of analogy as the essential feature of every intratextually constituted poetic code.

As with contact, Jakobson tried to ignore the fact that code is "double-sensed" (371). His need to deny the play of a poetic code was quite clearly motivated, for to the extent that a poem defines its linguistic means and exhibits a kind of unique linguistic code of its own, it lies beyond the norms of its natural language and of linguistic science. Except perhaps for some Dada texts, no poem is ever entirely beyond such norms, but on the other hand, as Jakobson himself insisted, a poem is a poem precisely by virtue of its deviation from these norms. It follows therefore that what he declared as constitutive of poetry is the very feature that decisively liberates poetics as a discipline from the discipline of linguistics.

Chapter 4
Tactics and Timing

Poetic imagination is not simply the capacity of the mind to use verbal cues to visualize an absent or non-existent object as though it were present. It assumes in advance an ability and willingness on the part of the reader to enter into the fictive process. Poetic play, which I recommended in Chapter 3 as a possible solution to several perplexing problems, obliges the reader to assume the voice and referential contexts of others while never relinquishing a sense of the habitual self, the real "me." This is the willing suspension of disbelief ("for the moment," as Coleridge wisely added) in the power of the self to become other selves.

The training that qualifies the reader to be this poetic player involves the learning of certain basic plays, or tactics. Since these are performed in language, poetic tactics are specializations of linguistic tactics, that is, syntactics. But unlike the syntax of speech and of what we in a print culture might term "disposable writing," poetic tactics are fashioned for a stored and repeatable verbal artifact, a *text*. Though, as I pointed out in Chapter 1, the storage mode (oral or graphic) is an important factor in the structure and content of a text, the very fact that it *is stored* and can be repeatedly retrieved differentiates it at every level of integration from that of unstored discourse. Because of this fundamental difference, poetic structures are not bound by tactical rules at all comparable in rigor to those of grammar. Accordingly, there is no compelling need for repeatable discourse to reveal its complete meaning at first hearing or perusal. It would have been an impressive announcement—that the grammar of poetry had finally been discovered—but if, as I have argued, the links are loose and determined by the aesthetics of play behavior, linguistic syntax can never be more than an available model, not a norm, for poetic tactics.

Since the primary difference between poetic and linguistic tactics stems from the iterative, textualized character of the former and the ongoing, speech-grounded character of the latter, the issue of time must also be addressed. We seem to enter another sort of temporal state when we enter the play of reading. What has been written belongs to the past, yet as we begin reading a text we project its events into our immediate future, a future that, if we have read this text before, we paradoxically *remember.* The time of the actual reading and the time of the portrayed world of the text are the two different kinds of time we encounter in reading. The latter image-thronged time, often a complex weave of temporal perspectives, is the principal object of tactical structuration.

Hypotaxis

Webster's Third International Dictionary informs us that *hypotaxis* is "syntactic subordination (as by a conjunction)—opposed to *parataxis.*" In contrast to this scant definition it tells us a great deal about its correlative term, *parataxis:*

1a: coordinate ranging of clauses, phrases, or words one after another without coordinating connectives (as in "he laughed; she cried")—opposed to *hypotaxis*
b: the placing of a subordinate clause beside a main clause without subordinating connective (as in "I believe it is true; there is a man wants to see you")
2: the parataxic mode of experience.

This last cited word, *parataxic,* one discovers, is a psychological term that describes what it is like to experience the world "without subordinating connectives." This word is defined as

characterized by or relating to a mode of individual experience in which persons, events, and relationships are perceived as discrete phenomena, in which occurrences in the real world are seen as having no sequential or logical relationship, but in which all external stimuli have only idiosyncratic autistic significance.

Parataxis, as a rhetorical figure of speech, is literally a "side-by-side arrangement" of statements like "I came, I saw, I conquered." (The Senate was presumably expected to fill in the gaps Caesar left by supplying the logical connections.) Hypotaxis is an "underneath arrangement," that is, a layering of one statement upon another (cf. "After I came and saw the enemy, I conquered"). Military types have always been fond of parataxis (perhaps it reminds them of the Macedonian phallanx, perhaps it mimics the autism of definition 2). Diplomats, on the other hand, have been exceedingly fond of hypotactic discourse because it lays down conditions upon which further agreements can be negotiated.

Early Renaissance writers also seemed to delight in hypotaxis. They savored not only the rolling *cola* of the Ciceronian period but the complex sentence for its own sake. Consider this sentence of Boccaccio ("Simone and Pasquino"):

> Know then that no great while ago there dwelt in Florence a maid most fair, and, for her rank, debonair—she was but a poor man's daughter—whose name was Simona; and though she must needs win with her own hands the bread she ate, and maintain herself by spinning wool; yet was she not, therefore, of so poor a spirit, but that she dared to give harborage in her mind to Love, who for some time had sought to gain entrance there by means of the gracious deeds and words of a young man of her own order that went about distributing wool to spin for his master, a woolmonger.[1]

Here two lives are limned, two foregrounded figures balanced at either side of a sentence, their geographical setting and occupations ranged behind them, while between them Love appears as an agent of mutual attraction. There are coordinate clauses here, but the comprehensiveness of this sentence is made possible by the subordinate clauses and nonrestrictive elements that nest themselves one within the other.

Before we consider how this notion of superimposition is important to a theory of cognitive modes as it may be applied to poetic structure and imagery, we should look more closely at its linguistic application. As we all remember from traditional grammar, a "complex sentence" is characterized by "subordination" (this term is the Latinate equivalent of "hypotaxis"). A complex sentence is made up of a "main (or independent) clause" and one or more "subordinate (or dependent) clauses." Two examples, drawn from a traditional grammar handbook (Buckler and McAvoy 83, 323) are as follows:

> Although he had been warned against fighting, *he chose to defy his parents* when the neighbor's boy insulted him.

> Because we have been asking the wrong questions in this country, *we have been stifling education.*

The main, or independent clauses, here emphasized, can syntactically stand alone, whereas the other clauses, introduced by the connectives "although," "when," and "because," cannot stand alone. But from a semantic point of view this ascription of main and subordinate status, this hierarchy of value, is put in question.

In the first sample sentence the main clause is indeed the focal point, the climactic incident, the consequences of which will probably be stated in subsequent sentences, but the value of this clause is semantically dependent on what, from the syntactic point of view, are two dependent clauses. They set forth the conditions that give value to this climactic action. But the placement of these clauses is worth noting: the main clause is embedded out of sequence between two correctly sequenced events, a past perfect warning and a simple perfect insult. If this were presented in film, it would necessitate two possibly confusing "jump-cuts": a scene of parental admonishment, then a view of the boy's reddening face, clenched fists, and sudden lunge, then incomprehensibly the other boy's provocation. Perceptual visuality would have considerable difficulty with this sequence because it would not have the syntactical markers that verbal visuality has at its disposal: as a complex sentence, this scenario presents no problems to the reader, whose mind somehow unscrambles these three events and reassembles them into a single complex of *interdependent* meanings.

The second example, of which the authors say the "ideas here stand in cause-and-effect relationship," have no sequencing problem and therefore demonstrate how semantically dependent a syntactically *in*-dependent clause can be on a syntactically dependent clause. Asking the wrong questions is the underlying cause of a stifling education, but here "underlying" does not imply subordination, but rather its opposite—dominance and effectuation. As these examples illustrate, hypotactic structure when semantically analyzed reveals how multiple blocks of information become mutually associated. The "main" block lies on the top of, and is conditioned by, the lower-layered blocks.

Hypotaxis thus represents a quasi-three-dimensional model of real-world events. Unlike parataxis, which does not recognize the footprints and the foreshadowings of the absent within the perceptual present, hypotaxis creates a dynamic force-field in which entities amass meaning through association. Like a complex visual object or that series of discrete acoustic impulses that the human mind recognizes as a melody, the complex sentence is received as consecutive units, but is comprehended as a totality.

The dependence of the so-called main clause on the so-called subordinate clause is particularly apparent in the case of restrictive clauses, that is, subordinate clauses that significantly modify the main clause. But the non-restrictive clause is also an interesting form to study. As an elaboration, often descriptive, of elements in the main clause, it has an obviously important role to play in verbal imagery. An example from this traditional handbook, which its authors attribute to Sherwood Anderson (Buckler and McAvoy 195), is as follows:

On the Trunion Pike, where the road stretched away between berry fields now covered with dry brown leaves, the dust from passing wagons arose in clouds.

Set off by commas, the central clause is in the nature of a *parenthesis*; a fluent speaker when articulating such a construction intonationally acknowledges it as supplementary by lowering the pitch, then raising it to its normal range for the concluding clause. The relevance of parenthetical hypotaxis to literal imagery is apparent from the above example, but its equal relevance to figurative imagery emerges only if we open this non-restrictive clause after "road" and insert between commas another hypotactic element, for example the non-restrictive phrase "like a snake." Now suppose we modify the "snake" by adding a participial phrase "twisting and turning its gray, coiled length." If we were feeling particularly Homeric, we could detour into a herpetological simile that might stretch its hideous length through several sentences before returning us to Trunion Pike. But, having announced by the word "like" the parenthetical nature of this excursus, we would expect our reader to construe this snake as belonging to a context semantically parallel to, but not actually copresent with, the principal referent. Which is to say: No legless reptile crawls upon Trunion Pike.

Footnotes and endnotes are parenthetical addenda that book pagination introduced. Texts stored in memory or in papyrus scrolls had no footnotes and so their authors had to insert these addenda directly into the text following the cue-sentence. The sometimes rambling style of Herodotus, for example, is a hypotactic consequence of his storage medium, the scroll. Modern translators (of his medium as well as his message) have sometimes decided to convert his note-like asides into footnotes.[2] Oral compositions show evidence of the same process. Not only were rhapsodes, or "song-stitchers," obliged to stitch explanatory elaborations directly into the text, but could do so only if these passages were brief and fitted the meter. If these were long, they had to be set-pieces interesting in themselves. The Homeric epics abound in such inflations. The story of how Odysseus received the scar on his leg is in the nature of what we would now call an extended footnote, a parenthetical excursus that could maintain its place in the epic only because this story of the boy's hunting with his grandfather "Lonewolf" has intrinsic narrative merit. Of course this is not its only merit: as an expanded moment in which his old nurse recollects the information, this remarkable flashback relates hypotactically to the present circumstance and sustains its suspenseful tone.

Hypotaxis is thus a means by which serial information is converted into parallel information. For readers, it requires the ability to retain a number of items in short-term memory until they can be integrated into a whole that is greater than, and different from, the sum of its parts. The complex sentence is therefore a homologue of the poetic text, the larger structures of which can include excursuses as in Homer and framing devices as in the *Arabian Nights,* the *Decameron,* and the *Canterbury Tales.* But before I address the proposition that cognitive modes are indeed hypotactic clauses writ large, I need to examine the correlative term, parataxis, and then construct the ways by which these two tactics are temporally ordered.

Parataxis

"Parataxis" may not be a word on every contemporary literary scholar's lips, but twentieth-century theory, like *Webster's,* has found much more to say about it than about its opposite principle, hypotaxis. Parataxis in fact is generally assumed to be a structural trait of Modernist poetics. Associating it with Ezra Pound's "ideogrammic method," the juxtapositions of T. S. Eliot, the minimalist prose of Gertrude Stein and Ernest Hemingway, and the dreamlike sequences of Surrealists, cultural historians also detect its traces in filmic montage, in collage and Cubism, and in aleatoric music. Some have interpreted its emergence in the twentieth century as a response to the ethical decontextualization of this century and the loss of those common cultural assumptions that connect and make meaningful any series of occurrences. For them Camus's Stranger is the new Everyman for whom the world is one vast, bewildering, sun-drenched parataxis "in which all external stimuli have only idiosyncratic autistic significance," to cite *Webster's* second definition of the word.

Such analyses are no less cogent simply because they have been repeated so often. But since our concern in this chapter must be upon the ways that cognitive modes affect poetic imagery and upon the tactics by which these modes are deployed in texts, we must focus here on the function of parataxis in the reading of texts.

In traditional grammar parataxis can be any arrangement of syntactically coequal elements, which may or may not be linked by coordinate conjunctions—for example, *and, but, yet, for, or,* and *nor.* But as a stylistic term, parataxis is generally taken to mean the linking of elements by *and* or the omission of connectives altogether. The relation between such elements must then be a product of their position in a linear sequence. An interesting analogy to this is that of a relatively noninflected language that depends on word order rather than bound morphemes, for example, case- and declension-endings. In this sense, English and Chinese are paratactic languages.

All languages, of course, are produced linearly as a series of sounds or graphic symbols and the medium of poetry is therefore serial. In his *Laokoon* (Chapter XVII) Lessing concluded that on these grounds poetry could not successfully portray "a bodily whole by its parts." That is, the reader could not hold an extended, serialized inventory of parts in mind long enough to integrate them into a whole as a composite image. The "*coexistence* of the physical object would come into collision with the *consecutiveness* of speech" and the whole would necessarily be dismembered into its verbalized parts.

There are surely limits to the capacity of most minds to store details while waiting to assemble them as a single complex image and surely many of Lessing's contemporaries had become so enamoured of the "pleasures of imagination" as to push to the limits their readers' long-suffering short-term memories. Yet Lessing's poetic norms seem to derive from the essentially oral traditions of epic and drama. As I proposed in my first chapter, these genres cannot successfully accommodate extended description, for in oral performance not only the consecutiveness of speech, but also, more importantly, the coexistence of visual percepts, collides with mental imaging.

How broad indeed is our attention span when we confront the "consecutiveness of speech"? Even if it is centered on a letter or phoneme or syllable, it also has to be broad enough to include the word these elements compose and the phrase this word is part of; otherwise, discourse would seem meaningless. Must it not span the clause also, and the sentence? These questions are important because, if parataxis is a stylistic factor in reader response, it is so only to the extent that a present segment of text is separable as a unit from preceding and succeeding segments—so separable that it seems logically disconnected. When we come upon such a passage, we must sense a discontinuity, a "place of indeterminacy," as Ingarden termed this disjunction.

When moments occur, they are not chasms into which the reader falls but rather occasions for bridge construction, as Wolfgang Iser has proposed in *The Act of Reading* and elsewhere. The mind has no difficulty briefly holding together two passages at the same time. If they are logically related, they will cohere by common associative links. If they are logically opposed, they will seem to connect by antithesis or negation. If they appear to have no conceivable connection and the second passage seems an absolute non sequitur to the first, the reader's mind will still connect them by some associative bond. The impulse to find—or impose—coherence on texts is a human instinct. We all know, for example, that children (and adults too), when they encounter a word in a song that they do not know or do not hear clearly, substitute their own near-homophone just to preserve the coherence of the oral text. Written texts are less amenable to such emendation, but readers nevertheless insist that such disparate passages be linked somehow, if not entirely rationalized.

One reason for this anti-paratactic tendency lies in the nature of the human "present." William James called it "specious" because he recognized that not all of it was actually present at any single point in time. It was "no knife-edge," he said, but a saddle-back, with a certain breadth of its own in which we sit perched and from which we look into two directions into time. The unit of composition of our perception of time is a *duration,* with a bow and a stern, as it were—a rearward and a forward-looking end. (I, 609)

Edmund Husserl in his *Phenomenology of Internal Time-Consciousness* named this rearward present the "retentional consciousness" (or "primary memory"), the forward-looking present the "protentional consciousness," and the immediate, punctal present the "impressional consciousness" (57–60). Ingarden and Iser, when they speak of the two ever changing horizons that follow the reader moving through the text, refer to the limits of retention and protention.

Why, one might ask, have paratactic constructions that so stretch our readerly horizons emerged so pervasively in twentieth-century poetry. As I argued in Chapter 1, literacy has certainly increased the capacity of texts and readers to store and retrieve extended imagery. It has also made it possible to read and reread shorter texts and through this process of familiarization forge (in both senses of this word) links between ostensibly unrelated passages. Writing (and especially print), since it places an entire text in a reader's hands, implies a greater degree of coherence and completion than that of a spoken text existing only in vocalized time. Can a set of seemingly disconnected items really be disconnected if they appear as components of what we visually perceive as a single text? Are they contextless because no subordinate clause states the conditions of their existence, or in their destitution do these orphaned items pitch in and offer themselves as context for one another? "Bare lists of words are found suggestive to an imaginative and excited mind," as Ralph Waldo Emerson observed and the Surrealists demonstrated. Paratactic writing is not an inducement to parataxic anomie. On the contrary, it is an invitation to the reader to participate actively in the completion of the structure.

A celebrated example of parataxis appears in Pound's "In a Station of the Metro." The faces he saw in that station become linked in this two-line poem with:

Petals on a wet, black bough.

There is no more paratactic punctuation mark than a semicolon, which Pound used to couple these two images. It is as noncommittal as a connecting marker can be, so why do we treat that inarticulate semicolon as though it signaled "metaphor"? Perhaps because we are used to metaphorical constructions, perhaps because we suspect Pound is imitating some elliptical Chinese or Japanese poetic style. But, if when we analyze our responses we end with the question "What else can the poet be doing anyway?" we acknowledge our assumption that poets have intentional tactics that they hope their readers can follow and that poems are made up of parts that do things together. When in this instance we choose to construe these two lines as the two terms of a metaphor, we do so undirected by the text but with what we have come to assume is the encouragement of this Modernist maker of parataxis.

The fact that we are undirected by the text and that we throw ourselves and our associative assumptions into the breach between juxtaposed elements of discourse produces in us an experience that seems somehow different each time we reread such texts. We *hypothesize* some principle of relation—and "hypothesize" (to put under, or suppose, i.e., sub-pose) is a legitimate verb to accompany "hypotaxis."

Barbara Herrnstein Smith, assessing the function of hypothesis in her study of poetic closure, states that, "if the conclusion confirms the hypothesis suggested by the work's thematic structure, closure will be to that extent secure" (120). When such a closure occurs, the reader can look back and note with aesthetic satisfaction the "retrospective patterning" (119) that has logically prepared her for this ending. But what if she has already read this text? In this case retrospection is not the only factor, nor is hypothesis the only means of anticipating closure. *Pro*spective patterning is also a significant factor, since the reader (the "real 'me'") cannot altogether expunge from her memory her knowledge of outcomes and endings.

Smith's focus on this left-to-right process, like Stanley Fish's in *Surprised by Sin* and his early essay "Affective Stylistics," illuminates the vicissitudes of the initial reading. But, while the medium of poetry is indeed consecutive and time-like, a poem is not unidirectional and only one of its readings can be "initial." It is not meant to be a once-and-for-all-time encounter; if it were, it would not be stored *as a text*. Whether it is stored in memory, in writing, or in some other modality, a text, like the rubrics of a ritual, is meant to be reused again and again. This repeatedness, which is a condition of their reception, becomes a property of texts, inseparable from their thematic content. The fact that any reader can know, simply by reading the play once, that Agamemnon will be murdered in his bath affects the meaning of his appearance and his speeches when he enters Argos. Who, for that matter, even at its premiere, did not know the fate of Agamemnon and of the whole House of Atreus? These *mythoi* were already collectively stored memorial texts. Only the dramatis personae could not be sure of this play's closure—none of them, that is, except Cassandra. Unlike the others who, locked within the flow of time, were ignorant of what even the tiniest fraction of the next second would bring, Cassandra was like the reader to whom this text was already known. In short, we resemble fictive personae in our ignorance of our own future, but not in our knowledge of *their* future, which at any point in the unfolding narrative we, as privileged witnesses, can know with absolute certainty. What appears to A as an unfathomable occurrence, we understand as the contrivance of B; what seems a minor risk, C, we know as the stroke of doom, D. Confined to the linear, unidirectional time-line of their lives, fictive personae strive to make sense out of the paratactic consecutiveness of events; we, however, as *re*readers look down from our divine vantage point at a world ceaselessly turning in cyclic recurrence and glimpse the hypotactic relations that underlie such events. Fate, *fatum* in Latin, means the thing already said. The textual storage of what has already been said thus bestows upon us the privilege of replaying fate—the fate of others, not our own.

We can respond to this advantage in one of three ways: (1) by stressing our under-standing of the under-arrangement, that is, the hypotaxis, of events; (2) by stressing our bewilderment at the unpredictable shifts of paratactic occurrences; or (3) by attempting to experience understanding and bewilderment at the same time. The first response is one that conceptualizes formal synchrony; the second attempts to restrict itself to each moment as it is diachronically revealed to a persona or to the reader-as-persona; the third accepts the paradoxical motto, the *Aixo era y non era* of poetic play, and assumes a prior knowledge and a present ignorance of text, which is the privilege of retaining a "real 'me'" while becoming an "alien 'me.'"

The second response has an interesting relation to the two structural principles we have been considering in this chapter. The assumption of ignorance, that is, the bracketing of prior acquaintance with a text, creates a role for the rereader as the central character in a once-in-a-lifetime adventure. Like Dante and unlike Vergil or Beatrice, to whom the Other World was a familiar script, the reader is constantly making hypotactic assumptions—hypotheses—in the course of encountering paratactic experiences. Some of these guesses are correct, thanks to the hints authorially provided, but many of them are incorrect. Correct or not, this readerly engagement in problem-solving enlightens the reader only if and when the text solves the problem it has seemingly posed. The supreme dénouement, of course, is the closure. But for a reader who knows the closure and anticipates each gap, surprise and efforts to hypothesize and anticipate can only be functions of poetic play, not actual efforts in problem-solving.

The Structure of Kairotic Play

The Greeks made a distinction between "time" as the continuous flow of change and "a time" as a recognizable segment of that flow. The former they called "chronos," the latter "kairos." To be in chronos was to be consigned to an indefinite temporal flux that continuously swept one from one instant to another. Of course, like moderns, the ancients recognized a certain "psychic" breadth to this instant: in one's memory and imagination one was not bound as a galley slave to the present and did not live one's life in the utter bewilderment of parataxis. One reason for this was that nature is rhythmic and, by offering us time in cyclical units of days, nights, and seasons, permits us to convert it into chronometric units. Another reason is that the individual memory organizes time into episodes, events with beginnings, middles, and ends, each episode framed by a shadowy margin of forgotten experience. The third reason is that culture, as a collective memory, has provided means of storing and retrieving episodes and other valuable reserves of information so that we may repossess these bounded paradigms of experience whenever we have need of them.

These repeatable units of time, snatched from the oblivious flow of chronos, are the time of ritual, drama, narrative, song, and dance. Each constitutes a kairos, the "time" the mother means when she says "Once upon a *time*." It is also what the child understands as "story*time*." When the child says "Tell me the story about the . . ." and names his favorite tale, he means he wants his parent to perform for and with him a kairos (the telling) about the kairos (the bounded events that comprise the tale) and, as he listens in the half dark he imagines those two kairoi merging into one. This willing suspension of disbelief in the difference between the action of portrayal (*mimēsis*) and the portrayed action (*mimēma*) is what I mean by kairotic play.

The delight we experience in kairos may be partly a response to our liberation from chronos. A saddle on which we sit as we ride, a boat in which we sail—William James's images place us in motion through a space that sweeps toward and past us. We anticipate the arrival and mark the recession of objects that we so briefly encounter—or that encounter us, since such conjunctures are relative. Our conscious present may not be an indivisible mathematical point, but it is what we mean by a "point" in the sense of a locus, as when we speak of a "vantage point" or "a point in our lives." Our consciousness of linear time, or chronos, is therefore that of a series of points, moments of attention to the objects of the ongoing present. Our "now" position, our vantage point, may have breadth, but so does a prison cell: we can never remove ourselves from this position nor be certain either of what will happen next or of the meaning of what is now happening until we know the future, which we can only know when this narrow present has added its tiny interval to the long past.

Never to know the meaning of "now"—this is our fate, living as we must in this paratactic universe. We may never know till later the significance to others of a word or gesture that we make. A parent never knows which piggyback ride is the last he will ever give his child or the last bedtime story he will ever read: it comes and goes unsolemnized by reflexion. Every surviving child will see a parent for a last time, but rarely is this last glimpse recognized for what it is. The now that we perceive and can in some respects modify has scant significance for us. We blunder upon it and improvise a response to it. Its significance is only retrospectively assigned. Only in memory can we construe—correctly or not—its place in a hypotactic system of causes and consequences.

Kairos, on the other hand, is a durational totality all of whose temporal points are knowable and retrievable. Each of its points are tinged with the known meaning of all its points. This whole is saturated with meaning at every point, at every "now" along its passage from beginning, through middle, and to end. The persona or personae represented in the kairos rarely possess this extraordinary knowledge: if, as is usually the case, they are restricted to chronos, we pity them their blind subjection to dramatic irony and fear for them as we fear for ourselves, similarly vulnerable. The uniqueness of kairotic play lies in its abrogation (for us as readers, at least) of the laws of chronos. Its pleasure for us lies in the liberation of the mind from the strait confines of linear time and in the opening and saturation of the moment with meaning.

Before we consider the tactics of poems, the ways in which blocks of verbal cues are offered to the reader's imagination, it might be useful to observe the ways in which these two time-concepts affect our experience of poetic structure.

Augustine explores these "times" in the well-known passage in *The Confessions* (11.28), beginning "Dicturus sum canticum, quod novi":

I am about to recite a Psalm that I am familiar with. Before I begin, my anticipation [*expectatio*] extends [*tenditur*] over the whole of it, but once I have begun reading, whatever I have separated off into the past extends into my memory. Thus the life of this activity of mine now stretches in two directions [*distenditur*], into memory in respect to what I have recited and into anticipation in respect to what I am about to recite. My attention, on the other hand, remains ever in the present and it is by virtue of attention that that which was future is propelled across to become the past. The more this action is performed, the shorter is my anticipation and the longer is my memory; when finally my whole anticipation is consumed, then the whole completed activity will have crossed into memory.

This process by which the attentional present moves through a familiar text occurs at the level of particular portions and even at that of particular syllables. The process he describes in this passage is a distinct combination of the two times, a chronos of linear progression through the words of the text and a kairos of performing this total composition. Since this is one that he has already become familiar with, his reading is a linear progression through a kairos.

At the other scale of magnitude, Augustine goes on to add, a human life and the life of humankind on the earth can equally be read as a text. He implies, of course, that this reading can only be from the vantage point of God, who as author knows the script of history and knows even when and where he will revise it. Human chronos, that interminable chain of days and nights, is from the height of Augustine's God a single kairos, or a sequence of seven kairoi, a cosmic week, as he suggests in the *City of God*. But a viewer privileged with such a vantage point *could* pretend to belong among the poor folk who do not know the full script. This empathetic projection of oneself into the time-bound blindness of these others is a compassionate act of play that Christianity celebrates in its mystery of the Incarnation.[3]

Cognitive Modes

Writing for solitary reading installs the single subject at a godlike height above the world of fictive objects, a knower separate from a known. As I proposed in my discussion of the Jakobsonian addresser and addressee, the reader, though impersonating all the fictive personae and their points of views, remains forever situated at a here and now from which he or she conducts the poetic play, projecting referents along two axes, an Inner-Outer axis and a Past-Present-Future axis.

The importance of the reader as participant in the reenactment of texts has been adequately demonstrated over the past two decades, but the contribution of the solitary reader to the determination of literary form has not been sufficiently explored. What I am suggesting is that, as literature gradually dispensed with specifically oral conventions derived from storytelling and drama, the underlying action that it began to exhibit, the underlying structure that it assumed, became that of the *turning of attention* within the mind of the implied reader. The turning of the "mind's eye" thus became the primary action of the modern poem or novel and the cognitive modes became the primary planes of experience upon which the play of reference is projected. Since this surface play of plot, character, and setting is absolutely essential to poiesis, I do not say that writing is "about" reading, that its single theme is its own construal, but I would maintain that its "deep structure" is precisely that.

Though traces of the Inner-Outer axis (see my diagram, page 59) with its synchronous, space-like projection may be found in literate antiquity, it seems to have come first into prominence during the Renaissance only with the emergence of the new literate subjectivity. The temporal axis, however, appears fully formed quite early and seems to have been one of the first by-products of scribal literacy. Its presence in Mesopotamia and Egypt marked the first shift from an exclusively cyclic notion of time to one of increasingly unidirectional linearity and historicity. The Hebrew Scriptures are probably our most complete record of this early shift and, as religious traditions that placed a sacred value upon writing, Judaism and Christianity made meditation along this axis a particular obligation. All believers were expected to examine their consciences by reviewing their personal pasts, to introspect their present attitudes and affections, and to anticipate weal or woe as consequences of their acts. The Greeks were perhaps less acutely time-conscious, but Aristotle, for one, divided rhetorical compositions into three classes: forensic (the determination of past conduct), epideictic (the pointing out of some present circumstance), and deliberative (the proposal of some future course of action), and the early grammarians were quick to point out how verbs were temporally inflected.

The six cognitive modes that are generated from the intersection of these two axes have both a tactical and a constitutive importance in the study of imagery. As constitutive, they determine the kind of image—its provenance and degree of elaboration (I will examine these issues in the next three chapters). Their tactical importance lies in the manner in which they produce layered sequences of imagery and in so doing incorporate verbal visuality into poetic texts. It is this tactical function that we are concerned with here.

As I described them in Chapter 3, these modes are categories of knowledge that we maintain carefully discriminated. We have learned to distinguish them in our minds and know that an inability to distinguish the inner from the outer and the past, present, and future from one another is to risk profound disorientation. I will describe these modes in somewhat more detail now and follow this with texts that exemplify their tactical deployment.

Retrospection is the reviewing of retrieved experience. When we retrospect persons and places we do so in the form of *episodes* that we can locate, albeit approximately, at particular times and places. As we recall such an episode, we sometimes say we can "see it now," for even incidental details seem to emerge in this particular mode. Retrospection is the primary mode of all narration.

The mode I have named *Assertion* is rather a belief or opinion than an experience. Since we recognize an item of Assertion as something stored in memory, we understand that its acquisition occurred in the past, but we can seldom specify the time and place in which it was learned. It is a conclusion that may be based on many experiences or accepted simply on the authority of others. The principles that we assert serve as the paradigms by which we recognize and interpret objects of *Perception* and, in the process of storing them for later retrospective retrieval, label them as elements of particular episodes. Such Retrospections are then available to us when we need to demonstrate an asserted generalization. The imagery of Assertion is schematic, not particularized, as is those of Retrospection. Things that are asserted do not have the particular space-time locus of Retrospection and represent habitual, predictable phenomena—the "way things are," the *rerum natura*.

Perception we know as such when the object of our consciousness is not something we are retrieving from the past, projecting into the future, or imagining, but is an outer array of stimuli that is at this very moment urging its presence on us. (This is a simple-minded observation, I know, but in discussing the cognitive modes we are dealing with Simple-Mind itself and need sometimes to get down to its level of discrimination.) Perceptual stimuli so saturate our waking senses that all but a few of them must be buffered, sidetracked, or simply blocked out; otherwise our central nervous system would be overwhelmed. Perception is not a passive imprinting but a complex kind of *doing*. We may be exposed to innumerable objects, but after all, as our parents told us, we can only *do* one thing at a time. Perception, when it appears in writing, requires that the reader pretend to be sensing (usually *seeing*) some situation presented here and now. We distinguish it from the other here-and-now cognition that I have called *Introspection* by recognizing the latter as deriving from an inner store from which it seems to spring forth spontaneously in response to some triggering circumstance. An Introspection is therefore what one might loosely term an interior perception. (The Schoolmen, taking Aristotle as their authority, believed that such *visiones* were received by *sensus interni*, inner senses equipped to register the subtler lineaments of spirit.) An important use of Introspection in discourse is the presentation of metaphorical vehicles—images that emerge suddenly in iconic response to other images, schemata, or abstractions. It also appears as fantasies, visions, and the like. Reading is actually a semiotic conversion of Perception into Introspection: this is what the "real 'me' " does. But since poetic play entails the impersonation of "alien 'me's,' " who are able to display the full complement of six cognitive modes, we need to view the text as a play-script that prompts fictive acts of cognitive projection, including play versions of Perception and Introspection.

The two future modes, Expectation and Judgment, are, like the future self, supposititious and composed of elements less clearly categorized than those of the other modes. *Expectation,* literally "looking out" (from the present to the future), includes prediction and willed intention and may best be regarded as a projection of the Retrospective Mode from the Already into the Not Yet. That is to say, we tend to conceptualize the future as a mirror-image of the past to which we add contingency, freedom, and consequently a degree of unpredictability. As the "outer" aspect of the future, Expectation involves suppositions about the world of objects among which, and to which, we, as subjects, also appear as objects. *Judgment,* finally, is our own "inner" evaluation of a proposed action or an anticipated happening in terms of its subjective consequences. It, too, is a mirror-image realm, but it mirrors that store of beliefs I have called Assertion. If we project an action and then judge it according to any standard—efficiency, pleasure, ethical worth, and so on—we apply to it axioms stored as general knowledge.

Problem-solving is one procedure that involves, and so can illustrate, all six modes. For example: I intend to take my car and go to town to do shopping (Expectation). When I turn the ignition key, I hear a slight wheeze, notice the dashboard lights are dim, hear a tapping behind the glove compartment, but hear no other sound from beneath the hood (Perception). These perceptual data I take to be symptoms of some condition that will stand in the way of my expectations. To diagnose them I must find in my store of general knowledge a cause that can account for them (Assertion). I may propose several possible causes, for example, leaving the car lights on overnight, having damp sparkplugs, having a frozen battery, having corroded battery terminals, and so on. I may phone a friend who, recalling a similar occurrence (Retrospection), may ask how that tapping sounded. In response I hit upon a simile and tell him that it sounded like a woodpecker (Introspection). He might then advise me to check for corrosion inside the connector on the positive pole of the battery. After I clean this out, the engine responds immediately to my ignition key. Later, when I telephone him to thank him, my friend advises me that "to stay on the safe side" I should invest in a new connector (Judgment).

Poems, however, are seldom about conditions that can be so effectively corrected. Poetry makes nothing happen, as W. H. Auden once said, but by defining the incorrigible and the ineluctable it does stake the boundaries of the humanly possible. The language of literature does not insert itself into linear time as the language of an owner's manual is meant to do. Poetic structure is never a series of discrete steps that results in accomplishing one thing or another, nor is it a series of discrete steps that achieves a climax or conclusion, though some poetic texts assume a paratactic guise. As the rubrics of a kairotic performance, a poetic text is usually found to be a series of overlaid cognitive modes.

I illustrate in the next figure this hypotactic structure, using Keats's familiar text. We *know* that the fundamental analogy is that between reading and traveling and that the main topic, as announced in the title, is the poet's discovery of Chapman's translation, yet we are seduced as we read this text even for the hundredth time to promote the second term of this metaphor to something more than a serviceable vehicle for bookish enthusiasm. A tactical analysis reveals how the poet has arranged his cognitive modes in such a way as to background his tenor and foreground his vehicle.

As my diagram points out, the octave is composed of two retrospective blocks, the travel-of-discovery vehicle of the metaphor superimposed on the tenor, the direct reference to Chapman. (This eighth line seems to continue the vehicle—Keats does not say "Till I read Chapman's version of the Greek"—but, if we take this line as a restatement of the title, we can regard it as the necessary emergence of the tenor from its seclusion.) The vehicle (lines 1–7) pretends to be the tenor by virtue of its extension from one retrospected time to an even earlier time and by its dominant position in the tactical arrangement, that is, by its timing in the kairos of the poetic performance. Only at the fourth and sixth lines does tropical meaning seem to show through what might otherwise seem some persona's straight autobiographical statements. With line 8 we understand clearly that these two retrospective blocks, these two quite different "pasts," are mediated by another layer, the introspective mode that asks and answers the question: what do I imagine this feeling to be like?

The sestet pivots into an overt simile; that is to say, into an overt presentation of Introspection. A simple simile (or metaphor) takes for its vehicle a noun or noun phrase (or implies one through some other part of speech). This simple form correlates a generic referent or some type with the tenor, for example, "like *some* watcher of the skies" when he is performing some suitably exciting astronomical activity, "Or like stout Cortez," a typical explorer of the "realms of gold." At this point we have an introspective block laid down upon the retrospective base. But Keats is not content with a simple metaphorical cross-reference. He has a sestet to complete and what more elegant way to do so than by creating his own Homeric simile, plus an epic caesura (fourth foot of line 12) tossed in for good measure? When Cortez takes as modification an adverbial clause that places him in a time-bound episode, we have Introspection itself accepting an overlay of Retrospection.[4]

The hypotactic structure that reveals itself in cognitive analysis is one that requires the reader to entertain three levels of discourse simulta-

84 Chapter 4

>   RETROSPECTION
>   ON FIRST LOOKING INTO CHAPMAN'S HOMER
>
>> INTROSPECTION (*vehicle of the metaphor*)
>>
>>> RETROSPECTION
>>> Much have I traveled in the realms of gold
>>> And many goodly states and kingdoms seen
>>> Round many western islands have I been
>>> Which bards in fealty to Apollo hold.
>>
>>> RETROSPECTION (*past perfect*)
>>> Oft of one wide expanse had I been told
>>> That deep-browed Homer ruled as his demesne;
>>> Yet did I never breathe its pure serene
>
> RETROSPECTION (cont..) (*tenor of the metaphor*)
>   Till I heard Chapman speak out loud and bold
>   Then felt I
>
>> INTROSPECTION (*another set of vehicles*)
>>   like some watcher of the skies
>>   When a new planet swims into his ken;
>>   Or like stout Cortez
>>
>>> RETROSPECTION (*embedded in the later vehicle*)
>>>   when with eagle eyes
>>>   He stared at the Pacific—and all his men
>>>   Looked at each other with a wild surmise—
>>>   Silent upon a peak in Darien.

neously. Two are generated by the analogy, the normal relation of tenor and vehicle that in simile, metaphor, and allegory are made to overlap. The first (in this instance) is retrospective and the second introspective (which is always the mode of metaphor-vehicles). The third level, superimposed upon the second, is again retrospective. From a technical point of view one of the interesting factors in this text is the relative dominance of these retrospective elaborations of Introspection, elaborations that invest the vehicle of the metaphor with the semblance of more experiential actuality than the actual experience that occasioned the poem. But, of course, this imaginative actualization is the thematic core of this sonnet: his first looking into Chapman's Homer was the triggering circumstance, but the event the poet meant to celebrate was the "then *felt* I" experience.

This leads us to one final consideration.

Affect and Cognition

To many the term "cognition" has a cold and bloodless connotation and represents an approach to poetic texts that is inappropriately analytical. The rhetoricians of classical Greece and Rome and of the Renaissance were concerned with the affect that texts produced in readers, Jonathan Culler asserts, but "modern reader-oriented critics [are] cognitive rather than affective" and the cognitive critic, he adds, "cannot tolerate ambiguity but wants to reduce poems to univocal meanings" (*Pursuit of Signs* 47). And Harold Bloom asks: "But what can a cognitive or epistemological moment in a poem be?"—if, as he maintains, the poem is an act of will rather than intellect (387).

I touched briefly upon this question of affect in Chapter 2, but mainly to point out how problematical this topic is to philosophy, to literary theory, and even to psychology. To speak of "cognitive modes" in relation to poetry is inevitably to raise the question of the supposed opposite of cognition, the "feelings" that most persons report experiencing in the process of reading literature.

As I mentioned in Chapter 2, the theory of the Association of Ideas attempted to discover logical laws to account for illogical procedures of thought, that is, cognition vitiated by habit, prejudice, laziness, and *feelings*. These "lower" tendencies, as an early eighteenth-century rationalist version of Original Sin, were believed to run constantly counter to the logical sequentiality of ideas. But some thinkers, as that century proceeded, began to regard some "feelings" as noble, for example, the feelings of sympathy with humankind and of awe in the presence of the sublime. When such feelings interrupted one's "train of thought," one ought to yield to them as to an invasion of grace.[5]

Coleridge, in a letter to Southey (see above, Chapter 2, page 30), compared feelings to a breeze and ideas, that is, imaged concepts, to the ruffled leaves of a forest. What this suggests is that feelings can exist independent of their objects or at least without conscious objective correlatives. Whether or not this "free floating" condition characterizes human affectivity on some level, it does not appear to characterize the affects that readers of poetic texts experience, which are prompted rather by the moving leaves than by the disembodied breeze. But the question Coleridge raises may be: How can one account for sudden shifts from one associative train to another? These leaves do not all stream out from their stems forever in one direction; something is there at work that impels them now in one direction, now in another, something that seems to suffer its own turmoil, its own vicissitudes.

In the last chapter I suggested that the dialogic structure of thought could account for those shifts we encounter even in what superficially seems monologic poetic discourse. Whenever the speaker in a poetic text comes to an impasse of some sort or has exhausted a line of argument—in any case has not satisfactorily explored or taken a satisfactory stance toward the overall topic—she may need to satisfy her real or implied interlocutor or inner conversant by taking a different tack and trying again. The clearest indication of a shift is a conjunction or adverb that marks a contradiction. The two lines that begin the final stanza of Robert Frost's "Stopping by Woods on a Snowy Evening" suggest, in the space between them, the conversant's input.

> The woods are lovely, dark, and deep.
> But I have promises to keep. . . .

"But" indicates a definite reversal of direction for Frost. The breeze of feeling suddenly veers elsewhere as cognitive modality shifts from Perception to Judgment, that is, from a present scene to an assessment of the (future) consequences of some contemplated action that is left unspecified. Conjunctions and conjunctive adverbs (e.g., *yet, still, though*), negations, and abrupt changes of tense and subject often mark shifts that are not only cognitive, *but affective* as well.

The relation between these two functions is intimate. What we think about arouses our feelings—not only in poetic texts but in everyday experience as well. We do not go about resonating like Aeolian harps, nor, I suspect, did Coleridge. We think about things that we desire and things that we fear and our affective states are responses to these objects of consciousness. Since these stimuli are *objects of consciousness,* our responses are to the acts of consciousness in which we problematize our being-in-the-world. In other words, affect is a response to cognition.

This response is not, however, epiphenomenal, a heat produced, as it were, by the friction of thinking. Affect might better be regarded as an organismic response to the recognition of an impasse in thought. Such an impasse is encountered whenever the mind moves from one cognitive mode to another, for, though these modes are indispensable constituents of thought, they represent to the mind mutually irreconcilable states of being. By the differences that define them as zones of consciousness these six modes do not permit objects to flow unaltered between them. Beliefs and opinions stored as Assertion never quite match up with experiences stored as Retrospection; the subjective images of Introspection never correspond exactly with the objects of Perception; the future that we forecast in Expectation never perfectly satisfies the values of personal Judgment. The past is irretrievable in the present and the future never arrives.

Feelings are unavoidable in the poetic process. For if the contents of these cognitive modes seem not to clash, we are unlikely to sit down and write poems about this uncomplicated bliss. We do not need to take such extraordinary measures. But if, when we think about what we desire, what we fear, what we desire and fear we will not get, or what we fear and desire to evade—if, when we engage in such thought, these discrepancies seem important, we may be moved to write a poem or to read a poem that articulates this situation.

The advantage that poiesis enjoys in dealing with such problematic situations is a consequence of its kairotic constitution. The person who is perplexed or troubled by needing to think out a problem and needing to do so within and across irreconcilable cognitive modes is, as all of us are, time-bound in chronos—shackled to a here and now between an outer other of contingencies and an inner other of unconscious impulses, between a remembered past and an anticipated future. But I, as reader of a poem, am only partly in chronos. The "real 'me,'" having begun the reading, is moving unidirectionally through the words, and will eventually end this interval of verbal play. This persona is still confined to linear time, but by virtue of the doubleness of poetic play the "alien 'me,'" including all the personae I imaginatively impersonate, is a self that liberates the "real 'me'" from its imprisoning "now" and permits it to float in godlike ease across these dissociating chasms.[6]

When ordinarily unassociated elements are juxtaposed, they constitute a "place of indeterminacy" (Ingarden) that the reader is called upon to determine. But if this determination is not logically possible, if the relation between the two is undecidable, something else appears in this gap. Eliot and Pound spoke of "emotion." Allen Ginsberg, who transposed Pound's "ideogrammic method" into a new key in "Howl," spoke of those like himself,

> who dreamt and made incarnate gaps in Time and Space through
>   images juxtaposed, and trapped the archangel of the soul between 2 visual images and joined the elemental verbs and set the noun and dash of consciousness together jumping with sensation of Pater Omnipotens Aeterna Deus
> to recreate the syntax and measure of poor human prose. (ll. 74–75)

The "archangel of the soul" is certainly one way to describe the epiphanic entity that is glimpsed in the ellipsis, the "dash of consciousness." The affectivity we experience in the kairotic play of poetry is one of surface clashes—juxtaposed elements from single words to whole sentences, but those blocks of discourse that I have termed cognitive modes, being the largest semantic blocks that can be juxtaposed (and as irreconcilables cannot *not* be juxtaposed) create the greatest impact, the deepest chasm, and the most profound affect. But surface discontinuities are insufficient to account for the affect we experience in the reading of poems. The tactics of poetry are not those of prose (*oratio prorsa,* or straight-ahead discourse); they are those of verse (*versus,* turned and repeated discourse). The archangel with his unimaginable aura of feeling appears in a paratactic gap superimposed upon other rhetorical levels that combine with it to form a hypotactic complex, a polyphony of depth-resonances that echo back their meanings to the surface.

Those who, like Culler and Bloom, have questioned "cognitive" approaches to poetry have aimed their criticism at hermeneutical interpreters who have tried to reduce the meaning of texts to logic and univocality. I trust it is clear that this has not been my aim. In proposing this theory of cognitive modes I have tried to fashion a technique of describing poetic structure, its tactics and timing, and to propose a means of accounting for the *a*logicality of poetic discourse and the multiplicity of poetic affect. Cognition, that much abused term, is paradoxically the key to affect and therefore to the meaning of that other abused term, *mood.* The affective moods we sense as we read a poem are, I submit, the functions of the clash of incompatible cognitive modes.

Chapter 5
Simulations of Perception

We have arrived at a point at which we can begin to form a definition of the "*poetics* of the mind's eye." Verbal *poiesis* is the making (up) of units of discourse that, since they are stored and retrieved, are radically different from ongoing speech and "disposable" writing. They may not be demonstrably different in stylistic form and semantic content from a soap ad or a congressman's press release, but it is their iterative character—their human use as play-equipment, as kairotic rubrics—that finally entitles them to the status of "poetic" or "literary" texts. If enough readers chose to reread the ad or the press release again and again or at least glimpsed in them characteristics that might repay such attention, these too would become poetry. If they did achieve this status, they would be treated as instruments of ludic behavior requiring imaginative use. (As disposable writing, such texts might be glanced at with unconscious scepticism, but as poetry they would be read with a conscious suspension of scepticism: they would be treated as incredible in either case but for different reasons.)

We can distinguish, logically at least, two concurrent levels of imaginative use. At one level, logically prior, I imagine myself the "alien 'me'" represented in the text as saying these words or having these thoughts and being this alien *subject*. Subsumed within this ludic subjectivity I can distinguish at another level another set of entities, namely, alien *objects,* for no poem's persona can exist as a consciousness without objects of consciousness or know himself except in terms of his attentional objects and the tactics by which he mentally engages them. These objects can be abstractions or concrete representations in non-visual sense modalities, but, since we have decided to restrict ourselves to the visual, we will consider only the "mind's eye"—not the "mind's ear" or the "mind's nose," and so on. Through the operation of my "mind's eye," or visual imagination, I form images that correspond to this persona's visual experience, that is, to what this persona indicates as the objects of his visual attention whether recollected, directly perceived, intuited, or projected into the future. The alien subject that, willingly suspending all disbelief, I imagine myself to be dictates the kind of objects I am invited to imagine and the tactics by which I project these imaged objects into cognitive modes. As I suggested in Chapter 4, the cognitive modes into which a given image is projected determine its character, particularly in respect to vividness and elaboration.

In the next three chapters I will focus on four of the six modes: first perception, then the two memory modes of retrospection and assertion, and finally introspection. (Since the six terms I have been using to designate these modes have somewhat special definitions, I have up to now capitalized them. Henceforth, however, I will refer to them in the less conspicuous lower case.) Much of what might be said of expectation and judgment may be inferred from the discussion of these other four; moreover, the writings in which these two modes are paramount are now of somewhat marginal interest as literature, for example, oracles, apocalyptic texts, Talmudic writings, and applications of case law to specific situations. The order I have chosen has some expository advantages: some of what can be said of perception applies to retrospection and assertion and a discussion of these memory modes prepares us to examine the dynamics of introspection. But all the while we must keep in mind that these modes are subtly synergistic and that in the tactics of discourse they embed themselves within one another with great speed and facility.

In this chapter we will examine textual situations in which we are asked to simulate immediate perceptions, perceptions unfiltered through memory and its filing systems. Of course this is an ideal immediacy: rarely if ever do we physically observe an object without recognizing it as X or Y, without viewing it through learned attitudes (convention) or personal acquaintance with it (experience). Poets who urge upon us a set of percepts usually want us to *try* to bypass our cross-referenced memory systems and to contemplate before we question or define. Accordingly, as we examine such poetry, we will assess the dependency of imaging on the routines of perception—of the "mind's eye" on the "body's eye"—and note how verbal cues prompt this imitative play.

We logically begin our inquiry into the imagery of particular cognitive modes with a consideration of perceptual imaging, because it is the model upon which retrospective imaging is constructed. If a text asks us to pretend we are remembering a set of once perceived events, we simulate retrospection, which means that we pretend to revisualize past perceptions. The processes of perception are modified in retrospection but substantially replicated. A rhetorical shift from past tense narration into the historical present preserves the imaginal focus on dramatic events but considerably intensifies the illusion of perceptual presence. Conversely, the imaging of retrospection may be understood, partly at least, as a diminished form of perception. Before we consider retrospection, it is therefore useful for us to examine texts that prompt us to imitate immediate visual perceptions. For demonstration purposes I will select examples from the poetry of William Carlos Williams.

Disguised Rituals of the Eye

Over the past twenty-five years cognitive psychologists have amassed an impressive amount of data that supports the conclusion that mental imaging is indeed a close simulation of visual perception and not a separate form of iconic display (the so-called "pictures-in-the-head" metaphor). Stephen Kosslyn, one of the leading researchers in this field, in summarizing his findings in 1983 stated that the mind "contains" a "depictive medium" or "mental matrix" that has "grain"; as a result, for example, some imaged objects can be too small to have visual resolution. This medium, which he likens to a cathode ray tube (a television or computer monitor screen), has size and shape ("scope") but variable sharpness:

Evidently the grain in the medium is not constant at every location; rather, images are sharpest in the center and fade off gradually toward the edges. . . . [A]t the highest degree of acuity the medium is circular. At the lower degrees of acuity (that is, around the edges), it gradually flattens out into an ellipse that is wider than it is tall. (*Ghosts*, 65–66)

This flattening of the imaginal field he attributes to the horizontal separation of the eyes (71).

Kosslyn and his associates have also discovered that imaging is just as active a process as perceiving. In visual perception ocular movement is not an option but an absolute requirement. If the muscles of the eye are artificially forced to fixate very long upon an object, that object fades and eventually disappears. Our angle of vision normally "drifts" and must be continually refreshed by saccadic and so-called "microsaccadic" corrections. One of Kosslyn's discoveries was that when experimental subjects are constrained to image the same small sector of their imaginal field, objects within that sector quickly disappear. Just as in visual perception, an imager must shift her inner "gaze" and continually return to details in order to maintain the clarity of an image.

Roger Shepard's experiments with three-dimensional block drawings have revealed how the mind takes a visual percept and transforms its appearance by rotating it in imaginal space—and *through time*.

The now classic experiment in its simplest form is this: a subject is shown a series of paired drawings and asked in each case if the three-dimensional shapes are identical; to find if the pair match, the subject must reorient one shape by "mentally rotating" it, a task that must be performed sometimes in the two dimensions of the pictorial plane, sometimes in depth, sometimes in both. That such tasks take time to perform would probably surprise no one—psychologists, it sometimes seems, are always taking what everyone supposes are truly facts and proving them factually true. What made the findings of Shepard and his colleagues remarkable was that they revealed an extremely close correlation between the reaction time (from 1 to 5 seconds) and the orientational difference of the paired drawings (from 0 to 180 degrees). To Allan Paivio, the dean of image-researchers, these chronometric experiments suggested that "mental representations must contain a dynamic component that functions internally much as perceptual-motor processes do when applied to the concrete world of objects and events" (Nicholas, ed., 63).

The connection of mental imagery to motor processes is well established. One practical example is the mnemonic device of the "mental walk," attributed to Simonides of Ceos (556–468 BC): an orator would first commit to memory the details of a place—a temple or street—then associate key image-words of his speech with the series of images he would perceive if he were walking in an orderly fashion through that environment. The fact that this is not an act of visual imaging but also one of motor imaging is usually neglected when considering this mnemonic: it is, after all, a mental *walk*.

Kinesthesia and tactility are senses that seem to enhance visual perception and visual imaging. Mental rotation experiments with congenitally blind subjects replicate Shepard's conclusions but indicate that these two non-visual senses can also "imagine" spatial transformations (Carpenter and Eisenberg). The small child says "Let me see that" and we teasingly show the object to her, turning it about, but she keeps holding out her hand as though her sense of sight were partly in her hands. As we walk about our world, our legs carry us around and behind objects, our neck pivots our head, our hands touch textures and mold themselves to the contours they grip, our muscles weigh the heft of things: we "see" with our entire body. As Donald Hebb stated:

> Except with very familiar objects, perceiving is not a one-stage, single-shot affair. It usually involves (a) a sensory event; (b) a motor output, the adjustment of eye, head, or hand to see, hear or feel better; (c) the resulting feedback; further motor output, further feedback, and so on. (Nicholas, ed., 142)[1]

To the extent that imaging replicates visual perception, it also replicates the exploratory behavior of the entire motor system. It would seem to me, therefore, that Kosslyn's cathode ray tube metaphor and the computer models of the researchers into artificial intelligence have their limitations when applied to mental imagery.

Of all the motoric operations that accompany sight one particular set is crucial to perception and, according to Donald Hebb at least, to imaging also. These are the tiny, but exceedingly swift and accurate, movements of the eyes themselves. In his 1968 article "Concerning Imagery" (reprinted in Nicholas, ed., 139–153) Hebb argued that an image is a "reinstatement" of a percept and therefore replicates the sequential process by which separate focuses or "part-images" are produced and integrated into a complete image. In imaging, a "part-image does not excite another directly, but excites the motor system, which in turn excites the next part image" (Nicholas, ed., 145).

Hebb was taken to task by Kosslyn and others for apparently maintaining that these same or similar contractions are overtly repeated in imaging. But when he spoke of overt eye movements in imaging, Hebb seems to have had in mind the afterimage phenomenon that we experience when, after staring at a given figure, we close our eyes or turn them to a neutral surface and then observe an image of the figure that seems to hover in space, similar to the imagery that eidetikers are said to experience. If this figure, when perceived, was large enough to require separate focuses (or "part-perceptions"), its image would seem to require separate eye movements, overtly performed even beneath closed lids. It is questionable, however, whether eye movements appropriate to immediate perception are a major feature of memory images, for some imaging dispenses with them altogether. Dream imagery, for example, is accompanied by its own type of movement (rapid eye movement, REM) and literary imaging is performed while the reader's eyes are wholly occupied with graphically cued eye movements, which would surely interfere with any possible "reinstatement" of overt perceptual procedures even when reading a text that prompts perceptual simulation. In the reading situation it is sufficiently clear that, if such motoric excitations occur, they do so in the cerebral cortex, not in the efferent nerves. In short, they too, like the images themselves, must be imagined.[2]

If one is a poet and has set oneself the task of reproducing in words, not the memory of experience or the flavor of things, but the excitement of immediate perception, then one has undertaken a truly formidable project. This is exactly what William Carlos Williams attempted to accomplish in his early poetry, though he acknowledged how difficult this was:

[T]he thing that stands eternally in the way of really good writing is always one: the virtual impossibility of lifting to the imagination those things which lie under the direct scrutiny of the senses, close to the nose. (J. H. Miller, ed., 11)

Yet, he would not abandon his project:

If I succeed in keeping myself objective enough, sensual enough, I can produce the factors, the concretions of materials by which others shall understand and so be led to use—that they may the better see, touch, taste, enjoy—their own world *differing as it may* from mine. (Miller, ed., 197)

Williams always insisted on our need to encounter the world sensuously and on the restorative virtues of written texts. Some of his most emphatic statements he wrote in the prose sections of *Spring and All* (1923). Between the myriad sensory stimuli of the here-and-now and our full attention to any of these stands the barrier of memory, abstraction, and irrelevant reverie—

Yesterday, tomorrow, Europe, Asia, Africa,—all things removed and impossible, the tower of the church at Seville, the Parthenon. (Miller, ed., 15)

"Yesterday, tomorrow," the cognitive modes of retrospection and expectation that project the mind into the temporally absent; "Europe, Asia, Africa," spatially absent entities that also imply retrospection and expectation because they cannot be "here" if they are not also "now"— such thoughts are, he says, the "vaporous fringe which distracts the attention from its agonized approaches to the moment." And what resource do we have with which to dissipate this "vaporous fringe"?

To refine, to clarify, to intensify the eternal moment in which we alone live there is but a single force—the imagination. (Miller, ed., 16)

Note that in invoking this sacred name "imagination," Williams could not have meant the same thing that Coleridge or Mallarmé or Stevens meant by the word. The imagination that he here opposes to the "beautiful illusion" is our ability to perceive direct, immediate impressions of our world and to employ verbal means, as writer and as reader, to imitate such perception. The imagination takes as its proper facilitating instrument the poetic text and thereby serves to train the perceiver in the discovery of our world. But if it "fails to release the senses," to engage the "sympathies, the intelligence [of the reader] in its selective world, [it] fails at the elucidation" of that world. Imagination, as Williams uses the term, is therefore a skill that subsumes both the sensory perception of stimulus-objects and the mental visualization of images, a skill that fashions art as its instrument: "In the composition, the artist does exactly what every eye must do with life, fix the particular with the universality of his own personality" (Miller, ed., 17). The "particular" is presumably the uniqueness of the experience and the "universality" of one's "personality" is based on the eighteenth-century notion that at the deepest level of personhood we are all democratically similar and equal, virtually identical. Judging from Williams's own poetic practice, we might add that this perceptual imagination fixes this particular, universally recognized experience in the *present tense*, relegating the past to a poetics of memory that he rarely practiced, for example, narration and Wordsworthian meditation.

Being "anterior to technique" (Miller, ed., 17), this ability to perceive and visualize is the foundation upon which all literary art is built. When that foundation begins to rot, it must be renewed. At various points in his long writing career Williams undertook a number of "making-it-new" projects: an examination of local cultural meanings, a sensitization to American speech, and the fashioning of a new metric. His one ongoing project, however, was to uncover, clean, and display the raw materials of poetry—the particulars of experience, the *things*. What he most prized in poetry was its power to "revive the senses and force them to re-see, re-taste, re-smell and generally revalue all that it was believed had been seen, heard, smelled, and generally valued. By this means poetry has always in the past put its finger on reality" (Miller, ed., 235).

"Williams is the master of the glimpse," his younger friend Kenneth Burke wrote in 1922: "The process [of composition] is simply this: There is the eye, and there is the thing upon which the eye alights; while the relationship existing between the two is a poem" ("Heaven's First Law"). These glimpses Burke identified as "minute fixations" that mark the "shortest route between object and subject."

At the poet's death in 1963, Burke again stressed the function of perceptual imagery as a means by which the knower and the known coexist in phenomenological interpenetration: "Typically in his poems the eye (like a laying on of hands), by disguised rituals that are improvised constantly anew, inordinates us into the human nature of things" ("William Carlos Williams" 53). How are rituals disguised? we might ask. One normally thinks of a ritual as an extraordinary and meaningful ceremony, a recurrent kairos. A disguised ritual would therefore be an action that seems ordinary and without significance and may be so habitual as to escape notice. The disguised rituals of the eye to which Burke refers may well be disguised for the same reason that our eyes are unseen in the act of seeing. Not only do we not see our eyeballs when we see the world, but we are happily unaware of the various intricate operations that they perform in enabling us to maneuver successfully in visual space. But a poet who wished to reproduce sensory phenomena as they are perceived, a poet with more than a passing interest in human physiology, might well attempt to capture in his verbal medium some of the dynamics of visual perception.

These rituals of the eye, says Burke, are "like a laying on of hands," the physician's *tactus eruditus* translated into the language of ritual. For Williams, as for Whitman, the truly common sense, the *sensus communis* of ancient psychology, was a sense of touch in which body and mind united in intuitive vision. Poetry, he had said, had always striven to replicate perception, to "put its finger on reality" and thus palpate the world. Hillis Miller in his *Poets of Reality* reminds us that the magazine Williams edited in 1932 he titled *Contact* (316) and that for this poet "eyesight has a power to grip things in a tight embrace that is as much muscular as visual" (320). For Dr. Williams the old "eye-hand coordination" concept was no dry textbook concept.[3]

The highest art, as the old saying goes, is the art of concealing art. The most skillful performer is least aware of the instruments of performance, having extended into those instruments, be they eyes, hands, forceps, or paintbrush. The artistry of a poet of perceptual imagery lies in his or her ability to portray not only objects but the "disguised rituals" by which those objects are perceived, to activate not only our memory store of nameable genera and schemata but also our memory store of procedures.

Our task now is to defamiliarize the act of seeing, to see the eye in the various procedures of seeing, and to consider the degree to which language is capable of imitating this process.

Saccadic Movement on the Pictorial Plane

Our visual field is an oval lying on its side, outlined by our brows, cheekbones, and nose. It roughly measures 180 degrees in the horizontal projection and 150 degrees in the vertical. In order to see objects outside these limits we must shift this illuminated oval by changing the position of our head. This visual field is the product of binocular vision, a product, that is, of the partly overlapping views of the environment that each eye transmits to the brain. As we become aware of this oval window of light, however, we discover that it is not uniformly clear. In fact, all but a tiny area is blurred. That tiny area, only about the size of our thumbnail held at arm's length, represents that segment of the visual array that the lens of each eye projects onto the *macula*, a mass of color-sensitive cone cells at the back of each retina within which lies the thickly packed *fovea*, used for minute examination of objects. For present purposes I will generalize macular and foveal vision by referring to them both as "focal" vision.[4]

When we need to inspect an object, our attention seems to stream into this focal field and we are aware of little else. For minute work it contracts to a disk of clarity from 3 degrees to less than 1 degree in diameter (foveal vision). But when more global viewing is called for, this field can expand to 15 degrees (macular vision). (Authorities differ on these numbers slightly plus or minus.)

Beyond this circle lies the *peripheral field.* As the focal field blends into the peripheral, visual acuity drops off rapidly; objects lose color and definition and become fuzzy; to the far left and right of this surrounding field, shapes degenerate even further, losing their recognizable contours and appearing as shadowy blotches. Since most objects that concern us overflow the perimeters of focal vision, we must use certain of our eye muscles to rotate our eyes in such a way that information about important portions of those objects is projected onto the macular region of the retinas. We must, in other words, shift our focal field.

It takes a little effort for most of us to visualize this everyday visual process. One way might be to imagine we are using a flashlight in a dark room. We can never illuminate the entire room at once: all we can do is cast the narrow beam now here, now there. But we can still succeed in getting a sense of the contours and contents of the room because our short-term memory apparently forms one composite out of all these separate projections.[5]

Though this is very much the way our eyes orient us in visual space, this analogy is not sufficiently exact. The shifting movements of the eyes, called *saccades*, are sudden, unidirectional jerks. With our flashlight we could pan about the room as slowly and meanderingly as we liked, but when we actually shift our focal field in a saccade, our movement is so swift (up to 1,000 degrees per second) and bullet-like that we cannot slow down or veer from our trajectory for an interesting item: *we cannot even see it.* We see only when the saccade-driven focal field comes momentarily to rest in an optical *fixation.* We see most clearly then when we attend to our focal field, but, if we know what we are looking for, we can also attend to objects in our periphery (observing "out of the corner of the eye"). We can even keep all our visual options open and process information gathered from both focal and peripheral fields, the "wise passiveness" that Wordsworth celebrated and that Ulric Neisser called in 1967 the "preattentive level" of visual processing. If some detail of interest appears then in the peripheral field, we have only to judge it "interesting" subliminally for our visual axes to shift dartingly toward it. Peripheral vision may be likened to the outstretched palm that grazes the surface of the environment, focal vision to the thumb and fingers that reach out and close tightly upon an object.

Saccadic movement, then, is the eyes' prime technique for exploring visual space and perceiving shapes and relationships. It has been well documented since the 1930s that our eyes dart restlessly about our visual field in search of objects of interest, which, once we locate them, we target again and again for focal inspection. (See Buswell.) Our individual saccades are random, in the sense of "not rule-governed"; how often we repeatedly fixate on the salient features of objects is determined only by the degree of interest they arouse in us.

With the help of short-term memory the visual cortex can generate a complex spatial image all parts of which are understood to be simultaneously present—*understood* to be simultaneous, but *not imaged* simultaneously. This, I wish to stress, is an important distinction, for, from an operational point of view, saccadically driven vision has a temporal aspect similar to language and, to the extent that mental imagery replicates visual perception, it, too, is generated temporally. Lessing in his *Laokoon,* in chapter XVII, which I referred to in my last chapter, acknowledged this but denied its importance: the eye, he said, integrates the various fixations so quickly that the mind sees only total objects.[6] He concluded that the linguistic medium of poetry disqualifies it from delineating visual objects because the coexistence (*das Koexistierende*) of an object comes into collision with the consecutiveness of speech (*dem Konsekutiven der Rede*). The problem here lies in the assumption that coexistent parts are coinstantaneously perceived. If they were so perceived, then consecutive description could never reproduce them in their spatial coexistence. But since objects are perceived part by part, the consecutiveness of speech accords with the consecutiveness of visual perception. The difference between them is that visual perception on the level of saccades and fixations is *only* consecutive, whereas language is consecutive *and* sequential. That is, the order of words (in most languages) is meaningful, whereas the order of saccadic recurrence (in most visual acts) is not. How would one reproduce in language the multiple refixations of the gaze that the eyes perform when scrutinizing a landscape or a face? One would have to repeat oneself a great deal and the effect might remind one of a madrigal text or a canon, an extreme instance of Jakobson's principle of equivalence. Even at that, the text could not itself reproduce the peripheral field.

Language is a temporal medium, as Lessing said, but there are certain aspects of literature that seem to struggle against the unidirectionality of discursive time and to emulate the recurrent patterns of saccadic vision. First of all, the literary text constitutes a whole, completed, stored order of words, a repeatable verbal ritual of interreferential events, often underscored by recurrent themes, motifs, formulae, and such devices as foreshadowing and flashback. Second, literary texts normally rely on description to create setting and convey character, which elements, when they recur and evoke imagery, demonstrate a saccade-like redundancy. Finally, this redundancy is a function of the system of linguistic redundancy, which, as Jakobson and Halle (5) pointed out, characterizes most poetic texts.

The debate between literary spatializers, for example, Jakobson and his structuralist confreres, and temporalizers, for example, Derrida, Fish, and poststructuralists of every persuasion, has not helped to clarify the nature of the image. A generation before Derrida and Fish, Susanne Langer's distinction in *Feeling and Form* between "discursive" and visual form echoed Lessing's conclusion and reinforced assumptions that continued to block the advance of imagery study in twentieth-century poetics. Even that pioneer in the psychology of imagery, Allan Paivio, echoed what is essentially these dichotomous space-time premises in his *Imagery and Verbal Processes* (33), when, after quoting Langer approvingly, he contrasted visual and auditory perception, declaring visual perception a simultaneous process and language a sequential one.[7]

The question whether visual cognition is a simultaneous or a linear process has been hotly debated by cognitive psychologists over the past two decades. I would not now risk interdisciplinary life and limb by commenting on it, if its implications did not bear so very heavily upon my primary topic, the poetic imagination. The issues involved in this problem become significantly altered, I would suggest, as we move from a consideration of visual perception to visual imaging and then to verbally cued imaging.

To begin at the logical beginning, is visual perception a simultaneous process? Parallel processing occurs at the cellular level, as retinal cells pick up information simultaneously from all sectors of the visual field. But not all sectors are equally informative, because not all cells are equally discriminative. This is not to say that peripheral vision is *un*informative: we would be virtually immobilized if we saw our unpredictable environments through narrow macular tunnels. In familiar settings, again thanks to our retinal periphery, we can sit back satisfied that floor, ceiling, walls, and furniture are all there, arrayed before us in a near-hemispheric diorama and can be instantaneously glimpsed in a single *Augenblick*. But when this periphery presents to us objects that require inspection, this wide-angled simultaneity must yield to a narrow consecutiveness. Complex motor processes, that is, shifts of focus, must then be performed and separate fixations produced. The fact that the visual centers of the brain quickly integrate these shifted fixations into a fluent, seamless display does not contradict the fact that this "picture" of space is temporally produced. It would seem then that visuospatial perception is very much a spatiotemporal process.

As an imitation of visual perception, mental imagery is a much diminished thing. We will consider this diminishment in more detail in the next two chapters, but now it will suffice to say that image-formation is as consecutive and temporal an operation as visual perception, but unsupported by a stable stimulus-object. If we ask a friend to image a familiar object or scene, we do not expect her to open some inner eye and glimpse it instantaneously, all its elements displayed in spatial simultaneity. We ask, "Do you 'see' it?" and after a second or two perhaps she says, "Yes, I've got it." "Getting" a mental image takes time, as Roger Shepard's and Stephen Kosslyn's experiments have clearly demonstrated. Try, for example, visualizing a simple figure like a five-pointed star: the difficulty you have keeping all the points equally sharp and geometrically accurate indicates that imaging, like perceiving, is a process of consecutive focusing, but only more difficult. (See Kosslyn, *Image and Mind*, 234–239.)

Now what of verbally mediated mental images? If I might rephrase Lessing's dictum, I might say that the consecutiveness of visual perception collides with the sequentiality of language. The verbal medium is best at reproducing swift glimpses of things. Lessing understood this well. The labored description of large, complex units—the horrendous example he cites is of a flower garden—presents the reader with the tedious task of remembering details ABC while now considering details XYZ. The relative paucity of repetition in descriptive writing attenuates the emphasis that normal visual perception gains by repeated fixations, thus problematizing verbal visuality and differentiating it from perceptual visuality.

All literary imagery displays a text-determined sequentiality. When in the service of plot and represented action, this linear temporality puts no constraint on us. But texts that explicitly ask us to simulate actual, immediate visual perception force us to simulate optically unnatural acts. They expect us to lay aside our ocular freedom to inspect a scene by repeated saccades and fixations and require instead that we observe a text-governed order.

Returning now to the poetry of William Carlos Williams—to his "Red Wheelbarrow"—we will consider some of the ways texts direct the imaging process.

so much depends
upon

a red wheel
barrow

glazed with rain
water

beside the white
chickens.

(*Collected Earlier Poems,* henceforth *CEP,* 277)

If we were actually to perceive this scene from a distance of thirty or forty feet, we would probably have to make several short saccades in order to view each of its three major visual elements. The verbal format, however, simplifies this process somewhat by naming them—the red wheelbarrow, its rain-glazed surface, and the white chickens—thereby treating each of them as a separate fixation or cluster of fixations (a unitization that, by the way, is counterpointed by the fragmentation effect of the line-breaks). However one might imagine the complexity of saccadic movements in the hypothetically perceived scene, the text requires that the imager imagine a minimum of three fixations, linked by two saccades. The first image, the red wheelbarrow, suggests a rather large visual angle—the fully extended focal field of 12 degrees or perhaps a series of saccades sufficient to identify this object. This is followed by a saccadic shift from its contours and color to a detail of its surface texture. Finally a distinct saccade is indicated by the word "beside," which draws our simulated gaze laterally toward the white chickens. How many chickens do we "see"?—more than one and not a single chicken more than is needed to satisfy our compositional requirements for this pictorial exercise. Their plurality, it should be noted, calls for an optional number of simulated saccades.

Let us turn now to another short imagist text, "Nantucket" (*CEP,* 348), this time accompanied by a running commentary.

TEXT	SIMULATED PERCEPTS
Flowers through the window lavender and yellow	1. indeterminate number of saccades and fixations;
changed by white curtains—Smell of cleanliness—	2. flowers now partially occluded by diaphanous curtain;
Sunshine of late afternoon—On the glass tray	3. luminance visible on surfaces; 4. fixation; the preposition anticipating saccade to . . .
a glass pitcher, the tumbler turned down, by which	5. the pitcher, then 6. the tumbler (also on the

	tray?); preposition "by" anticipating saccade to . . .
a key is lying—And the immaculate white bed	7. the key; conjunction anticipating saccade to . . .
	8. the bed

I might also add that paratactic indicators, for example, dashes, as in this text, often represent saccades, saccadic parataxis and that indicates a gap within the perceptual process, a naturally occurring shift that reasserts the coexistence of parts-within-the-whole of a visual array. Conjunctions and prepositions also serve to mark suggest ocular shifts within a single imaginary space. This parataxis of the mind's eye thus indicates a hypotactic integration but one that is imagined or intuited as a peripheral field rather than spelled out on the page. I should also append a disclaimer: a perceptual analysis, such as this, is obviously not an adequate hermeneutical interpretation of this poetic text, nor is it intended to be. It is simply a demonstration of one aspect of its visual poiesis, namely, the readerly construction of its images.

Texts like "The Red Wheelbarrow" and "Nantucket" exemplify Williams's urge to rival in words the painter's and photographer's art of selecting and minutely fixating percepts on a two-dimensional pictorial plane. Three other fine examples are "To a Solitary Disciple," "Young Sycamore," and "Young Woman at a Window" (*CEP*, 167, 332, 369). These all have about them a quality of intense stillness, not only because the objects and persons portrayed are motionless but also because the imaginary viewer is scripted in a fixed position with a stabilized visual field.[8]

Yet even in the most motionless representation of portraiture or still life we can say there is swift motion—in the eye of the beholder. When we view the painted surface, these saccades are overt muscular responses; when we visualize from a written text, they are simulated by the imagination.[9] Accordingly, saccadic movement is the compositional key to Williams's even more obvious experiments in ekphrasis, for example, such early texts as "Winter Quiet," "Spring Strains," "Conquest," and "The Pot of Flowers " (*CEP* 141, 159, 172, 242) as well as the later *Pictures from Brueghel.*

Depth Perception and Vergence

To live in a three-dimensional world, however, we need to be able to gauge visual depth. One way we do so is by walking toward and away from objects, which appear to loom and shrink accordingly. We also note that nearer objects sometimes partly cover farther objects and that very distant ones seem hazy. But viewing a simple, stable array forty or fifty feet from us, we rely largely on adjusting our eyes so that their separate focal fields overlap perfectly. Unless this is accomplished, the percept our brain forms will be unclear. To avoid double vision when focusing on objects at various distances, our eyes must perform a delicate corrective procedure. In addition to conjugate movement (a rotation of the eyes in the same direction like a pair of yoked horses), our eyes can also rotate in a direction opposite to one another: the closer the object, the greater the degree of *con*vergence; the farther the object, the greater the degree of *di*vergence. The phenomenon is quite familiar: our eyes visibly "cross" when we try to maintain an object in focus as it approaches the bridge of our nose; after hours of close focusing, as in reading, we "rest our eyes" by looking out a window at a distant point, thereby relaxing the muscles of convergence and giving those of divergence a salutary stretch. This pair of opposite rotations has been aptly termed *vergence*.

The visual cue that activates the vergence response is the cue that activates all corrective eye movements—an unfocused percept. Whenever the angle of vergence is imprecise for a given object, that object will not be projected uniformly on the foveas of each eye and will appear blurred and double.[10] This adjustment for depth is part of our standard repertoire of perceptual skills. Combined, as it almost invariably is, with saccades, vergence allows us to zoom in on objects at various distances from the eye, to break, as it were, the pictorial plane and enter a three-dimensional environment. An analogy might help clarify the collaborative function of saccades and vergence. Suppose I am peering through a small hand telescope at the tiled roof of a red barn two hundred feet away. Should I decide to explore the hillside above and beyond it, I must perform two procedures: I must shift my angle of vision and readjust my scope for depth. In this rough analogy the telescopic field represents my focal field; the shift of angle, the saccade to the new fixation point; and the readjustment, the vergence.

The early poetic texts of Williams provide several striking examples of vergence. "Tree and Sky" and "The Tulip Bed" (*CEP*, 102, 221) display a carefully ordered series of perceptual imagery cues. In the former text the cues prompt the simulation of divergence, as the eyes slowly focus upward and outward to infinity. In the latter, the directions take us from the sunlit sky, through a small town, down a street, and into the calices of the tulips.

In the first half of "Spring and All" (*CEP*, 241) the fixations are the product of a rapid darting in three depth projections: vertical, frontal, and lateral.

104   Chapter 5

> By the road to the contagious hospital
> under the surge of the blue
> mottled clouds driven from the
> northeast—a cold wind. Beyond, the
> waste of broad, muddy fields
> brown with dried weeds, standing and fallen
>
> patches of standing water
> the scattering of tall trees
>
> All along the road the reddish
> purplish, forked, upstanding, twiggy
> stuff of bushes and small trees
> with dead, brown leaves under them
> leafless vines—
>
> Lifeless in appearance, sluggish
> dazed spring approaches— (ll. 1–15)

As usual, prepositions govern the principal shifts of focus. The one exception to this is the first preposition, "*By* the road," which merely establishes the vantage point of the invisible observer, who in the case of simulated perception is always the reader. The first real saccadic preposition tells us that if we cast our gaze upward from the road (probably by moving our head and with it our visual field), we will see that we are "*under* the surge of blue / mottled clouds." Then we are directed to look "*beyond* [the road]" and to perform a series of fixations that justify our concluding that over there lies a "waste of broad, muddy fields" within which we can discern (again serially because they are pluralized) "dried weeds, standing and fallen" and (further in the distance?) "patches of standing water / the scattering of tall trees." After this, we are asked to look "All *along* the road . . . ," from a relatively distant point where we see "bushes and small trees," to a closer and lower point where we discern more minute details, the "dead, brown leaves *under* them" and the "leafless vines." The final half of the poem is a set of generalizations based implicitly on these serial fixations, plus several single, rapidly flashed glimpses of plant growth.

Among these examples of vergence taken from the first half of "Spring and All" there are series or clusters of fixations but no instance of the zooming-in effect. To be zoomed in on, an object must be totally perceived in a single fixation; it must fit wholly within the focal field, that is, present a diameter of less than 3 degrees. If it appears larger than, say 15 degrees, it must be perceived in a series of fixations. A text ordinarily indicates serial fixation in two ways: *contextually,* by conveying an image that seems to be too large or too near the implied viewer to be perceived adequately in a single fixation (e.g., the waste of broad, muddy fields and the road), and *grammatically*, by simply using the plural form of nouns (e.g., the patches of standing water).

For some final examples of vergence, plus serial fixation and zooming in, let us turn to the tiny text "Between Walls" (*CEP*, 343). The title, which is syntactically part of the body of this text, initiates by its strong preposition a set of crisscrossing saccades over a yard of cinders.

Text	Simulated Percepts
the back wings of the	1. too large and plural; therefore serial fixations crisscross the space between vertical planes;
hospital where nothing	
will grow lie cinders	2. again, too large and plural; therefore serial fixations over horizontal plane (the angle of the viewer to this plane will necessitate several vergence adjustments);
in which shine the broken	3. "in which" indicates narrowing of the field and anticipates the fixing of an object of interest at a particular distance in depth;
pieces of a green bottle	4. a zooming in on this object (or a series of such zooming-in fixations)

Williams relied upon vergence, in combination with saccadic movement, to organize some rather more complex perceptual simulations. "View of a Lake" and "Blueflags" (*CEP*, 96, 225) also deserve mention as two exceptionally rich explorations of three-dimensional visual space.

The Imagery of Perceived Motion

So far we have been considering motion only in terms of eye movement. Now we come to consider eye movement complicated by the movement of objects and by the locomotion of the observer.

The analogy of poetry to painting, at least as old as Plato and Simonides, has obscured the fact that poetry can, and often does, represent moving objects. The motion picture as a narrative art form is perhaps most responsible for undermining the old distinction assumed by persons like Lessing and Henry James between action and description, between drama and scene, which are variations on the Newtonian absolutes of time and space. In 1934, looking back on his break with the early Imagists, Ezra Pound (*ABC* 52) cited this as an important aesthetic issue:

> The defeat of earlier imagist propaganda was not in misstatement but in incomplete statement. The diluters took the handiest and easiest meaning, and thought only of the STATIONARY image. If you can't think of imagism or phanopoeia as including the moving image, you will have to make a really needless division of fixed image and praxis or action.[11]

A year later Williams defined a poet as "a man / whose words will bite / their way home—being actual / having the form / of motion" (*CEP*, 68). And in 1944 he likened the poem to a machine: "As in all machines its movement is intrinsic, undulant, a physical more than a literary character" (J. H. Miller, ed., 256).

Moving images may be usefully divided into two classes: *gestural,* in which parts of an otherwise stationary object are in motion, and *translocal,* in which the entire object is observed in the act of moving relative to its environment. A cat, for example, may be observed licking its paws and preening itself, then suddenly racing across the lawn after a butterfly. For the human perceiver these are not just two degrees of motility; they induce two significantly different eye movements that the poet, if he or she is at all concerned with reproducing perceptual events, must manage carefully.

In simple terms, gestural motion transforms the still life or portrait into the "moving picture" and does so without a shifting of the visual field. In other words, the reader as imaginary viewer establishes a fixed positionpoint and from that point observes an otherwise immobile figure performing an action. This form of motion is ordinarily detected by serial fixations that, like the separate frames of a film, display a progressive displacement of the parts of the object. Williams's poetry contains numerous gestural vignettes: an old woman reaches into a bag, takes out a series of plums, and munches them; a big, young, bareheaded woman in an apron toes the sidewalk and takes a nail out of her shoe; a little girl bounces a ball, stops, runs her fingers through her hair, pulls up a stocking, lets her arms drop, waits . . . (*CEP*, 99, 101; *Collected Later Poems of William Carlos Williams,* henceforth *CLP,* 120).

What I have called translocal motion induces a totally different eye movement that psychologists have called *pursuit*. In contrast to saccadic movement, which is jagged, rapid, and often clustered in series, pursuit is smooth, considerably slower, and fixed upon one moving target at a time. When we use this movement to track a free-moving object, like a bird in flight, our target-object is fixed in our focal field, while its relatively stable background streams past in the opposite direction in a fluid blur (sometimes referred to as "retinal smear"). To keep that object comfortably in focus, the head is often turned in conjunction with the eyes, thus causing the entire visual field to shift.

Pursuit is a most difficult eye movement to simulate in the medium of poetry. It is not easy, nor perhaps is it very interesting, to describe a blur, yet peripheral blur is a necessary accompaniment to this specific eye movement. Williams's inventiveness seems to have been provoked by the difficulty of this problem. "Spring Strains" (*CEP*, 159), an early experiment that seems mostly concerned with the painterly fields of force generated by the massive shapes and colors of the scene, nevertheless includes those uncontainable, magical beings:

>   two blue-grey birds chasing
> a third struggle in circles, angles,
> swift convergings to a point that bursts
> instantly!

And again:

> On a tissue-thin monotone of blue-grey buds
> two blue-grey birds, chasing a third
> at full cry! Now they are
> flung outward and up—disappearing suddenly!

Note how their acceleration is described in terms of the observer's inability to maintain them in a visual field. But though a proper peripheral blur is indicated (the "tissue-thin monotone"), this is not true ocular pursuit, for no single observer could pursue these three birds simultaneously. Perhaps because of the difficulty of the task, the poet asks us to image the trajectories in terms of geometric afterimages.

It is quite difficult in poetry to convey an image in continuous realistic motion without making concrete reference to an environment. To present an image without reference to its environment is to present a figure without a ground.[12] (This question of groundless images we will consider in Chapter 7.) The difficulty of this effort is demonstrated by the little poem simply titled "Poem" (*CEP*, 340):

As the cat
climbed over
the top of

the jamcloset
first the right
forefoot

carefully
then the hind
stepped down

into the pit of
the empty
flowerpot

The syntax of "Poem" (one incomplete sentence without final punctuation) suggests that the motion of the cat is continuous and ongoing—and perhaps, that a poem has a similar "form of motion." Yet our simulated gaze is diverted from this cinematic action twice by prepositionally specified saccades to the peripheral ground: "over / the top of / the jamcloset" and "into the pit of / the empty / flowerpot." That is, the simulation of smooth pursuit eye movement is interrupted by these two saccadic fixations upon elements of the periphery that, being named, lose all semblance of the blur that is the normal ground against which moving targets are tracked. At these two points the cat's fluid movements are caught in, as it were, the still photographic frames of language. The result captures some of the arrested motion first viewed in Eadweard Muybridge's classic pre-cinema studies.[13]

The imagery of perceived motion includes a yet subtler perception of motion, a motion that is seldom perceived as such because it is the observer, and not the perceived objects, that produces the movement. If I stroll along with my gaze slightly unfocused, I may with a little effort become aware that my world behaves oddly. When I turn my head to the right, the contents of my visual field swim to the left. When I raise my head, the horizon plunges and, when I lower it, the horizon rises above it. And, as I move myself through space, stationary objects loom larger, jiggle and twist their contours as I pass, and shrink as I continue on my way.[14]

Fortunately, I have an internal hook-up that corrects all the wobbles, jumps, and contortions that would otherwise destabilize my visual field when I move. It is called the vestibulo-ocular mechanism, a set of nerve channels that link the semicircular canals of the inner ear, which govern balance, to the nerves that control the muscles of the eye. If, as I step along, I fixate my focal field on an object, my eyes automatically make rotational adjustments to compensate for the slightest jog of my head. Without such adjustments, the tiniest movement of my head would, like a jiggled movie camera, produce a dizzying and disorienting picture of the world.[15]

Yet these deformations of our visual field produced by locomotion, corrected though they are, are not neglected by the brain: the changes in our orientation toward an object give us valuable information about it. For one thing, three-dimensional objects that cannot be turned by us or will not revolve at our bidding require that we move about them. When our objects belong to our circumambient environment, the inevitable distortions in angle of vision experienced as we move about also inform us as to the relative distance of objects. This is the phenomenon of *motion parallax*. Simply put, nearer objects seem to flow past us more quickly than more distant ones. This means that an object that seems to move in a behindward direction as we move forward is judged closer to us than an object that, by comparison, seems to accompany us forward. Thus at night the moon always seems to travel with us as we go, while all stationary sublunar objects seem to move past us at a rate determined by our speed and their distance from us. Another obvious clue to relative distance in such a setting is *occlusion:* an object that seems to pass in front of another is deemed closer. Motion parallax and occlusion are the principal cues by which we judge the relative distances, for example, of hills and trees while traveling in the country and of moving objects when we steer a vehicle in traffic; they are our main sources of visual information.

Every attempt to reproduce these perceptual procedures in their phenomenological nakedness deautomatizes them and defamiliarizes the world of objects. A century and a half ago Emerson commented upon the curious effects produced by even "a small alteration in our local position."

We are strongly affected by seeing the shore from a moving ship, [or] from a balloon. . . . The least change in our point of view gives the world a pictorial air. The man who seldom rides needs only to get into a coach and traverse his own town, to turn the street into a puppet-show. (*Nature*, sec. iv, 43)

When our distance from objects alters we do not normally regard these objects as changing in size, even though their projection on our retinas enlarges and shrinks. But for the "man who seldom rides" this so-called "constancy phenomenon" no longer governs perception: distant people become puppets. And not only that: these fellow townspeople suddenly lose their stable reality (become, as he says, "unrealized"). And how strange a familiar countryside seems when viewed from a "railroad car." Invert your entire world, he cheerfully recommends, by looking at it through your legs "and how agreeable is the picture . . . !"[16]

Literature abounds in the paradoxical presentation of relative motion. Before examining two final exemplary texts of Williams, I will remark on two consecutive stanzas from "The Rime of the Ancient Mariner." The Mariner begins his narration with two interesting visual illusions produced by the same sort of movement Emerson was intrigued by:

> The ship was cheered, the harbor cleared
> Merrily did we drop
> Below the kirk, below the hill,
> Below the lighthouse top.
>
> The Sun came up upon the left,
> Out of the sea came he!
> And he shone bright, and on the right
> Went down into the sea. (ll. 21–28)

In a text so replete with the hallucinatory and the uncanny, these lines usually draw little attention. Yet, like the horn motif at the start of Wagner's *Flying Dutchman,* this mix of transferred epithet and personification introduces us to a world of strange truths. As the ship reaches the limit of the offing, the curvature of the earth makes the landmarks seem to sink, but the Mariner ominously transfers this occlusion phenomenon to his ship, which with characteristic time-lapse suddenness "drops." The second visual illusion is all the more profound because it is concealed in the pre-Copernican commonplace that it is the sun that moves from east to west and not the earth widdershins. The conclusion seems unavoidable: once the eyes are liberated from the executive mind, they are tools that deautomatize themselves and consequently defamiliarize the world. Once apperception yields to sensation and seeing actually becomes believing, the world that only a moment ago was known becomes suddenly new and strange. Then one becomes a "voyant"—not through a "dérèglement de tous les sens," but through their radical empowerment.

Though fascinated with the possibilities of language to evoke painterly imagery, Williams, as poet of the innocent, unhabituated eye, seems also to have been interested in reproducing the cinematic effects of moving points of view. One largely neglected text, "The Source" (*CEP,* 346), is a quite ambitious ocular exploration of space that makes an intriguing contrast on several levels with Frost's "Directive." It is divided into two sections: the first details a single visual field and includes clear indications of saccadic and vergent eye movements across what is essentially a pictorial plane. The second section recounts the changing views that appear as the implied observer *penetrates that pictorial plane.*

Section I is a very careful composition of the visual field. One imagines the observer in a fixed position, perhaps looking out his bedroom window. The excitement he seems to be feeling as he discovers this landscape in the morning light seems to suggest that he arrived at this farmhouse or cottage only the night before. The reader is instructed to visualize first a "slope of . . . heavy woods" that vanish in a "wall of mist" that lies below a peak over which "last night the moon—." The text stops abruptly: this is morning now and memory has no place in the immediate perceptual imagery that Williams is concerned now to convey. The eye movements that had been darting upward (saccadically) and away (vergently) are now set in reverse. Our new starting point is the margin of a pasture marked by "silhouettes of scrub / and balsams" and then, focusing nearer, we fixate on "three maples / . . . distinctly pressed / beside a red barn," the shingles of which are "cancelled" (occluded?) by an elm. This tree appears to occupy the foreground of this visual field, for it is close enough to reveal its lichened bark and "wisps of twigs" that "droop with sharp leaves."

Section II begins with one of Williams's casually abrupt transitions:

Beyond which lies
the profound detail of the woods
restless, distressed

soft underfoot
the low ferns

Suddenly we have been told to shift our gaze from the "fitfully" moving branches of the nearby elm back outward toward the woods and there to zoom in on an overwhelmingly replicated pattern of minute activity, an effect Williams had already achieved in the crowd scene of "At the Ball Game" (*CEP*, 284). Then with equal suddenness we are asked to enter through this pictorial plane into the depth dimension we have heretofore traversed only through ocular adjustments. (The process recalls the Taoist story of the ancient master who, having just unveiled his painted landscape before the Emperor and his assembled court, calmly strolls away into it and vanishes up a tiny brushwork path of pine trees.) The fact that this series of percepts could be viewed only by a walker, not some disembodied sensorium, should prompt us to simulate the appropriate sort of visual procedures, namely, fixations briefly stabilized by the vestibulo-ocular system and of objects continually occluding one another and being displaced by motion parallax. (Needless to say, a reader need not know these technical terms to perform this imitative play: after all we *do* these routines every time we get up and move about.) Responding to Williams's cues, we image separate, precariously sustained glimpses of roots, fungi, hoof prints, and cow dung amid shifting lines of trees, alder bushes, and, with mounting excitement, finally the source itself:

> An edge of bubbles stirs
> swiftness is moulded
> speed grows
>
> the profuse body advances
> over the stones unchanged

And suddenly, without punctuation, the poem ends with this Heraclitean vision of changeless change.

The often anthologized, but problematical, "Flowers by the Sea" is, I believe, one of the best examples of what Burke meant when he spoke of Williams's disguised rituals of the eye:

> When over the flowery, sharp pasture's
> edge, unseen, the salt ocean
>
> lifts its form—chicory and daisies
> tied, released, seem hardly flowers alone
>
> but color and movement—or the shape
> perhaps—of restlessness, whereas
>
> the sea is circled and sways
> peacefully upon its plantlike stem

This one-sentence text with its branching clauses seems to represent a process: when A happens, then B changes, which then alters A. It is a sort of feedback loop. This text has been variously interpreted as dreamlike, surrealistic, and ekphrastic,[17] but in the case of Williams we would do well to ask first whether a simpler, phenomenologically realistic interpretation is possible. (Cf. Husserl 116–117.)

In the first stage of this process we visualize a clearly focused horizontal line in the middle distance. The ocean is as yet "unseen" but anticipated both syntactically ("When over . . .") and perhaps olfactorily (by its "salt" smell). In the third line the dependent clause attains its resolution with the predicate "lifts its form." How, we might ask, does the ocean do this? Probably not by inundating the chicory and daisies, which would not be found in tidal salt marshes and are here, anyway, edging a pasture. The simplest explanation is that the implied observer is walking toward the flowers at the edge of a headland. The Ancient Mariner, looking backward while moving forward, watched as the "edge" of the sea occluded the land; Williams's observer, looking *and* moving forward, watches as the edge of the land discloses the sea. In the former situation the landmarks drop from sight; in the latter the seascape rises.

In the second stage of the process, as the unseen becomes seen, the flowers, at first "tied," become "released." They lose their identity as particular flowers and become "color and the movement—or the shape / perhaps—of restlessness." (Note once again Williams's interest in the "form of motion," the tension of the static and the dynamic.) Here too, I believe, we have the poet recounting in precise detail the operation of his eyes and prompting in the reader a set of images strictly determined by the sensory data—and marveling at the result like a person blind from childhood whose sight is suddenly restored. If we interpret "tied" as meaning visually fixated and "released" as unfocused, then, as the eyes diverge to view the distant ocean, the loss of definition that these flowers undergo is perfectly understandable. These nearby flowers, when unfocused by vergence, appear doubled and, no longer projected on the focal but rather on the peripheral areas of the retinas, lose their former contours and are reduced to a blur of color and movement.[18]

The final stage in this optical transformation is the synthesis of both images, the rounded horizon of the sea, with its distant details of swells and troughs, appearing to rest like a broad flower upon the "stem" of the wavy, unfocused foreground. The eyes are thus discovered to have composed a metaphor, the flowers having become sea-like, the sea flower-like—an interesting anticipation of one of the central metaphors in Williams's "Asphodel."

Translating Percepts into Language

Before I conclude this chapter on perceptual imagery, I need to address the fundamental question of how visual information, both perceptual and memorial, is linguistically encoded. Since the return of imagery to scientific respectability in the 1960s the question of its relation to propositional language has been hotly debated. I will not reiterate these arguments here but refer the interested reader to my bibliography, specifically to: Block, ed.; Carterette and Friedman, eds.; Dennett; Kosslyn (*Ghosts*); Morris and Hampson; Nicholas, ed.; Pylyshyn; Segal, ed.; Sheehan, ed.; and Yuille, ed. By whatever means the brain accomplishes the feat, it does seem well able to translate percepts and images into words and words into images. Whether language is based on images or images on language, whether or not the mind at some level decodes imaginal and verbal input into some common propositional code, some neuronal "mentalese," there is ample evidence that language and the visual system are compatible and collaborative. This working relationship I now wish to examine briefly.

The means at the disposal of language to communicate spatial information have always intrigued linguisticians. Leonard Talmy at the University of California at Berkeley has detailed some of the resemblances between language and vision. In his essay "How Language Structures Space" (in Pick and Acredolo, eds.) he demonstrates how language schematizes objects in their settings in terms of "points, bounded and unbounded lines, bounded and unbounded planes, and the like" (258). This level of language Talmy calls the "fine-textural level" of grammar; it is represented by the paradigm NOUN + PREPOSITION + NOUN as idealized forms in geometric relation. Such concatenations, he asserts, are usually made below the threshold of awareness, our attention being drawn normally to the lexical, or macroscopic, level at which schemata become full images and concepts. Talmy's "fine-textural level" would seem to be the level at which the "disguised rituals" of the eyes are performed, for in his basic paradigm we clearly recognize the linguistic equivalent of the linear shiftings of saccadic vision.

Let us for a moment consider some of the details of Talmy's theory. An important concept for him is "co-locational order," a set of Gestalt-like rules by which language places one referent in relation to another. His conclusions may be summarized as follows: a "primary object" is one whose spatial variables are to be determined. Relative to the "secondary object," this primary object is smaller and geometrically simpler; in addition, it is more salient or has appeared on the scene more recently. The secondary object acts as the reference object and has one or several of these characteristics: it has more familiar spatial features, is more permanently located, is larger, has greater geometric complexity, acts as the visual ground, or has appeared earlier on the scene.

He offers two examples of co-locational order: "the bike is near the house," which has co-locational order, and "the house is near the bike," which is deemed anomalous. (Clearly, however, this order is not a rigid sequence and should not be confounded with word order, for the primary object can follow the secondary without sounding awkwardly inverted or anomalous, as in "near the house stood the bike.") His main point is that language subserves our visual need to distinguish and situate figural objects in respect to ground objects (or, as he calls them, "reference objects" and "landmarks"). This linguistic trait he associates with our "predominant concern . . . with a smaller portion of focal interest within a broader field and . . . with a determination of that portion's spatial relation to the field, so that we can achieve direct sensory (or imaginal) contact with it" (233–234). Only slightly rephrased, Talmy's conclusions are that descriptive sentences guide the addressee to locate an object, or part of an object, in a relatively small focal field by relating that object to another object that occupies a larger area. Because of its relative size, this secondary object must be imaged either in a simulated succession of rapid saccades or in a simulated focal field that is enlarged and consequently less acutely focused, that is, the macular field at its widest extension.

Theorists of the past who tried to prove that all words were either consciously or subliminally imaged have easily proved that nouns are either image-cues or derived metaphorically from concrete referents, but these theorists had considerably more difficulty with the other parts of speech. Prepositions have been particularly resistant. How does one image "between" or "under" in isolation from nouns? The psychologist B. R. Bugelski makes this point when he argues that "a preposition cannot have meaning in and of itself. It always describes a so-called relationship between at least two things. A book is *on* a table. There is no need to image 'on' as a separate act" (66). This fact does not, however, prove that language is a code incompatible with visual imaging as a simulation of visual perception. If anything, it proves how faithfully the grammar of language actually translates the procedures of vision, for the principal eye movement, the saccade, is both a *separate* and an *undetectable* act. As I noted earlier, that part of the visual field over which a saccade passes *is not seen*. (Researchers into visual perception term this phenomenon "saccadic suppression.") "On," therefore, does cue a separate act—a simulated saccade—but without producing an image. The function of prepositions in verbal visuality depends on our memory of procedures, not of data, and is one of those innumerable motor programs that subserve the higher cognitive processes.

Zenon Pylyshyn's 1973 article "What the Mind's Eye Tells the Mind's Brain: A Critique of Mental Imagery" (reprinted in Nicholas, ed.) was regarded as a damaging frontal attack on advocates of imagery and analogue coding. Without restaging these polemics, I ought to note that "data-structure representation," which Pylyshyn says is a useful alternative theory to that of visual imaging, is based on a system of propositional "nodes" (Nicholas, ed., 23). Intent as he was to combat the "pictures-in-the-head" metaphor of imaging, a straw man model at best, he maintained that an information-processing model that included propositional networks could eliminate "all reference to *perceptual* processes" (34). I would submit, however, that these processes, those of vision at least, are themselves networks of nodes and links and that propositional language may indeed have patterned itself upon the evolutionarily antecedent processes of primate vision. If, as it seems to me, Pylyshyn's "nodes" correspond to nouns and fixations and his "links" correspond to predicates, prepositions, and saccades, the antagonism of proposition and visual perception is profoundly mistaken.

Even if, as I am proposing, the NOUN + PREPOSITION + NOUN structure of language neatly parallels the FIXATION + SACCADE + FIXATION order of visual perception and imaging, the comparison will be incomplete until we consider two further questions. They are these: (1) besides nouns and prepositions, do other parts of speech correlate with eye movements? and (2) since saccadic movements are random successions, not ordered sequences, what, therefore, have saccades to do with sentence structure, which in most languages is governed by rules of word order?

These are formidable objections, but let me suggest ways we might at least begin to address them. We must begin, it seems to me, by frankly admitting that not all sentences are imageable, at least not so to the extent that they cue simulated eye movements. "Jesse has considerable athletic potential" is rather low in imagery-value. "Jesse threw his baseball through the neighbor's picture-window" is the sort of sentence I wish to account for here. So saying, let me proceed with a few comments on other parts of speech.

First, let us account for the simpler word classes—simpler than verbs, that is. Adjectives, besides representing detached accidents of the nouns they modify, often add spatial extension to them and provide the imager with precise instructions on how to simulate eye movements, as in: *spiral* staircase, *sinuous* stream, *craggy* mountain range, *tall* tree, *long* road, and so on. Pronouns, besides standing for nouns, indicate the relationship of persons and things to the speaker. To use Talmy's terminology, "I" is always the secondary, or reference, object for other pronouns (and implicitly for other nouns as well) ranged at various distances, real and symbolic, about the speaker. Again, the displacement of objects in imaginal space implies simulated eye movement. This is also the case with conjunctions, when they are used in descriptive, rather than purely logical, contexts, and it applies more readily to coordinate than to subordinate and other conjunctive categories.

Verbs present greater, or perhaps I should say more interesting, problems. Like all parts of speech except nouns and pronouns, verbs are not in themselves imaged, yet they obviously play a role in the production of verbal imagery. Not all of them equally, of course. Like nouns and modifiers, they can intensify or flatten the imaginal effect, specify or generalize the meaning of a sentence. Here again I will limit my comments to verbs that designate the visible behavior of referents, that is, visually detectable changes in composition, disposition, and appearance, for example: growing, decaying; jumping, flying, striking; flickering, darkening, and so on. Such words instruct us to image particular nouns in particular ways—as agents or reactive recipients of action—and to visualize spatial objects in particular temporal processes. Of course, like absolute space and absolute time, pure nouns and pure verbs do not exist in the real world. As Ernest Fenollosa observed, "the eye sees nouns and verbs as one: things in motion, motion in things" (17).

It is quite significant that it is the verb that in most languages conveys temporal information, both through tense and through aspect, for example, imperfective, frequentative, durative, inchoative. It is also significant that in many languages, notably the Indo-European families, verbs attract prepositional prefixes, suggesting that they too are used to cue simulated saccades. But with or without prepositional or adverbial assistance, those verbs that indicate a temporal process plus a change of visual focus all imply eye movement. "Jesse's baseball smashed the neighbor's picture-window" is not as informative as the earlier example, but, given the proper context, it too can cue a simulation of saccadic, pursuit, and vergent eye movements.

There is perhaps no more convincing evidence of this function of verbs than that provided by the radio sports broadcast. Here, for the aficionado, the spatial setting is the known frame of reference upon which the unpredictable action is imaged in response to the verbal cues of the broadcaster. During intervals in the action the auditor resets the overall image of the playing area as an assemblage of noun-cued objects, but at moments of action he or she converts the broadcaster's phrases, verbs and prepositions especially, into the images of spatiotemporal process. At the moments of most intense action, when the pace of events becomes too rapid for normal grammatical discourse, sentences become truncated and words monosyllabic. At such moments verbs become verbals: a left jab, a line drive, a tag, a right sweep, a fast break, a spike. Such verbal nouns abbreviate a complex sequence of actions and interrelationships that in every case entail for the auditor, playing at being a spectator of players, a complex simulation of eye movements.

In this chapter I have begun to specify the imaginal objects of this focus and to propose evidence that this focusing is serial. The reason *why* it is serial is that imaginal language serializes the successivity of visual perception. This process of serialization is a kind of translation and, like any translation, is a give-and-take process. Literary imaging does not perfectly replicate the experience of immediate visual perception nor the imaging experience of retrospection. It bears resemblances to both procedural and propositional memory-retrieval, but it has its own characteristics. Some of them seem to dim its vividness and reduce its personal impact. Much is lost in this translation. Nevertheless, this linguistic medium into which visual information has been translated has its own extraordinary properties, which, as I will suggest in the next two chapters, permit poetry to imitate, and thus memorialize, extraordinary states of visual consciousness.

Chapter 6
Transformations of Memory

The poiesis of the mind's eye is a making inseparable from a doing. When such a performance is cued by the words of a text, it is an act of the imagination that simulates some of the patterns of visual perception. In this respect we have noted how not only the eye but the entire viewer, as well as the objects being viewed, can be cast into motion by the temporal flow of language. Because of the temporality inherent in human consciousness and in poetic texts, the way single images are formed cannot be studied in isolation from the way images are organized. Examination of such topics as the "association of ideas," the hypotactic layering of cognitive modes, and the simulation of saccadic visions have revealed some of the complex ways in which images are interwoven in the *texta* of consciousness and of writing. Now we consider how human memory interconnects images and how literary compositions adapt these mnemic linkages.

Memory enters into every act of consciousness, both of waking and of dreaming consciousness. Not only is memory the mother of the Muses, as the Greeks called her; she is also the mother of the modes. Her first and continually youngest child is perception, but her seemingly eldest children are retrospection and assertion. When we consciously access memory, we enter these latter modes and undertake one of these procedures. When we envision the future in the modes I have called expectation and judgment, we also rely on memory material and project it into a hypothetical Not Yet. Even when we perceive or introspect we draw on memory data, sometimes on data we did not know we possessed until some present circumstance triggered its spontaneous emergence.

Human memory in its processes of encoding, storage, and retrieval transforms perception into the stuff of retrospection. Events become simplified thereafter and only the most arousing details are clearly recollected. Margins of forgetfulness frame with darkness the small lit scenes of retrievable experience. But these scenes are not represented as static arrays simultaneously present in all their elements to the retrospecting imager. When we try to revisualize one of these episodes, reshaped as it may have become, we try to reproduce it as a perceptual event. We try to reexperience it as we once experienced it and from the same, or some plausibly similar, vantage point within its visible ambit. Those that I have presented in the last chapter as the perceptual processes of the "body's eye," simulated in texts for the benefit of the "mind's eye," are also simulated in autobiographical recollection and in those texts that simulate the retrospective mode.

In our remembrance of things past and its poetic simulation these percepts are reviewed over an unbridgeable gap in time. Unlike simulations of perception, those of recollected experience are therefore understood to be subject to the same sort of fadings, diminishments, and transformations that actual recollected experience undergoes. They may be tinged with regret, remorse, or nostalgia and be confabulated into heroic magnitude or Edenic felicity. Such affects, as we know, attach themselves to the images we summon to those sessions of sweet, silent thought. We also know that our past gets sorted out through time in terms of our belief systems and that we not only retrospect past episodes but also make general assertions about them. Assertion serves us, moreover, as a reconstructive resource: when we cannot precisely recall a particular episode from our past, we can often assert that such-and-such *must* have formed part of it.

These and other cognitive and poetic transformations of memory are the topics of this chapter. But before we can appreciate the ways in which retrospection transforms perception, the ways in which assertion transforms retrospected perception, and the ways in which poetic play transforms both these products, we must briefly return to the topic of the last chapter and observe how memory with its two modes collaborates with visual cognition in the immediate act of perception.

Stored Imagery

> He thought he saw a Buffalo
>   Upon the chimney piece;
> He looked again, and found it was
>   His Sister's Husband's Niece.
>
> "Unless you leave this house," he said,
>   "I'll send for the Police!"

All serious books have at least one gravely whimsical quote from Lewis Carroll. Having fulfilled my obligation with these lines from *Sylvie and Bruno,* let me proceed with two anecdotes.

I spend two to three months every summer at a cottage in a semi-wild countryside near the Shawangunk Mountains, eighty miles north of New York City. My house is situated on a naturally formed shale terrace overlooking a stream that comes down from the mountains. From my backyard, through the trees, I can see the stream as it appears, winding past a sandbar a hundred yards away and flowing directly toward the terrace; then I can see it swirling below me as it takes a right-angle turn to the left and proceeds past a file of trees downstream into the distance.

One summer morning, as I looked out, I saw upstream what seemed to be two young deer on the sandbar, one bent over drinking from the stream, the other staring at me, both perfectly motionless. I peered intently, excited by the thought that such wild things still felt welcome in my neighborhood. But after a minute or so, when they failed to move, I walked to the edge of the terrace and looked again from a slightly altered vantage point. What I now saw, in sudden and surprising clarity, were two broken tree branches that must have come down the stream during the recent heavy rainstorm and embedded themselves in the sandbar.

On another occasion I was in my backyard near the stream when I heard an unusual beating of the air. I looked toward its source and for an instant glimpsed what seemed to be a very large bird, six or seven feet in wing span, flying somewhat laboriously downstream. Through the lacing branches of the trees I could make out only a glint of its long plumage in the sunlight. What was it, I asked myself. That must have been a great blue heron, I answered myself, because that is the only bird of such size that flies that close to rivers in this region. I actually saw no blue tinge, no long crooked neck, no extended legs, but I was so satisfied nevertheless with my identification that I could now fully visualize *Ardea herodias* sweeping downstream past me.

Each of these anecdotes illustrates a different way in which perceiving and imaging interact in visual experience. In the first I was willing to entertain the happy thought that two fawns were there only a hundred yards away: for that reason I stressed in my visual interpretation the specifically deer-like shapes of what I saw. Never mind that the drinking fawn had in fact only two legs and the staring one boasted what hardly could be called a head: they were two fawns and any moment a doe would appear, give a snort, and the two would bound effortlessly into the brush along the bank. When this did not happen, I looked more closely and was forced to relinquish my first image-identification. By a process of empirical induction I discovered that they were very particularly gnarled elm branches and not the calendar-illustration stereotype I had imposed upon them. The second instance was quite different. Here the data were incomplete and had to be disambiguated through deduction before I could form a full mental image of the flapping creature.

In both instances, however, I had to retrieve from my memory certain images that I then proceeded to impose as paradigms on my ocular experiences. The first image-imposition was proved wrong upon further inspection of the particular data. In the Piagetian terms that Sydney Joelson Segal borrowed to describe this process, this constituted an initial "assimilation" (of percept into mental image) followed by a corrective "accommodation" (of mental image to percept). The second image-imposition, that of the heron, was a case of assimilation that was judged correct on logical grounds and because no further perceptual evidence was available. (See Segal, ed., 84.)

These two sorts of visual phenomena complicate the traditional commonsensical distinction between perception and fantasy. Subjective image-formation—in effect, fantasy—is essential to every act of perceptual recognition, that is, apperception. (Except when the context clearly indicates otherwise, whenever I speak of "perception" in this study, I mean the whole process of sensation, attention, and apperception.) As Segal remarked, "sensory input does not depict an external stimulus; it merely gives clues out of which the observer constructs a personal experience" (95). A subjective image is needed to integrate these sensory clues. When such an image plausibly matches the available sensory data, as in the case of my heron, we judge this event to be a correct perception. However, when the image proves to be a mismatch, as in the case of my "deer," or when we can locate no external stimulus to connect with the image, we call it a purely subjective image, or fantasy.

The possession of stored images is, then, an absolute prerequisite for our recognition of things. And the prerequisite for forming those images is our prior visual experience of them. That is, having already perceived certain items or aspects of our world, we now have stored in memory the data that will permit us to recognize these objects when we encounter them again.

The study of human memory is a vast field. Its concerns include representational codes, for example, words and images, encoding stages, for example, short- and long-term storage, techniques and problems in learning, and the varieties of memory disorders. For our present purposes, however, we need only concern ourselves with the organization of memory contents.

A basic preliminary distinction must be made between *procedural* and *propositional* memory. Procedural memory is our store of operational routines, our knowledge of how to respond to circumstances, how to use our body and external objects as instruments, and even how to marshall propositional memory to solve problems. Propositional memory organizes and stores those data that can be expressed in statements and imaginal displays to which truth or falsity can be attributed. Knowing *how* to shift from one cognitive mode to another is part of our procedural memory; knowing *what* to cognize is part of our propositional memory.

Propositions framed within any one of the six cognitive modes may be differentiated as relatively general or relatively particular in their reference, a scale that might have a statement such as "All men are mortal" at one pole and "I saw my Uncle Robert collapse and die last May 4 as he was transplanting marigolds to the plot alongside the walkway to his garage" at the other pole. We understand that there is a sharp difference between these two kinds of statement and that no smooth continuum of statements can be devised to link these poles and make any sense in natural language doing so (e.g., "Some mortal men are uncles"; "Some uncles who collapse are called Robert"; "Last May 4, 1,243.2 uncles died in the U.S.A."; etc.). The propositions we think, say, and write seem to cluster close to the poles of the general-categorical and the particular-anecdotal.

Does this mean that our memory is also organized into a store of general knowledge and beliefs and a store of particular lived experiences? One psychologist, Endel Tulving, has proposed just such a theory. In it he distinguishes between two subsystems of propositional memory, the *episodic* and the *semantic* (Tulving, *Elements* 8–9). Episodic memory is our long-term store of personal experiences, particular events that we can, if called upon, reconstruct or at least locate in our past and associate with some particular time and place. What we know of them we know because they actually happened to us. Semantic memory, however, forms its propositions in a quite different manner. As its name implies, semantic memory operates very much like language: it regularly takes verbally propositional forms, is quickly processed without the need for detailed imagery, and is conventionally maintained and transmitted. This latter memory constitutes our long-term memory store of general knowledge and belief—for example, that fire burns, that the earth rotates on its axis, that "receive" is spelled with an "ei," that animals with fat tails, long hind legs, and abdominal pouches are called "kangaroos." This memory may be termed *doxical*, that is, made up of beliefs not necessarily founded on personal experience. Of course, an item of semantic memory may have gotten there as a result of a significant personal experience, the first time, for example, that we realized the burning properties of fire. Usually, however, we do not identify such knowledge with particular episodes and so its expression is general, axiomatic, or proverbial as, for example, our knowledge that $2 + 3 = 5$ and that pride goeth before a fall.[1]

Retrospected Experience and Asserted Convention

To adapt Tulving's two subsystems of propositional memory to a study of poetic play and its play-scripts I will have to make some adjustments to them. In doing so I will have to take upon myself the responsibility for the consequences. Accordingly, I propose to refer to episodic and semantic memory by the less restrictive terms *experience* and *convention* and speak of their conscious representation as the cognitive modes. Of these modes, retrospection and assertion would, theoretically, bear the closest resemblance to the two storage systems that subserve them. If "experience" and "convention" (which Tulving, using his terms, proposes as storage systems "hard-wired" in the human central nervous system) were evident only when we retrospect experience and assert what we have conventionally assumed to be true, then it would be superfluous to add these categories. But, though they add their own characteristic modifications, the other four cognitive modes also draw upon experiential and conventional data. We need to keep this in mind as we consider the two cognitive modes that most closely reproduce "experience" and "convention."

Retrospection, as I have been using this term, is the representation of personally witnessed events stored as unique episodes. It is distinct from the very recent past (short-term memory or Husserl's "retentive consciousness") that is continuous with perception. As I will use this term, "retrospection" will refer to the retrieval and representation of past experience in the form of imagery chronologically arranged as an episode.

Assertion presents a somewhat more complicated problem: it is the retrieval and representation of general knowledge that we potentially share with others within our cultural community. As a body of knowledge inscribed *within* us and *upon* all our cultural artifacts, it exists in what D. W. Winnicott called the "intermediate area" between the experientially defined self and the world-as-other. Its principal vehicle is language, but it includes all public sign systems and their inscriptions.

Since conventional memory data are principally the internalization of culture, that is, of everything we recognize as collectively known, they are latent in every semiotic act. Their manifest form, assertion, is therefore always potentially present. For example, most of our everyday recognition of our world is accomplished with the help of verbally labeled image-stereotypes (like "deer" and "heron") stored in conventional memory. For me to know what I was seeing and to assert that knowledge to myself or to others I had to retrieve from this reservoir of data appropriately labeled schematic images that seemed to match the particular sense datum before me. The fact that in one instance I was mistaken and in the other only making an educated guess does not significantly alter a process in which the real-world truth of propositions is always, at best, problematical.

If we are walking in the woods and I say "I'm not sure what tree that is," I am announcing my present perception of a tree and confessing that, after scanning its details, I have failed to match this arboreal phenomenon with any identified schema I possess. My companion, who tells me it is a sweet gum tree, proves to have amassed a larger internalized field book file and by means of which he is able to match the bark, leaf, and bough structure of this solid, living organism to a certain schema and to a name, both of which are associative hooks to which further information has been attached. He could accomplish this because he could match imaginal to perceptual data, then proceed deductively: since this is a sweet gum tree, it typically grows to x feet high, is pollinated in y fashion, can be used for z purposes, and so on. All this he is able to do because conventional memory has dually coded this object—as a name and as a schema.

Since I am now remarking on the pervasive character of convention, I might mention that you are at this very moment engaged in matching perceptual data (graphic signs) with conventional data (signified concepts). Even the private, anecdotal narrations of retrospected experience must achieve their uniqueness through a verbal context woven out of conventional signifiers. Our lexicon, except for certain proper names, are types and the named world is an assemblage of tokens that correspond to these types. Put differently: we go out every day to jostle with tokens that we cannot know except as types.

The "coded sweet gum tree," for example, has no substance: it is a type, not a token. That particular tree may be stored in memory in all its sensory detail; as such it is stored as part of an experience that may be retrospected. But if this individual instance is to be understood as the token of a class of instances, it has to be stripped of its gnarled, ramose individuality and reduced to a type. Once it is issued its name and schema, that is, once it is encoded, it is stored in conventional memory. Since every schema, albeit abstract, resembles the shape of what it represents, it is said to employ an analog code. My friend's schema of the typical sweet gum tree might, for example, display a strongly branching structure in silhouette. This shape, despite its morphological resemblance to the perceived tree, is almost as much a conventional artifact as the *name* "sweet gum tree."

I say "almost" because schemata, though conventionalized, are not wholly conventional. They are generated by words but are not wholly arbitrary designations. Though words signify by digital coding, they often prompt the imagery of the analog code. It is important to distinguish the two codes invoked by linguistic convention, the relatively strong digital coding of language and the relatively weak, or "fuzzy," analog coding of schematic imagery, and it is equally important to distinguish the encoded schematic imagery of assertion from the richly detailed, *un*coded, incidental imagery of retrospection. Now suppose we consider some other distinctions between asserted convention and retrospected experience, especially as they bear on the issues of mental imagery and language.

One of the everyday dilemmas we face in using conventional coding resembles the hermeneutical circle: as soon as we decide to give a name to a sketchily perceived datum, that datum has an uncanny way of resembling what we call it.

"Do you see yonder cloud that's almost in shape of a camel?" asks Hamlet.

Polonius obligingly agrees: "By th' mass, and 'tis like a camel indeed."

"Methinks it is like a weasel."

Again the supple-minded old courtier matches a verbal cue to a mental image of another animal and applies a second template to the ambiguous figure in the sky. "It is backed like a weasel." (The comedic effects of this interchange are not based merely on Polonius's humoring of the "mad" prince: it is also based in the characterization of Polonius as dependent on what Segal would term assimilative cognition. His serviceability lies in his ability to perceive only the world that his or others' words define for him.)

Having forced two apparently capricious identifications upon this phenomenon, Hamlet may just as well venture a third: "Or like a whale?" and the old man may just as well mutter: "Very like a whale."

When I selected them from my mental menagerie, my own animals, the deer and the heron, were verbally labeled images retrieved from my (our) conventional lexicon. When, however, for the purposes of this chapter, I remembered them *anecdotally*, I drew these images forth from my experiential store. The imaginal differences are highly significant. As stored in convention, these animals were textbook fauna—schematic representations, isolated generic samples, in short: types. But as components of events subsequently stored in my experience, they became focal points in scenes of circumstantial richness, elements in a detailed narration. Though my identifications left much to be desired as to accuracy, my retrospected memory retained the record of particular stimuli and of the efforts I then and there made to test my surmises. But how accurate was my retrospection? In my reconstruction of these episodes I may indeed have added other details that I might not have noticed then but that I know would have been present in those settings. I may, in other words, have embellished these recollections with confabulated imagery. This accords perfectly with the "style" of retrospection: it is richly particularized with imagery, but, as any judge or trial attorney knows all too well, it is notoriously unreliable.

As we consider the differences between the two types of memory, another distinction arises. The images of assertion, being unconditioned by circumstance, seem to belong to a timeless, Platonic realm of archetypes. They seem so, perhaps, because they are the pictorial counterparts of words and participate, to the extent that mental images may do so, in the fixity of conventional signs. Not only do they belong to no particular moment of time, they belong to no particular imager. The schematic images of assertion seem to be possessed collectively, as are words. When I retrospect a past episode, however, I seem to travel alone backward in time, to relive a portion of my own personal past, to re-present it in its unique eventuality. It is a particular—not a general and collective—knowledge that I then mentally rehearse and it is a particular, privately possessed time that I reenter.

Having identified convention with assertion and experience with retrospection, I must account for one problem: the former pair (convention and assertion) I have characterized as an *inner*-past projection and the latter pair (experience and retrospection) as an *outer*-past projection. The apparent contradiction here is that the former pair is associated with collectively stored information, whereas the latter is associated with privately stored information. My response to that objection is that collectively and privately stored kinds of *information* are probably inextricably meshed in human memory—they certainly blend into one another in verbal utterance—but that cognitive modes are kinds of *representation*. That is, these "places" into which information is projected, places each of which exhibits distinct characteristics of its own, need bear no resemblance to their manner of storage. Though the retrospective mode presents the unique, privately stored data that differentiate a self from every other self, it is "outer" insofar as it represents oneself "having experiences" within a particular time-space context of outer-world objects. The content of assertion, though for the most part garnered as kinds of information from the outside world and constituted by the environing culture, is nonetheless *represented* as general knowledge distinguishable from particular outer-world experiences. In short, we say we have confronted ABC experiences, but know "in our heart" that XYZ is true.

Turning now to literature, we recognize in these two modes of memory storage, and in the cognitive modes of retrospection and assertion by which they are expressed, the bases of what we might term the two master-genres, *narrative* and *gnomic*. Narrative and those literary genres that use narration as a framing device or point of departure (as is often the case even in lyric poems) imitate the procedures of experiential memory and its representational format, retrospection. Referring to a piece of literature as "imaginative writing" is usually an acknowledgment of its kinship with storytelling, that is, with the recall and recounting of personally experienced episodes. The alternative form of literature is *gnomic*, which deals with doxical matters—general lessons, common knowledge, and uncommon wisdom derived from long years, even ages, of lived experience. It is patterned, in other words, on the procedures of conventional memory and its representational format, assertion.

These two "master-genres" are marked by distinctive grammatical features of tense and mood. The natural tense for the recounting of experience is the past and the so-called "historical present." The tenses associated with conventional assertion are (1) the present, in such apodictic expressions as "time flies" and "water seeks its own level"; and (2) the future, in such deductive predictions as "murder will out." The mood normally associated with retrospective discourse is, of course, the indicative, whereas assertive discourse employs a wider range of sentence types: primarily the indicative, but also the imperative, the obligative, and the interrogative (for use in the rhetorical question, that device so beloved of gnomic writers).

If the communication of knowledge is based on memory-retrieval and if memory data are stored in two very distinct modes, then all discourse may be differentiated in terms of experiential and conventional structure. As the representation of stored data, the cognitive modes of retrospection and assertion will directly reflect the experiential and conventional memory, but, as I have already suggested, insofar as the other four modes need to access stored data, they too will display characteristics of these two memory systems. For example, expectations and judgments will express themselves in conventional, generic terms insofar as these hypotheses are based on stated principles, but in experiential particularity insofar as these principles are applied to particular circumstances. Perception and introspection, because of their immediacy, will always be unique in respect to sense data and affect and will therefore announce themselves as memorable experiences for subsequent retrospection, but, as objects that must first be recognized and may often be named, they are knowable only as tokens contained within the system of types stored in conventional memory.

Literate genres are rarely unmixed in respect to these two memory codes, but these two oral genres, (folk) narrative and gnome, exhibit a relatively pure descent. Narrative-based compositions will always be longer than gnomic compositions. Founded upon experiential memory, or more properly on a simulation of this memory mode, narrative has the mnemonic advantages of rich imagery and causal sequence. Gnomes, on the other hand, being low in image value and temporally indeterminate, are normally stored as simple units; only in a literate culture do such *sententiae* join to form paragraphs and become philosophical discourse.

Though these two memory modes generate distinct forms of literary discourse, they frequently appear in the same work. The animal fable, a literate transcription of an oral form (for example, Aesop or the Panchatantra) has its narrative and separate gnomic moral. It is more often the case in a literary work that one form of discourse (or mastergenre) provides the matrix within which the other form is embedded. The epic allows for the occasional gnomic formula or set-piece; the didactic or philosophical work allows for the insertion of narrative exempla or mythic analogies. In all such cases the tonal break in the text is definite and unmistakable.

Retrospective Imaging

Since narration is characterized by the verbal encoding of retrospection, it is important for us to understand the special characteristics of the images we form when we revisualize our own privately experienced and stored past. My assumption, of course, is that the imagery evoked by narrative texts, or indeed by any literary texts that presents a passage in the retrospective mode, simulates the actual accessing of experiential memory, that is, requires me as reader to pretend, in poetic play, to recollect the past of the "alien 'me'" I pretend to be.

Retrospective imaging draws upon data that had to have been unique and arousing when first perceived, else they would not have imprinted themselves so vividly that they could now be recalled as an episodic unit. Certain childhood experiences or one's first exposure to a strange city can leave one with impressions so vivid that a multitude of circumstantial details seem inseparably linked with every aspect of it. An item stored in conventional memory, however, was either learned secondhand or was so thoroughly overlearned by repetitive experience that one need not, or cannot, recall the circumstances in which one first learned it.

Retrospective imagery reproduces perception in some very interesting ways. As we have already noted, the imager not only comes equipped with a record of the incidental input signals, but, thanks to the marvels of neuronal engineering, is also provided with a scale-model reproduction of the visual field on which to sight these objects. And if this were not convenient enough, the imager is granted, through procedural memory, the ability to scan this field, simulating, that is, imaging, some of the same oculomotor routines he or she would normally use in perceiving a given array of stimulus-objects, including even the motor routines that move the body through three-dimensional space. In short, there is abundant and compelling evidence that retrospective imaging is a procedure that simulates not only the perceptual object(s) but also the perceptual processes themselves. The display that we view in retrospective imaging is therefore a composite of the input signals associated with a given episode plus the procedural routines (oculomotor and kinesthetic) that might plausibly have been employed in that original perceptual event. In effect, retrospective imaging operates like perceptual imaging except for two features, absence and familiarity. That is, retrospective images come classified as events retrieved from memory that represent conditions no longer existing and, having been already experienced, are assumed to be already familiar to us.

Let me be more specific. If I set myself the task of recollecting my college graduation, I must effortfully call up a life experience. (Conventional retrieval is relatively automatic—I know something or I don't and, either way, my assertion in untentative—but experiential retrospection is a more difficult task, often provoking head-scratching and facial tension.) I must "go back" some thirty years to a warm New England June afternoon. But as soon as I begin to insert myself into that time and place, I realize I must reconstruct that scene.

The problem lies with retrospection. I must try to focus on the unique features of that occasion, but since such memory traces are notoriously unstable and subject to decay, I need to supplement those temporally unique features with generic elements. Because four years at a small, remote Catholic college in the late 1950s loaded my mind with more conventional—alas—than experiential information, I must now call up my overlearned knowledge of the landscape, buildings, persons, and all that I associate with those four dim years, whether or not these items originally constituted some experiential chunk labeled "graduation day." In short, to fill out this mental reenactment I must confabulate enough details to make my recollection a passably complete "episode."

When I do this, my mind's eye moves its focus back and forth from experiential detail to conventional knowledge—from what I know I remember to what I remember I know. If my mind's eye were a presiding judge, I would be accepting alternately eyewitness evidence and expert testimony from the same source; then, combining these two very different sets of data into a coherent narrative, I (and the jury) would be obliged to produce a plausible reconstruction of the event—a deductive procedure traditionally permitted to a gentleman sleuth, but not, certainly not, to a conscientious judge. Most of us, I would venture to say, would rather have a vivid, fictionalized past than a dull, incoherent chronicle of facts. The wishes and biases that distort convention we tend to insert into our recollections as confabulated imagery. These subjective factors persuade me to accept whatever hearsay evidence I like, as long as it vividly bridges gaps in the eyewitness accounts: if for example I had heard some scandalous rumor about Professor X, I might in my reconstruction of this scene visualize him on the dais leering into his folded hands, savoring forever his secret turpitude.[2]

Now let us suppose a somewhat different situation, one somewhat closer to a literary situation. Suppose I have just found among my memorabilia the graduation program and discover that there on the back are notes jotted down during the guest speaker's unmemorable oration, notes that record a twenty-one-year-old's sardonic description of this scene. As I read them, first one, then another focus is represented to my mind, but except for its determinate order this textualized scene is no less "episodic," no less believed in, than my earlier unaided recollection. Such journal entries, serving as *aide-mémoires,* may enhance retrospective imaging but in no way alter its essential character.

Despite all this outrageous confabulation, however, we would like to believe that our retrospective imaging corresponds to eyewitness evidence and that its information has been purified as much as possible from the general ideas and biases of asserted convention. Even when we acknowledge the unavoidable conflation of the two memory systems, we identify retrospected reports as good faith attempts to recover the past. Retrospective imaging is a fact-based fiction, but, though a fiction, it is not encountered with a temporary willing suspension of disbelief. Quite the contrary, its performance is a strenuous effort to repossess a permanent personal past that can be wholly believed in. Poetic imaging of course frankly acknowledges the fictive character of this fusion of recollected information and therefore requires this suspension of disbelief.

Now that we have reminded ourselves of how creative retrospection can be, let us return to my graduation day and observe the processes of retrospective imaging at work.

When I begin to image this event, I first have to place myself somewhere in that setting. I do not hover over a schema of that campus: I choose, in a very literal sense, a point of view. The visual object I have in focus from that point may be a particular person or a tree or of a part of the Administration Building; I may thereupon choose to zoom in on a distant object, focus on my graduation program, view the assembled faculty behind the podium in a somewhat wider visual angle, or move my mental gaze in a series of overlapping fixations across the entire scene. I can even move my head and make a panoramic scan of 360 degrees and, if a tree is in my way, I can simply walk around it.

There is a potential plenitude of detail in this retrospected format that is derived not only from the vividness of the original impressions but also from the back-up support of conventional and procedural memory. As my example illustrates, though I may no longer be able to trust the accuracy of my retrospection of a particular event, conventional memory comes to my aid by reconstructing an overlearned grid of landmarks and a plausible set of characters. This grid is especially helpful, because it allows me to simulate a large visual field including a peripheral field in which objects appear before they can be targeted for focal attention.

The availability of a peripheral field in retrospection is of utmost importance, because this feature, as I will indicate in Chapter 7, distinguishes actual retrospective imaging from the verbally cued simulation of this cognitive mode. When we revisualize our own past, not-yet-focused-upon objects in a given setting "appear" on the fuzzy periphery well outside the 15 or so degree circle of focal clarity. We know they belong there. Even if retrospection cannot absolutely vouch for their presence, conventional memory asserts that they *should have been there.* Though I know that my account of my graduation day is only one possible reconstruction of the event and that other alumni may have other and more factual evidence, I believe it fairly represents what happened and, as they say in court, is "true, to the best of my recollection."

Now let us relate retrospective imaging to another famous Coleridgean formula and begin with Coleridge's contrast of primary and secondary imaginations. "The primary IMAGINATION" Coleridge defines as "the living power and prime Agent of human Perception, and as a repetition in the finite mind of the eternal act of creation in the infinite I AM" (*Biographia Literaria,* XIII). By this term he seems to mean visual perception—the visual experience we have when we encounter the world directly. To simulate perception, that is, to experience "perceptual imagery," would therefore be to imagine the process that Coleridge here calls primary imagination.

"Secondary imagination" he calls

an echo of the former, co-existing with the conscious will, yet still as identical with the primary in the *kind* of its agency, and differing only in *degree,* and in the *mode* of its operation. It dissolves, diffuses, dissipates, in order to recreate; or where this process is rendered impossible, yet still at all events it struggles to idealize and to unify. It is essentially *vital,* even as all objects (as objects) are essentially fixed and dead. (*Biographia,* vol. 1, p. 202)

Let me try now to gloss this classic statement with some of the terms I have been using. "Secondary imagination" is an echo, that is, a distant simulation, of perception. Its imagery, being willed, is unlike perception, which for Coleridge meant simply a beholding of what the Creator had determined to be there and not a mere semblance. Coleridge would no doubt classify a text that simulated a direct, present-tense perception as a product of the secondary imagination, which is identical with perception only in the "*kind* of its agency" (visual consciousness and the here-and-now of Augustine's *praesens attentio*). The simulation of perception, which I analyzed in the last chapter, replicates the procedures of visual perception, yet its performance differs significantly "in *degree*" (of vividness and verisimilitude) "and in the *mode* of its operation" (i.e., it operates in the absence of stimulus-objects and may be cued by language). Secondary imagination, or poetic play, also bears a considerable resemblance to actual retrospection, which works with the "objects . . . essentially fixed and dead" that are filed away in memory storage, but unlike actual retrospection, it is not based on these laws of association and preempts the contents of memory, dissolving, diffusing, and dissipating private experiences in order to "recreate" demiurgically a world consonant with the transcendental Reason.

This distinction between the imaging of actual retrospection and that which is simulated in poetic play corresponds to Kant's distinction between the *reproductive* and *productive* imaginations (*Critique of Judgment*). Both types of imagination were understood as the retrieval of memory data, predominantly visual memory data; reproductive imagination was the simple recollection of one's lived experience and productive imagination was the "creative" reconstruction of one's stored knowledge, a thoroughly fictive procedure.

This distinction, however, is not quite so clear-cut in practice. Retrospection can, but rarely does, reproduce perceptual experience without distortion and confabulation. As my graduation day example illustrates, as soon as I tried to retrieve a coherent record of that ceremony, I discovered that the details of that event had had done to them precisely what Coleridge said his "secondary imagination" does: they had been so dissolved, diffused, and dissipated that I, by virtue of some "esemplastic" power, was obliged to recreate that event. I did not so much reproduce that event as I *produced* it. Again, the crucial distinction is one of belief. Justifiably or not, I believe my own retrospective imaging (reproductive imagination), whereas my deliberate conflation of convention and experience I recognize as a fiction, an "embroidering" of the truth, a poiesis of memory, that I entertain only through a willing suspension of disbelief.

Nominative Images and the Transformations of Experience

When we compare the universe of language with the universe of sense perception, we immediately note that the part of speech that corresponds to perceptual objects is the noun. The images of such objects as we retrieve from memory storage in response to textual cues may therefore be termed nominative images. The question we must first address is, How do the two basic modes of storage and recall determine the image value of nouns?

Our first impulse may be to assume a correlation between common nouns and commonly shared convention and between proper nouns and personal experience. After all, a proper noun is "the name of an individual person, place or object, as opposed to a common noun which refers to any one of all things denoted by the noun. Thus, *John, Eiffel Tower, The Tyrol, London,* are proper nouns, whereas *boy, building, city,* are common nouns" (Hartmann and Stork 187).

Unfortunately this simple, logical distinction does not correlate with the "two memories" and the imaging of their cognitive modes. It should be obvious that the mere mention of a particular person, place, or thing does not guarantee its image value even if it does happen to occur within a narrative context. In Eliot's *Waste Land,* for example, many proper nouns are mentioned—Stetson, Mrs. Equitone, Jerusalem, Athens, Alexandria, and so on. Though these are unique entities and proper nouns, we are not invited to imagine them in the experiential detail with which we imagine the nameless typist in her room or the dull canal behind the gas-house. Proper nouns, like "Mrs. Equitone," lose much of their uniqueness when they are used metonymically to represent a class, or can be so spatially extensive, like "London," as to lie beyond the scope of any visualization. On the other hand, common nouns have only to be deictically specified and modified by descriptive detail to become fully individuated. A text has only to assume the cognitive mode of retrospection to suffuse a common noun in the full light of particularity.

Consider Browning's poem "Memorabilia." Its context is a dialogue. The speaker's interlocutor has evidently just told him a story of having once met Shelley. Though "Shelley" is as proper a name as any, its mention does not seem to lead the speaker or us to imagine this episode, for in the very midst of his friend's narration the speaker unpredictably recalls a unique event from his own experience.

1

Ah, did you once see Shelley plain,
    And did he stop and speak to you
And did you speak to him again?
    How strange it seems and new!

2

But you were living before that,
    And also you are living after;
And the memory I started at—
    My starting moves your laughter.

3

I crossed a moor, with a name of its own
    And a certain use in the world no doubt,
Yet a hands-breadth of it shines alone
    'Mid the blank miles round about.

4

For there I picked up on the heather
    And there I put inside my breast
A moulted feather, an eagle-feather!
    Well, I forget the rest.

Nothing—not Shelley, not the particular nameable but unnamed moor—emerges in the speaker's mind in such imaginal detail as does this single feather. Experience and convention, the two storage modes that subserve the six cognitive modes, are so fundamentally distinct that it is they, not the lexical properness, commonness, or concreteness, that determine the vividness of verbal images.

Turning to assertion, the principal mode of convention, we again discover that cognitive factors override linguistic indices. In texts that imitate the retrieval of general knowledge, nouns that otherwise denote objects equally concrete as Browning's eagle feather fail to evoke particularized imagery. Any reader may decide to focus upon them long enough to do so, but this would distort their function as *genera.* Consider this example of gnomic writing from Enion's lament at the close of Blake's *Four Zoas: Night the Second:*

> I am made to sow the thistle for wheat, the nettle
> for a nourishing dainty.
> I have planted a false oath in the earth: it has
> brought forth a poison tree.
> I have chosen the serpent for a councillor & the dog
> For a schoolmaster to my children.
> . . . .
> What is the price of Experience? Do men buy it
> for a song
> Or wisdom for a dance in the street? No it is
> bought with the price
> of all that a man hath: his house, his
> wife, his children.
> Wisdom is sold in the desolate market where none
> come to buy
> And in the withered field where the farmer
> plows for bread in vain. (pl. 35, ll. 1–4, 11–15)

Thistle, wheat, serpent, dog, schoolmaster, children—these are rapidly mentioned as though items in an inventory, synecdochal aspects of a larger human circumstance. The gnomic convention does not invite us to imagine the classroom in which the dog is lecturing to the speaker's children or the dance in the street that purchases wisdom. At most these are brief, fragmentary glimpses.

The nouns here, as in much of Blake's poetry, lack the high imagery value we associate with retrospection and the literature based on this mode. Despite this, I must add, his poetry is often able, even in its most generalizing passages, to exhibit imagery value because these gnomic utterances are usually spoken by dramatic characters, mythic personae who speak out of the passionate necessity of particular circumstances. We often image these speakers more clearly than the referents of their words. Moreover, we auditorily "image" the speaker's vocal tone, texture, and timbre; Blake helps us do so with such auditory cues as "she wailed," "he burst forth," "he answered her with tenderness," and so on, and thus helps us concretize these "visionary forms dramatic." Such writing, which is formally epic, has much also in common with closet drama and the novel.

Proper nouns are not necessarily imaged in any more particularity than common nouns. They are so imaged only when the cognitive mode in which they appear presents them as experiences, that is, when we the readers have had or, suspending disbelief, assume to have had a personal encounter with their particular referents. The proper nouns that prompt the most particularized imagery appear in the contexts of actual conversations, for example, when two persons gossip about an acquaintance, or when a writer does so in a personal letter.

Narrative, by reproducing the retrospective mode and endowing nouns with particularity, also, paradoxically, lends them generality. The narrative is accepted as relevant to the collective experience to the extent that its indicated meanings are not functionally restricted to a private frame of reference. It must, in other words, operate on two levels. One is that of simple narration, with or without the particularization of proper nouns. The other is that of general principles, the special province of gnomic utterance and convention (represented in the assertive mode). The outer format of experiential narrative is carefully retained—the text appears to record events that happened to someone, were stored, then recalled—but the inner content (the tenor, the *dianoia,* what the reader "comes away with") resembles the assertions of convention. The two modes and the two master-genres that derive from them are thus grasped together in a narrative spectrum that extends from particularized story to generalized myth.

As we have seen, the play frame inscribed about narrative tells us that, though the text portrays experiences other than our own, we may pretend these are our own and that the world thus portrayed, strange as it may be, is the familiar world of this self or these selves that we temporarily pretend to be.[3] While in the grip of story or myth we become familiarized with the unfamiliar and, when we return to our quotidian world, that ordinary place may now appear strangely reshaped.

To conclude: narrative, like any text, must be encoded and decoded by conventions, both literary and linguistic, but, as verbal play dictates in such scripts, convention must create a staging and select a cast that will simulate the retrospection—the "reliving"—of experience. Yet narrative does not simply reproduce the lived past in some diminished ersatz form, as Plato declared. In the process of conventional encoding the experiential format of retrospection becomes charged with the covert signification of conventional knowledge and belief, that is, of assertions that hermeneutics subsequently undertakes to reveal. Conventional content is less apparent in story, more apparent in myth, but across the narrative spectrum we find convention outwardly imitating experience in the retrospective mode, while inwardly conveying its own conventional message. Narrative, transformed in this way by the interpretation of memory systems and their primary cognitive modes, I propose to call *parable*.

The Transformations of Convention

If experience and convention are complementary memory systems, we might expect a certain symmetry in their operations. That is, if experience crosses over into convention, the opposite shift might also occur, in which case straight conventional discourse might carry at times a covert experiential content.

That conventional memory can form itself into "speech acts" and be stored in experiential memory is clear. For example, an especially kind or an especially abusive spoken word, though drawn from the public lexicon, one may store in memory as a component of a particular, privately experienced episode. But if there is to be found a transformation of the statements of conventional memory comparable to the verbal transformation of experience outlined above, one would expect it to take the form of a privatization of the discourse of common knowledge. One would look for a play-script in which the mind is expected to "grasp together" a discourse the outer format of which declares itself to be the contents of conventional memory, while the inner message indicates that this is the unique, private, verbal exploration of the author.

This transformation of convention occurs when a simple axiom of common knowledge is appropriated by an individual and made suddenly strange. Employing a linguistic model, Riffaterre (*Semiotics*) termed this phenomenon "ungrammaticality." Appealing to the structures of cognition and epistemology, I will term it *paradox* (*para-doxon*, i.e., contrary to received opinion or, more simply, "beyond belief"). Just as parable entails a grasping together in the mind of the reader of two parallel significations (privately experienced events implying collectively valid principles), paradox requires that a reader consider the statement at hand and at the same time possess in conventional memory the proposition or assumption that is being challenged by it or infused with a different value. The paradoxical, to make its point, depends on the doxical. Nineteenth-century New Englanders, to cite one example, responding more acutely to Thoreau's wordplay than do most contemporary readers, no doubt stiffened or guffawed when they read the language of the pulpit inverted and transvalued in such phrasing as: "Our manners have been corrupted by communication with the saints. Our hymn-books resound with a melodious cursing of God and enduring Him forever" (*Walden,* from ch. 1).

Paradox as a privatization of public convention also includes parody, which at its most effective strikes not merely at stylistic pretentions but at the pretentions of power that style naturalizes and protects. It does so, as Bakhtin notes, by presenting two voices in simultaneous dialogic opposition. In the example above we detect binaurally, as it were, Thoreau's voice and that of his doxological Other.

Paradox, even though it does not always take the derisory form of parody, often provokes the mind's laughter of surprise and as such has been a powerful rhetorical instrument in the development of ideas. Western science was inaugurated with the enigmatic pronouncements of the Pre-Socratics. That one can step but once into the same river was a paradox that revealed one neglected aspect of our world. No less paradoxical were such statements as "the earth is round," "the earth revolves about the sun," and "matter is a form of energy." The Christian paradoxes that in one form or another convey the thought that only by sacrificing one's own life can one save it had to have seemed absurd in a late classical culture obsessed with issues of prudence, comfort, and the avoidance of moral distress. That the last shall be first and the first shall be last, that the meek shall inherit the earth—these made sense only within the context of an apocalyptic scenario of history. These were "dark sayings" that were deliberately *para doxa,* contrary to prevailing exoteric beliefs and were intelligible only to those who shared the then esoteric *doxa,* or dogmata, upon which they were based. In a Christianized Europe these paradoxes eventually became the unquestioned first principles of the conventional memory store of every believer.

The path by which a paradox normally attains doxical status is marked by the proverb, a discourse composed of discrete units, as compared with the contingent organization of narrative. The terse assertions of the conventional memory and the schemata they prompt seem separated from us and from one another by a space-like distance. The contents of this memory mode are assumed to be universally valid and as true tomorrow as they were yesterday. Though some of them are obviously drawn from experience, they become distillations of such experiences, generalizations eventually detached from all empirical circumstances. Detachment is indeed the affect we most readily associate with this mode—a Montaignesque stepping back from the ungovernable flux of personal history represented in the retrospection of experience. As was stated earlier, the texts that externalize the contents of conventional memory are gnomic in style, the purest instance of which is the proverb, either in the collected or in the logical form.

A good example of the collected form is the biblical book of Proverbs, a reading of which will demonstrate the problems of sequencing an essentially atemporal set of texts. The editors obviously attempted to impose an order of sorts on this collection, but due to the special nature of gnomic utterance they could not hope to succeed: redundancies and nonce categories abound. A similar problem is presented by Blake's "Auguries of Innocence." In David Erdman's edition of *The Poetry and Prose of William Blake* the editor speaks of the manuscript as a "fair copy but a hasty one, with much mending of letters" and adds:

> It is conceivable that Blake, at greater leisure, might have rearranged the lines (as was his wont) in a less desultory sequence. Following the lead of John Sampson . . . , who printed the text in ms order followed by a "revised version for those who may prefer to read the poem as a whole, instead of as a number of disconnected proverb-couplets," . . . I have presented a thematically grouped rearrangement after the ms transcript. I concede that Blake may have wished each reader to cope with this "Riddle" by himself. (778)

I would argue, however, that the "Auguries," like the Book of Proverbs, is indeed a number of disconnected proverb-couplets that can never be rearranged into a "poem," if by that term one means a meditative lyric, or even a lyrical sequence.

The logical form of gnomic writing as exemplified by the proverb is what we know as philosophical writing, including the literary essay. This writing is the product of a different sort of crossover, one in which convention maintains its impersonal detachment, while organizing its propositions in a purposive sequence. Conventional knowledge, in other words, ventures forth on a series of experiences of its own, tracking down proofs of its own hypotheses and assimilating evidence as it pursues its quest for certainty. This mobilization of propositions, not sustainable before the technology of writing, has allowed the assertive mode with its weak imagery an independence from and indeed a dominance over the discourse of retrospection. Critical discourse thus supersedes mythic discourse.

Just as the literary transformations of experience, which I have broadly labeled "parable," range from "story" (as the least transformed) to "myth" (as the most transformed into collective relevance), so also the transformations of convention, which I have called "paradox," may be seen to range along a scale from "wit," as the least, to "anomaly," as the most privatized.

Alexander Pope's classic definition of wit is quite revealing:

> True Wit is Nature to advantage dressed,
> What oft was thought, but ne'er so well expressed:
> Something, whose truth convinced at sight we find,
> That gives us back the image of our mind.
> ("Essay on Criticism," II, 97–100)

This is not a reconceptualization of Nature but an improved restatement of it, not an invitation to a new world view but rather a reconfirmation of the principles already represented in our conventional body of knowledge. It is a verbal mirror upon the highly polished surface of which we see the "image of our mind"—the schematic imagery of conventional memory. Having stored axioms, definitions, and schemata, this memory mode contributes to wit a wealth of public (conventional) stereotypes. Wit scrutinizes these, refurbishes some, explodes others, corrects some, and sharpens the point of yet others. Serving the purposes of humor and satire, wit thus caters broadly to a public fondly attached to its own "notions," a collectivity that constitutes a group within, but separate from, the larger community that otherwise shares with it the same language, institutions, and conventional assumptions. It identifies an "us," as distinct from, and usually superior to, a "them." Erving Goffman speaks of a "we rationale" as typical of such games (*Encounters* 18).

The most extreme form of paradox, that is, the most thorough expropriation of the public resources of conventional memory, is anomaly. This includes the very private language of schizophrenics and of those writers who deliberately experiment with and explore the limits of language. The most famous linguistic anomaly, most famous among linguisticians, at least, is Chomsky's "green ideas sleep furiously." It is often cited to demonstrate that a sentence may be grammatically correct but semantically meaningless.[4]

These two kinds of stored data, experience and convention, as we have seen, are represented in their purest form by retrospection and assertion. The literary genres these cognitive modes ostensibly dominate are narration and gnome. But, as we have recognized, literature tends to transform these modes by subtly infusing each with the spirit of the other. As outer formats, retrospection and assertion have unambiguous markers, but retrospected narrative always contains a degree of generalized convention, and asserted gnome always implies a degree of privatized experience.

Memory, as a bimodal, transformative system of storage and representation, is thus the mother of the Muses. In non-mythic terms this means that memory processes determine the genres of literary discourse.

Chapter 7
Introspection and the Visionary Imagination

The cognitive mode I have called "introspection" is the inwardly projected complement of perception. The visual attention, or "mind's eye," situated at the perpetual midpoint of the here-and-now, rotates outward, as it were, to focus on the there-and-now of the perceived world or inward to intuit the there-and-now of introspected percept-like appearances that emerge from some inner store. As perception is to outer presence, introspection is to inner: the *thereness* of perception and introspection is their deictic aspect, their *right there!*ness. This aspect of presence distinguishes the imagery of these two modes from that of the other four modes, which are zones of temporal, as well as spatial, absence, or *then*-and-thereness. Though, like the five other modes, introspection is an everyday psychological phenomenon, it is, of all the modes, most readily identified as "poetic."

In everyday consciousness how do we recognize a visual event as an introspected image? Perhaps by some sort of process of elimination, a split-second operation that, if slowed down, might involve four decisions. First of all, we discriminate between a percept and a mental image. (We have an obvious need to do so, for if we do not make a correct discrimination, we misperceive and if we *can*not make this discrimination, we fall into that state of derangement in which objectivity and subjectivity collapse into one another.) Suppose we decide X is a mental image and not a percept: now our second discrimination is between images effortlessly retrieved through retrospection and those, like this image, that suddenly emerge into consciousness. A retrospected image is marked in regard to time and place and is normally accompanied by a peripheral field rich in detail, but an introspected image stands alone or, as is more often the case, hovers in an empty imaginal field. Third, the introspected image must be discriminated from that conventional image that we may term the abstract type:

although it resembles this type in its lack of experiential detail, the introspected image exhibits a degree of percept-like vividness and animation that no conventional type ever attains to. Finally, we must distinguish this image from those associated with expectation and judgment: though introspected imagery has in the past been assumed to be prognosticative or admonitory, we cannot regard this one as such unless we assume a transmitter of this image who knows the future or posit an inner faculty that is similarly prescient.

Daydreams and deliberative wish-fulfillment fantasies are common introspective events, but sudden spontaneous images have about them an aura of the uncanny. Even the incurious will ask, "What was it that made me suddenly think of that" or "Why did that image just pop into my mind?" The need to explain its presence has led some to connect it with some absent cause. Those who favor psychoanalytical, over extrasensory, explanations place the cause of this unforeseen effect in the past as a trace stored among repressed memories, especially those of childhood, which recurs, often in some disguised form, in waking consciousness and in dreams.

In this concluding chapter we will consider the actions of the mind's eye, that here-and-now center of visual consciousness, when in response to verbal cues it forms images without our questioning either their provenance or their logic. Within poetic play we are regularly called upon to imagine ourselves as others who, though located in particular places and times, imagine purely mental entities that seem strangely timeless and placeless—images without referential contexts of their own, images that simply *appear.* A particular function of this introspective mode is metaphor. A general function is reading itself. When we are swept up in poetic play, we are not focally aware that it is we who are conjuring these images out of thin air and in the inner present of the introspective mode. Insofar as it is an art, imaginative reading is essentially the art of introspection. If these images seem to us to be familiar representations of the outer world, we are little affected by their phantasmic nature. But when a poetic text actually asks us to imagine phantasms, that is, visionary and oneiric entities, it reenforces and overtly displays the introspective, innerworldly character of the medium.

Metaphor as Introspective Transfer

According to Roman Jakobson's now familiar tropology, metonymy and metaphor are the two poles of language. Metonymy becomes the pure expression of contiguity, that is, an indexical relation of signifiers to signifieds that includes association by sequence, cause/effect, contemporaneity, and (subsuming synecdoche) part/whole. Thus broadly defined, metonymy has come to denote a tendency to inventory our world, to designate tokens of types, and to represent by the use of selected items a larger contexture of referents. Metonymy may appear as significant detail in the discourse of any of the six cognitive modes but in some situations this outer-worldly trope proves inadequate. Some topics, such as affects, moods, and complex concepts, provoke that other linguistic pole, metaphor. At such moments the metonymic contexture, in whatever cognitive mode it happens to be woven, is suddenly ruptured by introspection and an item is introduced solely on the basis of its similarity to a metonymically ungraspable concept. Using I. A. Richards's two terms, we might say that a problematic tenor has invoked a vehicle and the two together have become a metaphor.

Translated into Jakobsonian terms, the cognitive modes are categories into which referential context is distributed. Introspected referents are no exception. But when introspected referents are declared to be equivalent to other referents and are projected into the axis of combination, they momentarily foreground what I have called the analogic code, which produces a number of glossings and iterations that notably include metaphor.

John Dyer, in the following passage from "Grongar Hill," supplies a simple example of this process. He first describes a distant slope as a very innocent eye might see it. "Streaks of meadows" project themselves tinily on the retina and so we underestimate their true size:

See on the mountain's southern side,	114
Where the prospect opens wide,	115
Where the evening gilds the tide,	116
How close and small the hedges lie!	117
What streaks of meadows cross the eye!	118
A step *methinks* may pass the stream,	119
So little distant dangers seem;	120
So we mistake the future's face,	121
Eyed through Hope's deluding glass.	122

(emphasis added)

"Methinks" is our cue that we are about to turn from the simulation of immediate perceptual experience to that of the inner world of thought. The first turning of the mind's eye occurs at line 120 as a shift from the cognitive mode of perception to that of assertion ("So little . . ."). Here the lessons of convention come to supplement perceptual imagery and convert a sensory revel into a parable on self-delusion. At the second turning (121) an allegorical vignette is intro-

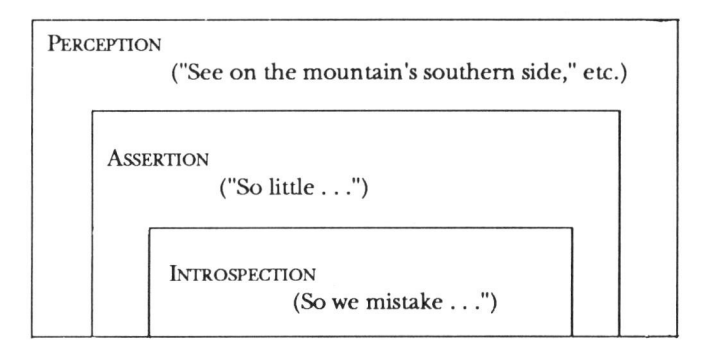

```
┌─────────────────────────────────────────────────────┐
│ PERCEPTION                                          │
│        ("See on the mountain's southern side," etc.)│
│   ┌─────────────────────────────────────────────┐   │
│   │ ASSERTION                                   │   │
│   │        ("So little . . .")                  │   │
│   │   ┌─────────────────────────────────────┐   │   │
│   │   │ INTROSPECTION                       │   │   │
│   │   │        (So we mistake . . .")       │   │   │
│   │   └─────────────────────────────────────┘   │   │
│   └─────────────────────────────────────────────┘   │
└─────────────────────────────────────────────────────┘
```

duced, in which Hope uses an optical device to view the "face" of the future. At this second turning we shift to information that could neither be perceived nor asserted (as a known fact or a belief), but could only have been envisioned by the inwardly gazing mind's eye in the form of an emblem fancy. In structure this introspective insertion is an implied metaphor (more specifically: personification) within a simile-metaphor, as shown in the diagram. The natural description is morally enriched by the addition of the abstract statement (the vehicle of this rather unmetaphor-like metaphor); then this abstraction is animated by personification: the future has a face and Hope is a landscape enthusiast with perhaps a "Claude glass" (see Gifford, 19–20).

This brings us to an interesting paradox. For the actual reader (the "real 'me'" who is trying to construe the meaning of the text) the second term (or vehicle) of most metaphors is usually experienced more vividly than the first term (or tenor), which is often indicated by a quite abstract word or phrase. The very opposite is the case for the metaphor-maker. The poet intuits the meaning that the wording of the tenor so inadequately embodies. At least the poet knows how inadequate this wording is for the reader and knows that the deeper resources of introspection must be drawn upon to articulate some aspect of this intimately apprehended meaning. Tenor and vehicle form the base line by which this partial meaning can be triangulated. The reader who in poetic play assumes the persona of the "alien 'me'" must also regard this unspoken meaning to which this vehicle points as an inchoately known entity. To Burns and to this latter persona "My luve" is much more concrete and specific than "a [just any] red, red rose." Paradoxically the generic rose is used to specify this already specific woman and her meaning for this specific man.

This need for generic terms of comparison seems to have precluded retrospection as a normal source of vehicles. The fact that retrospected images, vivid as they can be made to seem to the reader through narrative and extended description, are privately possessed impressions normally disqualifies them. At these moments when metonymic discourse requires metaphoric supplementation the vivid concreteness of vehicles is secondary to their immediate recognition value both to the reader and to the poet, who also needs an ad hoc verbal handle on his elusive tenor. For this reason it is the common lexicon of conventional types that poets access for perhaps 99 percent of all metaphor-vehicles.

This same lexicon is of course our first resource when we engage in referential and metonymic discourse: whenever I seek to name what I perceive or conceptualize, its name strives to emerge from that buried word-hoard, which some have called the verbal unconscious, and is combined with other words to produce phrases, clauses, and sentences. When, in metaphorical thinking, I seek to call up an item that shares some quality with the present object of attention, I can often accomplish this with the same swiftness I experience when I use simple lexical recall to name a percept. Introspection, the standard mode of metaphor-vehicles, drawing as it does on this common code, expresses itself in the same conventional diction as assertion.

Let us see once again how metaphor may be understood as one function of the mind's eye moving across a verbalized field of objects.

IT IS A BEAUTEOUS EVENING

It is a beauteous evening, calm and free,
The holy time is quiet as a Nun
Breathless with adoration; the broad sun
Is sinking down in its tranquility;
The gentleness of heaven broods o'er the Sea:
Listen! the mighty Being is awake,
And doth with his eternal motion make
A sound like thunder—everlastingly.
Dear Child! dear Girl! that walkest with me here,
If thou appear untouched by solemn thought,
Thy nature is not therefore less divine:
Thou liest in Abraham's bosom all the year,
And worship'st at the Temple's inner shrine,
God being with thee when we know it not.

Here Wordsworth imitates direct present-tense perception and asks us to pretend we are with him on the beach. If we *were* there with him, we would perhaps not need to be told it was a beauteous evening—such scene-setting is simply a rubric of the perceptual imagery play-script. But the speaker's attention, and our mind's eye with it, quickly turns from this global contemplation of the evening to the image of a person not actually present with us on the beach. A nun appears suddenly out of a conventional store of schemata and for one moment becomes conceptually fused with the evening, yielding up her qualities of breathlessness and adoration to the quiet of this scene and then, wraith-like, vanishing as the mind's eye turns back to the simulated percepts of the body's eye. The setting sun and the sea, and with them this entire outer world, are only briefly sighted, however, before the mind's eye turns again, this time to the contents of a mythic text, namely, the biblical story of creation in which "the Spirit of God brooded upon the face of the waters" and created light out of darkness. The image of a giant bird incubating the sea, implicit in this allusion, then quickens the sea, which, though visible and audible, is invested with some degree of consciousness through the implied metaphor of personification.

The sestet introduces a person who, unlike the nun, is part of the perceptual imagery. She is addressed in the here-and-now, but, even if she had not been present, her invocation in the vocative imitates speech addressed to a perceptually present auditor. We must not forget that during the imitative play of poetry the reality of reference is not an issue in question and that, as readers, our primary demand of a text is that it indicate from passage to passage which of several cognitive processes we are to simulate. Here the speaker's companion is not extensively described; we image her simply as a girl who seems untouched by the solemn thought experienced by the speaker, that is, unable to supplement her perception by turning her mind's eye toward the contents of the "philosophic mind" with its conventional and experiential memory stores that the years had brought to the poet. No matter, he says to her: Since the contents of my memory actually exist, at least for the purposes of this sonnet, you are really not here, weighed down with the weary weight of all this unintelligible, merely perceived, world. You are in Abraham's bosom and are worshiping God in the Holy of Holies of the Temple in Jerusalem. We cannot tell, of course, exactly when this occurs and you yourself are probably unaware of it.

Wordsworth's references to the bosom of Abraham and the Temple's inner shrine are implied metaphors that rather bizarrely identify this light-spirited girl first as some dead and sainted Lady Lazarus (Luke 16:22–23), then as a Jewish high priestess. All these anomalies notwithstanding, Wordsworth has succeeded by tropical legerdemain in transposing his companion from the perceived world to the mental cloister of conventional memory, where she can be merged with the "Nun / Breathless with adoration," the image of woman that had appeared spontaneously in the second line. The resemblance between these two metaphorical females, the nun and the Jewish worshiper, illustrates the way several introspected images, when they function as metaphor-vehicles in the same text, can serve to develop a system of metonyms, here indicative of female rapture. The poet performs as a pianist who fingers a surface melody of great variety with his right hand while returning again and again to the same lower chords with his left. Wordsworth's introspective subtext here suggests a preconscious wish that his companion was not this "dear child," this "dear girl," but rather a female counterpart of himself and uses this fourteen-line spell to transform her into this.

To sum up our discussion so far: introspection is the sudden looking inward and the sudden, relatively effortless retrieval of conventional schemata. The triggering context, which in metaphor is the tenor, is to the metaphor-maker the intimately experienced concept that for some reason cannot be adequately verbalized without reference to a catalogue of commonly coded conventional objects. These schemata, when invested with the spontaneous, apparition-like vividness of introspection, acquire the dynamic character of experiential images, that is, of visions that "happen to one." When we speak of an "image" in the metaphor we are usually speaking of this introspected entity. Because of the extraordinary cognitive mode that evokes it, this image is also extraordinary, assuming the character more of a *phasma,* or apparition, than of a *phantasma,* or mental image.

Reading as Introspection

The metaphor-vehicle is a moment at which the introspective mode intersects with a tenor-dominated plane of discourse. The manifestation of this mode is concentrated and sudden. It appears and then is gone, though it may later reappear in some disguised or displaced form. This emergence of introspection, like that of the other modes, is a hypotactic function of poetic play. But there is a more fundamental function of this mode, a function logically prior to poetic play. This is the introspective procedure of construing verbal signs at the level of lexeme and syntagm.

If we were to examine the sequence of procedures by which our mind processes a poetic text, we might find that every reception of a poem (as distinct from a rehearsal from memory) must begin in the cognitive mode of perception. We see graphemes or hear phonemes. These sensory elements are not, however, factors in verbal semiosis until we construe their semantic content as words and sentences. This construal is a function of introspection, the process by which we consult our linguistic code, access the signifieds of verbal signifiers, and form an understanding of the message. Generated by this introspective activity, our understanding may then form concepts and images and focus on them as projected into any one, or any series, of cognitive modes, including introspection. Having passed through a sensory and a semantic stage, corresponding to the perceptual and the introspective modes, the poetic message is now revealed to the mind's eye and dis-played multimodally upon the inner stage of the imagination.

The first decoding of verbal signs, this first dawning of our understanding of a perceived message, is thus the product of the introspective mode. As a receptive act, it is either completed or not completed; the message is either delivered word for word or some of it is omitted or misconstrued. Assuming linguistic competence and attentiveness on the part of the reader, this relay of textual data is normally completed at what we may term the "primary introspective stage." This is the stage at which the play-script is conned and its particular directions understood. In an initial reading this stage of comprehension tends to overlap and interfere with the final stage, that of poetic play, but, once one has become familiar with the text, one can afford to enter with all one's focal attention into the play of enacting it within the theater of the mind's eye.

Yet even when one can successfully maintain the play set toward the message, one finds that this poetic message has been imbued with the peremptory character of the primary introspective stage. This is especially true of verbal visuality: when we form particular mental images in response to textual cues, we cannot comfortably rely on our own particular stored experience of these objects. That is, when we imagine what we read, we cannot fall back on the rich contextual information that usually accompanies our own retrospected images. An individual's own retrospective imaging, as my commencement day example (Chapter 6) was meant to demonstrate, is relatively freewheeling and hit-or-miss. It is supposed, of course, to be constrained by the contents of one's experiential store, but because that system is subject to blurring and loss ("forgetting"), retrospection is regularly embellished by confabulation, edited by repression, and sometimes wholly revised by "cover memories." Moreover, in the act of retrieval, such aspects as object-selection, point of view, and duration of focus are subject to the whim of the retrospecter.

This freedom is not, however, transferrable to the poetic imagery activated in reading, even when the cognitive mode that is to be simulated is retrospection. For a reader the imaging procedure is strictly determined by verbal cues. True, one *can* linger over one word and stop to visualize it in variously detailed ways and, true, as Roland

Barthes advocated, one *can* alter the order of the text and go back five pages to reread a relevant passage. One can indeed do lots of things while ostensibly reading: daydream about similar events from one's own experience, as Gaston Bachelard recommended, critically evaluate the work, congratulate oneself on having gotten to page 256, or try to eavesdrop on one's teenage daughter's phone conversation. My point is that reading a literary text, far from being an improvisatory act, is rather like playing an instrument beneath the brow of Toscanini: one is obliged to play the notes as written. As readers, we are required to process the lexical information as it is given and are similarly obliged to image the imageable words as the context in its left-to-right sequence instructs us. A respect for the temporality of verbal notation does not, however, rigidly constrain us as poetic interpreters.

While it is true, as Iser, echoing Ingarden, has maintained, that gaps often appear between discontinuous blocks of literary discourse and call upon the reader to supply associative hypotheses but not to insert supererogatory data—certainly not the insertion of uncued images. Suppose that while reading Gerald Manley Hopkins's "Spring and Fall" one insisted on imagining a pain-wracked Jesuit interrogating a snuffling, freckled little Margaret. Such gratuitous images are not only irrelevant here but are obstructive to the reading of a poem that so strives to deprivatize human sorrow.

To declare that reading is a process of responding to verbal cues seems perhaps to belabor the obvious, but the implications of that definition for the literary imagination have not yet, it seems to me, been sufficiently explored. To begin with, the imaging cues we receive from texts are often quite minimal—bare, unadorned nouns that, even when they do receive modification, receive only a single swipe with a paintbrush or a single twist from the shaper's hand. Since all words, except proper nouns, are generic, it is generic meaning, that is, the contents of conventional memory, that is effectuated by texts. This generic conventionality, moreover, is public; it is no one's personal property. If, like diary entries, texts bore cues to our own experiential memory, they would prompt experiential imaging. As actual retrospecters we would have no trouble then supplying incidental details for each noun, imaging objects focally, *while being aware, albeit dimly, of other objects in a peripheral field of approximately 120 degrees diameter.* If an episode had taken place in a location so well learned by us that it has become for us a conventionalized setting, peripheral tracking is further enhanced. If, for example, we try to recall a conversation we had yesterday in our kitchen, we can visualize our interlocutor in a broad field in which, if we fixate the refrigerator, we do not "see" its image hovering in a void. We *know* that to its left is the sink and seem to

Introspection and the Visionary Imagination 151

glimpse its scooped shape in our left peripheral field even while we fixate serially on the rectangular contours of the refrigerator. The simple fact that literary texts are not drawn from the reader's experiential store (nor for that matter very often drawn wholesale from the *author*'s experience) means that the figures that they induce in the minds of readers are foregrounded upon a necessarily absent background. Verbal visuality, when governed by a written text, evokes a world of uncanny strangeness. Thus literary texts, when the reader performs them, have a defamiliarizing function that operates at a level far more fundamental than mere stylistic deviation. The portrayed world of the poem is "made strange" because to the reader it is indeed strange.

To put it bluntly, when we enter the imaginary space of a text, we don't know where we are. We orient ourselves only in reference to the few landmarks we are given—nouns situated in a void. These nouns are fashioned into an assumed visuospatial network by prepositions, verbs, and adverbs, but are displayed to us only in the linear, unidirectional sequence of word order. Not having actually perceived this scene ourselves, we have no peripheral field in which to detect and target an object as our next image. The fact that the speaker may be narrating events from experiential memory does not help one bit to orient us, because this is his, not our, experience: we can imitate the procedural format of retrospection, but we can never supplement another's retrospection by drawing on the contents of that person's memory. As the implied addresser several enters or reenters *his* world and names its objects, our peripheral field is as blank as the white space that surrounds each printed character and, as for our next image, that comes when and only when the text determines. To the speaker this may be the most familiar of all settings, but to us it is a place where absolutely anything might lurk before suddenly exploding into view. The saccades and fixations, observed in visual perception and simulated in the act of imaging, are in the literary texts verbally cued and syntactically bound and thus never left to the reader's volition.

Reading is a rule-governed behavior. It draws upon a culturally determined repertoire of readerly responses, but it also obeys procedural constraints that we might well regard as hard-wired and common to the social discourse of all natural languages. Any transfer of information from one mind to another, Saussure's *circuit de la parole*, constitutes a transfer of data from the experiential or conventional memory system of an addresser to the conventional, *and only the conventional*, system of an addressee.

Let me illustrate this by conjuring up a scene from the good old days before grammarians, when language was not yet an object of metalin-

152 Chapter 7

guistic anxiety but rather a tool used to confront what were at that time more pressing anxieties. Let us suppose it is a steamy summer afternoon in 40,000 BC. One man runs up to another and in the local idiom announces: "A little while ago I saw a sabretooth tiger at the water hole!" The addressee reacts by consulting his store of conventional knowledge and forming a quasi-retrospective image of this tiger, which, since *he* did not actually see the beast, must be in fact an introspected image, projected as the generic "sabretooth tiger" into the immediate past. If the speaker had said: "I see a large, haggard, slavering sabretooth tiger parting the tall grass behind you," this description would cue in the addressee a rapid introspective train of quasi-*perceptual* images. On both these hypothetical occasions, the addressee, receiving his information secondhand, quickly "makes up" an image appropriate to the verbal cues of the speaker. Since this addressee has not seen this particular tiger in the past nor sees it now, both images are introspected. The first, having been filtered through the addresser's experiential memory, appears to the addressee's mind's eye in a retrospective format, while the second, being presented as an immediate transcript of the addresser's perception, appears in a perceptual format. It is important to recognize that despite the fact that these two images refer to a particular, concrete object, the addressee, having no firsthand experience of them, must construct them out of commonly coded, generic materials.

There will be subsequent occasions, of course, in which the two friends will converse and one will prompt the other to retrieve common experiential memory. "Ah, it was terrible, wasn't it, when that sabretooth tiger chased us both over the mountain" or "What exactly did you do, when we split up and it chose to leap after you?"[1] Mutual reminiscence and direct interrogation may prompt retrospection, but, even so, the prompt itself is intelligible to the addressee only as it is initially construed by recourse to conventional memory.

Mutual reminiscence and direct interrogation are not, however, ordinarily encountered in the reading of literary texts. Neither oral nor written texts are addressed to the particular experiential store of a particular person, but are composed and transmitted as utterances meant for a collective audience. They are not conversation, but news dispatches, and are often as urgently conveyed as reports of tigers. A reader of a literary text thus shares with his or her prehistoric forebears this simple relation between verbal cue and cognitive response. As the image of the tiger would appear to emerge from an indistinct ground, so also every noun in a literary information-exchange appears virtually out of nowhere to hover momentarily before the gaze of the mind's eye. Like Blake's "Tyger," forged from spare parts, every poetic noun is drawn from the image-bin of convention, and, once produced, glows self-illumined against a ground as undefined as "the forests of the night."

The featureless character of this ground upon which verbally communicated images are projected is of immense significance. This blank periphery corresponds to the undifferentiated whiteness of the page upon which the graphic signs become inscribed. It is like a white desert upon which mirages appear. It is also like the silence or white sound that surrounds and isolates words and phrases of spoken discourse. In this distinction of figure-and-ground, we see once again how language as a storage medium and vehicle for poetic imaging is admirably suited to this task. We also detect a relationship here between literature and sensory deprivation states.

"Notice What This Poem Is Not Doing"

Neurobiologists tell us that at every moment of waking consciousness many more neurons are engaged in inhibiting input than in registering it. The activity of reading anything requires that we filter out not only all extraneous environmental stimuli, but all constructions not specifically induced by the text. Reading a poetic text requires even greater concentration, because its imaginary world is so minimally furnished with referents.

The differences between spontaneous imaging and text-cued imaging are quite important. Closing our eyes sometimes helps us to form images; the darkness that this creates can be the condition for the drifting in of certain lighted figures out of the dimness. Imagination, by the way, has often been likened to illumination. (The Greeks believed that *phantasia* was derived from *phaos*, or *phos*, "light.") If we choose to retrospect experiential memory or assert a sequence of conventional thought, we control to a great extent the distribution and intensity of this light. If we fail to assert this control, we may find ourselves entering into a reverie in which figures appear, fade, and transform themselves in bizarre ways. If, in this state, we decide to collaborate with our spontaneous images, partly overseeing their behavior and partly respecting their autonomy, we enter into a creative process of imaging. This we also do as writers. But as readers of a literary text, we are neither passive witnesses to nor active inventors of our fantasies but are directed absolutely by its verbal cues. The text is a statement that creates a world, object by object, *ex nihilo*. Where the light of the imagination is instructed to fall, there suddenly a noun-object emerges conjured like magic from the darkness. William Stafford suggests an analogy between the gradual illumination of a landscape by the morning sun and the verbal "nomination" of an imagined world:

NOTICE WHAT THIS POEM IS NOT DOING

The light along the hills in the morning
comes down slowly, naming the trees
white, then coasting the ground for stones to nominate.

Notice what this poem is not doing.

A house, a house, a barn, the old
quarry, where the river shrugs—
how much of this place is yours?

Notice what the poem is not doing.

Every person has taken a stone
to hold, and catch the sun. The carving
says, "Not here, but called away."

Notice what this poem is not doing.

The sun, the earth, the sky, all wait.
The crows and redbirds talk. The light
along the hills has come, has found you.

Notice what the poem has not done.

In most poems we are invited to view a setting over the shoulder of a speaker, a bona fide witness who is (re)experiencing particular events in a particular set of circumstances. If that witness is recounting past events, we normally assume he is now relying on experiential memory and is "reliving" those events with the circumstantial amplitude of that memory system. Though the witness contributes to our visualization perhaps only the barest of details, we intellectually assume that there is a wealth of incidental detail that he or she recalls, or could recall, a huge variety of shapes and colors that implicitly fill the background upon which each successive noun-object is placed. Stafford's speaker, however, does not permit the reader to identify with the authorial consciousness of a speaker who is presently perceiving or retrospecting having perceived this scene. The speaker pointedly reminds the reader that this is a poem by asking: "how much of this place is yours?" We are compelled to answer: "only what we are given, nothing else."

This is a somewhat unusual text, granted. Most literary texts invite the reader to pretend they are accounts drawn from his or her own experiential store. They do not challenge this fiction. Yet the point this text so uncompromisingly makes is that no literary text is ever actually drawn from the *reader*'s experience. The text-cued simulation of experience is a play that imitates, but is radically different from actual perception and retrospection. Such experiential accounts are as problematical to us as letters drawn from corked bottles washed up on the beach.

Suppose we take Stafford's challenge. Just what is every poem *not* doing? It is not supplying us with a peripheral space, a ground upon which to locate the figural images it cues. This leads us to another question: by not conforming to the expectations of ordinary consciousness, what *is* every poem doing? It is, I would suggest, accomplishing a feat that is visually quite extraordinary. Imbued as it is by the starkly determinate character of the primary introspective stage, every text presents a world in which figures, or fragments of figures, hover upon empty grounds, a bizarre world of floating synecdoches, of undulant Goyaesque phantoms. Whether or not they thematically exploit this aspect of the medium, every poetic text simply by virtue of its medium simulates visionary events.

Let us examine the implications of these statements. If the visual field available to the reader's imagination is noun-determined and limited to one small focal field at a time, is the result simply and necessarily a series of groundless figures? Yes and no. Yes, because no block of written words can simulate the blurred multeity of the peripheral field—every time an imageable noun appears, it must be imaged as a focalized figure. This is an all-or-nothing process. On the other hand, *after* it is read, it does not entirely vanish. As Ingarden (124–145) and Iser (*Act*, 140–151) have pointed out, the memory traces of verbal images form a kind of implicit ground upon which further images may be placed. We do not revisualize them, but, if the setting remains the same, we retain a tacit understanding that these entities are still "there," and, if we reread the text, we may anticipate their reappearance and sense their presence hovering somewhere in the recollected future of the text.

Having granted that memory furnishes an *assumed* ground for text-cued imagery, I wish to emphasize that this is not the same as an imaged ground. The difference between believing that such-and-such a room, previously described, continues to enclose the character I am now imaging is not the same as peripherally imaging that room as a ground for that figure. This difference is the fundamental difference between simulated vision and simulated belief. A text that bases itself in the sense data of consensual reality, like Browning's "My Last Duchess" or Frost's "Death of the Hired Man," requires of the reader the belief in the presence of a peripheral ground, composed partly of the objects mentioned in the text and partly by objects deemed appropriate to the setting. On the other hand, a text that describes the unfamiliar, like *Paradise Lost* or "The Rime of the Ancient Mariner," relies so heavily on the reader's willingness to suspend disbelief in the immediately presented images that a belief in the continuance of a stable peripheral ground is often allowed to lapse. In either case, however, objects not referred to by the text cannot be imaged in any simulation of the visual field nor can the peripheral ground ever be used to locate objects for focal attention unless and until the text "nominates" them and thereby conjures them out of the peripheral emptiness as focalized objects.

The data-reduced condition of texts and the sensorily deprived condition of reading bear an intriguing resemblance to the condition most poets find conducive to composition. Philosophy may be produced near the sensory hubbub of the *agora* or at the outdoor table of a Parisian café (non-imagistic cognition can tolerate a good deal of visual and auditory "noise," as long as there is no linguistic interference), but a literature of imagery can be produced and received only in a visually non-interferent environment. Moreover, a radically non-interferent environment, as the many experiments with sensory deprivation have proved, itself promotes rich and spontaneous image-formation. The "sensory deprivation" conditions that writers have sought out are not those of the classic laboratory experiments with their tanks of saline solution and elaborate means of barring visual, auditory, and tactile input. What I have in mind might more accurately, though less dramatically, be termed "conditions of visual deficiency." These conditions may be classified as follows:

1. *Visual deprivation* (absence of photic stimulation), e.g., darkness, dimness, blindness, closed eyes, etc. Hypnagogic and dream imagery are common products of this condition; hallucinations may sometimes also occur. (See Lewin, Vernon, and West.)
2. *Homogeneous visual fields* (photic stimulation but absence of features), e.g., fog, blue sky, etc. Ganzfeld phenomena characterize this condition. (See Avant.)
3. *Randomized visual fields* (photic stimulation and the presence of features, but the absence of good gestalts), e.g., wilderness settings, the surface of the sea, cloud formations, a starlit sky, a snow covered landscape, etc. This is a less extreme ganzfeld condition, one of uniform or unstable figuration, rather than one of homogeneous ground.

These conditions, circumstances, and places seem to promote the poiesis of literary images. They are also situations in which susceptible people, poets or not, have always tended to "have visions," quasi-perceptual experiences in which the functions of the mind's eye seem to enforce themselves upon the body's eye. The visionary event, related as it is to eidetic and hallucinatory imaging, is our most vivid type of spontaneous mental imagery. It is also, I would submit, the paradigm of poetic imagery.

Visionary Imaging

Our central nervous system evolved to help us survive in a world of lurking predators and swift-footed prey, both camouflaged in dense foliage, a habitat in which fine distinctions and split-second decisions can mean either life or death. Total, even partial, visual deficiency is a condition we try to avoid in our waking experience. During this time we are usually actively engaged in steering our course through a three-dimensional environment so rich with heterogeneous visual detail that our visual system is constantly busy responding to stimuli and locating distinct "things," that is, figures, within a peripheral ground of other things.

Thus figure/ground differentiation, characteristic of all human sense modalities, but most acute in vision, is fundamental to survival and is so essential to waking consciousness that when a differentiated sensory field is not available, the central nervous system becomes disoriented. This became defined as a problem for airplane pilots in the 1930s. When confronted by a figureless homogeneous ground, for example, cloud cover over the ocean or dense fog, the aeronauts' visual cortex, in its relentless demand for activity, would in time stimulate itself, thereby generating images and projecting them upon that field. Of course, though explanations vary, all peoples at all times have recognized this phenomenon. Most have noted that illness and fasting seem to facilitate these images. In a time of crisis or stress these may take fearful or comforting or merely enigmatic forms. These images, which "look like" identifiable objects, landscapes, and human shapes, may seem thematically interrelated, for our need to impose coherence on such spontaneous images is apparently as innate as our need to produce them. But, since they lack a spatially definite ground, the distance and size of these projections cannot be adequately assessed: they float, hover, and appear to loom.

Sometimes an actual stimulus-object within or close to the eye may trigger an "uncanny" visual experience. (Horatio, the skeptic, applies this diagnosis to King Hamlet's ghost, when he calls it a "mote . . . to trouble the mind's eye.") In extreme cases, entoptic phenomena, for example, phosphenes, *muscae volitantes*, and incipient eye disorders, have provided the matrices for some rather frightening hallucinations (see Horowitz). Coleridge, writing in November, 1803, gives us an interesting example of how in a state of visual deficiency a minimal stimulus once engendered a "vision":

A pretty optical fact occurred this morning. As I was just returning from Fletcher's, up the back lane and just in sight of the river, I saw, floating high in the air, somewhere over Banks's, a noble kite. I continued gazing at it for some time, when, turning round, I saw at an equidistance, on my right, that is, over the middle of our field, a pair of kites floating about. I looked at them for some seconds, when it occurred to me that I had never before seen two kites together, and instantly the vision disappeared. It was neither more nor less than two pair of leaves, each pair on a separate stalk, on a young fruit tree that grew on the other side of the wall, not two yards from my eye. The leaves being alternate, did, when I looked at them as leaves, strikingly resemble wings, and they were the only leaves on the tree. The magnitude was given by the imagined distance, that distance by the former adjustment of the eye, which *remained* in consequence of the deep impression, the length of time I had been looking at the kite, the pleasure, etc., and [the fact that] a new object [had] impressed itself on the eye. (entry no. 1668)

The "optical fact" was that his eyes, having rotated outward to focus upon objects at the greatest distance from them, could not see the twigs to which the leaves adhered. Moreover, the sky provided no usable depth clues. Unable to gauge these objects' distance from him, he could not assess their size and so the paired leaves became assimilated to the mental image of birds in hovering flight. (Cf. the "shape . . . of restlessness" of the flowers similarly unfocused in Williams's "Flowers by the Sea," page 112.)

The other factor he mentions is the "deep impression" made upon him when, earlier, he had observed the actual bird. Like me when I "saw" my two deer, Coleridge "saw" two subsequent birds partly because they were already in his preconscious thoughts: he *wished* to see them. The "occurred" to him as spontaneous thoughts that embody themselves in any likely visual object that happens to be available. "Such tricks hath strong imagination" and as Shakespeare's Theseus describes in *A Midsummer-Night's Dream* V.1.18 the relation between the actual stimulus-object and the subjective image is that of a spontaneous visual metaphor. The tenor is the given, in Coleridge's case the two pairs of leaves, and the vehicle is the schema, the birds, that spontaneously emerges from his conventional store.[2] If, as I propose, we locate the origins of tropes in the functioning of ordinary consciousness, we can place the origin of verbal metaphor in what I have called spontaneous visual metaphor, that is, misconstruction. From a purely factual point of view it was as much an error for Coleridge to identify these paired leaves with two kites in flight as it was for Pound to identify faces glimpsed in the Paris metro as petals on a wet, black bough. Both are misconstructions of perception, but misconstructions in the service of introspective gnosis.

Of the visual conditions that facilitate visionary introspection, the sky with its ambiguous depth warrants serious consideration. We have perhaps too readily accepted the notion that supernatural beings are associated with the sky and with celestial phenomena simply because the earth is the place of mortality and mutability, the brutish, blood-begrimed arena of "Nature." There may be some truth to this, but our consideration of the poetic imagination and its fondness for homogeneous visual fields suggests that objects viewed upon a ground of sky—sun, moon,[3] stars, planets, comets, clouds, birds, and so on—exert a special power over us because they resemble the visionary images we, or the more eidetically skilled of us, are capable of projecting from the unconscious upon that screen of boundless depth. When, in apocalyptic parlance, "the heavens are opened," it is perhaps inner, not outer, space that begins to reveal its secrets.

The empty sky apparently held a fascination for W. B. Yeats. After having completed his poem "The Dolls" and perhaps still under its spell, he says:

I looked up one day into the blue of the sky, and suddenly imagined, as if lost in the blue of the sky, stiff figures in procession. I remembered that they were the habitual image suggested by blue sky, and looking for a second fable called them "The Magi". . . . (449)

THE MAGI

Now as at all times I can see in the mind's eye,
In their stiff, painted clothes, the pale unsatisfied ones
Appear and disappear in the blue depth of the sky
With all their ancient faces like rain-beaten stones,
And their helms of silver hovering side by side,
And all their eyes still fixed, hoping to find once more,
Being by Calvary's turbulence unsatisfied,
The uncontrollable mystery on the bestial floor.

How far away do we imagine these Magi to be? Twenty feet, a hundred feet? If they are as far away as the sky (and how far away is that anyway?), they must be projections of monstrous proportion. Or are they tiny, eyelash-high puppets? We cannot decide, and this, I suggest, accounts for their *unearthly* character.

The earthly and the unearthly—these categories of phenomena are visually discriminated. The place upon which an object rests is its minimal relation to a visual ground. Ultimately every earthly thing, being subject to gravity, comes to rest on the surface of our planet and thus becomes very literally "grounded." By a rough and ready trigonometry we can judge the size and distance of any given object, once we can see its point of basal tangency. Even uncontrollable mysteries, once they are grounded, become genuine earthly incarnations. But the images that emerge during the play of the poetic imagination are uncontrollable mysteries of quite another order. Yeats's "bestial floor," like his Magi—even like Williams's wheelbarrow and white chickens—is an image that *as an image* floats in a void, featureless except for this lone presence. Poetic images that do not hover, that represent themselves as concrete objects perceived or recollected, are only pretending to be such. All poetic images are possessed of the power to fly and do so because, like visionary spirits, they are groundless. The highest art, as the old saying has it, is the art that conceals art. This usually means that the highest art is the art of concealing the painfully self-conscious process of poiesis. Now, before ending this chapter I wish to rework this motto slightly and adapt it to our terms of discourse.

In *The Critique of Pure Reason* (A140–143) Kant asserted that our knowledge of the world could not possibly be stored in the form of particular, concrete images. How could we know what a triangle or a dog was, if what we had to depend on was a variety of tokens of these types? Some image-like entity must exist in thought that, in such cases at least, can never be encountered in experience. He called this generalized entity the *schema*.

This schematism of our understanding in respect to appearances and mere forms is a concealed art [*eine verborgene Kunst*] in the depths of the human soul whose real mode of operations we are not likely to persuade nature to reveal to our gaze. This much only can we say: the *image* [*das Bild*] is a product of the empirical faculty of reproductive imagination; the *schema* of sensible concepts, such as figures in space, is a product and, as it were, a monogram, of pure *a priori* imagination, through which and in accordance with which images initially become possible. (190)

However we choose to account for this schematism, as a transcendental monogram of experience, a simplification of Hobbes's "decayed sense," or a higher order of cognitive computation, the "concealed art" by which it operates must be a profound concern for the student of poetic imaging. Poets, as specialists in the productive imagination, must work with these schemata through the mediation of conventional signs, and yet disguise these schemata as more or less concrete images. If, then, we regard the *concealed* art as the receptivity of the poet (and the reader, too) to the promptings of the preconscious schemata and of the public myths we share with our community, the *concealing* art becomes the ability to invest this conventional material with the appearance of privately lived experience. This "highest art," this "art of concealing art" is then the poetic play that incarnates conventional materials in experiential contexts, or, to use Kant's terms, schemata in images.

Overtly visionary texts, like "The Magi," are useful to us because they capture the schema in the act, as it were, of metamorphosing into the image and thus serve to reveal something of what is concealed beneath the concealing art. With such texts in mind, I will comment generally on the relation between these two "arts"—the art of introspective poiesis by which schemata manifest themselves and the art by which they are projected as images into other cognitive modes.

1. *Percept-like display.* Visions, that is, vivid spontaneous imagery, simulate actual perception; visionary texts imitate this simulation. Texts may do so by using the present tense and asking us to simulate here-and-now events or they may purport to recount these extraordinary happenings after the fact (see "Experiential format" below). In other words, the poet must choose between a reliving and a retelling of this experientially stored happening. Texts may rivet our attention to these visionary displays as though they were purely outer-world percepts, as surrealist texts often do, or gloss the apparitional percepts with interpretive metaphor and allusion, as Yeats does when he identifies the figures in terms of Christian iconography and myth. In any case, they ask us as vicarious visionaries to simulate the active participation of the eyes in contemplating a percept-like event.

2. *Experiential format.* Whether or not the text represents the vision as unfolding in the present or recollected from the past, vivid introspective episodes, when written down, inevitably bear the marks of retrospected experience, for example, gaps and selective recall. Temporal distance from the events also necessitates some degree of confabulation, that is, recourse to general information stored in conventional memory. Yeats's "Now as at all times" indicates that this vision is not only here-and-now but has also been stored many times over in experiential memory. He seems to have identified these images in the past and recognizes them "now" as old, familiar haunters of the World Soul. If he had chosen to relive (perceptually) or retell (retrospectively) the first appearance of these "pale unsatisfied ones," his text would have displayed the strongly narrative structure of a personal episode. (Timeless as these visitations may seem, they become events within the sequence of time, as Eliot points out in "Burnt Norton," 80–90.)

3. *Conventional provenance.* Since neither visionary nor textually cued images derive from specific experiences but are evoked directly from

the conventional store, they are essentially schemata—tokens of types. They may be elaborated in detail; that is, common nouns may be infinitely modified without losing their underlying generality. Lacking the particularities of concrete experience, schemata often present themselves with pale, stiff expressions and in conventional clothing, as for example the masks of ritual performance and classical drama and the icons of traditional religious art. Yeats himself referred to the underlying impersonality not only of this vision, but of *all thought:* "The fable for this poem came into my head while I was giving some lectures in Dublin. I had noticed once again how all thought among us is frozen into 'something other than human life'" (449). Clearly the poet implies that, uncanny as it is, culturally determined as it also is, this vision nevertheless truthfully reflects somehow the fundamental character of human thought, as distinct from sensory experience. It is as though the conventions we encorporate were a classical underworld, inhabited by shades that have drunk of Lethe and have forgotten their experiential pasts. It is as though we, the living, our consciousness stirred by perception and clinging to the selfhood that stored experience seems to substantiate, are tasked to resurrect these wraiths with the spell-like play of words.

Yeats's vision of the Magi strikingly illustrates two other aspects of verbally cued imagery: two-dimensionality and successive order. If the three paragraphs above deal with the game rules that govern the play of visionary imaging and of verbal poiesis generally, then the two paragraphs that follow deal with what may be considered the "ground rules" that apply to the imaginal medium itself within which the mind's eye executes its performances.

4. *Two-dimensionality.* Part of the condition I have referred to as "imaginal deficiency" is the flattening of mental images. The lack of an operative peripheral field in verbally cued imaging I have already discussed, but here I should say a word about the lack of binocular stereopsis. The term "mind's eye" is appropriately singular: this "eye" simulates the movements of the body's eyes, but its success is only partial because it is "monocular." If I cup a hand over one eye, my environment suddenly shrinks in depth. Of course, I happen to know that these trees are not espaliered to my window and I have only to move my head an inch to detect through motion parallax the true relative distance of things. Yet, if I was not already personally familiar with my environment, if I viewed it from a fixed position-point, and if I had the use of only one eye, what I saw would assume the flatness of a picture.[4] "Ut pictura poesis," a much abused phrase, can be somewhat rehabilitated if we note that verbally cued images are indeed viewed on a quasi-pictorial plane and that, despite the sometimes successful ef-

forts of writer and reader to animate them and project them into the third dimension, these images are, like Yeats's Magi, essentially "stiff" and "painted"—resembling the icons of Byzantine art that Yeats in another poem invoked as "sages standing in God's holy fire / As in the gold mosaic of a wall." This two-dimensionality is related to the hovering and looming effects of schemata as they metamorphose into images (cf. his "Among School Children": "Her present image floats into my mind,"—l. 25, and his "Byzantium": "Before me floats an image, man or shade, / Shade more than man, more image than a shade, ll. 9–10).

5. *Successive order.* Another matrical ground rule that Yeats's apparition typifies is processional form. The Magi appear "with all their helms of silver hovering side by side." (Cf. Pound's "The Return" in which the apparitions "return, one, and by one.") This disjunct adjacency further prevents the imager from assigning relative depth to these figures, for, if one figure were permitted to overlap another, the partially occluded Magus could serve as the ground for his companion and thus suggest that the imager place this trio in the ordinary world of visuospatial perception and experiential memory. The procedural rules of visionary experience, which are the rules of poetic imagination generally, preclude such simultaneous displays. The semantic memory wielding its ready-made instrument, language, knows to proceed in only one way: consecutively, one word after another, each bordered by the silence of phonemic difference—one apparition after the other, each situated in the void of what has not been said.

Recalling the Dead

As I suggested earlier, even when we project an image into the past or into the future we do so in the introspective present. The schemata that comprise the visual contents of what we know as the past and the future are not so much absent as filed away in a storeroom that is forever present to us. In the tenth book of his *Confessions,* Augustine furnishes us with an introspection of the act of introspection:

I will go beyond that particular power of my nature [perception]; mounting step by step toward Him Who made me, I now come into the fields and vast palaces of memory in which are found the storerooms of the innumerable images that have been conveyed there from all sorts of sensory experiences. Therein lies stored whatever we think about, no matter how we may have amplified, diminished, or altered it from what our senses had initially experienced. There these images are, plus whatever else has been consigned and reserved that forgetfulness has not yet engulfed and buried [*sepelivit*].

When I enter there and call for whatever I wish to be brought forth, some items instantly come forth, while others need to be searched for longer and fetched, as it were, from their more secret refuges. Some charge out in hordes and, while some quite different item is the target of my search, they lunge forward as though to say "Are we perhaps the ones?" These I drive off with the hand of my heart from the face of my remembrance [*manu cordis a facie recordationis*] until what I wish should emerge out of the mist [*enubiletur*] and come into view from its hidden recesses.

Other items readily organize themselves on demand in an unflurried series, those ahead yielding to those behind and, so doing, departing from sight, though nonetheless ready to return whenever I wish. This same process occurs whenever I recite a text from memory. (10.12)

A few pages later he reflects on the implications of this power of memorial introspection:

I enact these things within myself, in the huge fore-court [*aula*] of my memory. In here, sky, earth, and sea are present to me together with all that I have managed to sense in these environments, all but what I have forgotten.... When I speak to myself, the images of everything I speak of are present to me out of the storehouse of memory: I would simply have nothing to speak about, were these images absent. (10.14)

Great is the power of memory, something awesome, my God, a deep and boundless manifoldness [*multiplicitas*]. This is what mind is and what I myself am. My God, what am I then? What is my nature?—life variable, multimodal [*multimoda*] and absolutely immeasurable. (10.26)

These descriptions of Augustine's visit to the "huge forecourt of memory" become all the more interesting when juxtaposed with the following passages from the eleventh book of the Odyssey, the so-called Nekuia, the ritual of consulting the dead (ll. 34–43, 48–52, 82–98).

And when I had besought the tribes of the dead with prayers and vows, then I took the sheep and cut their throats into the pit. And the black-clouded blood poured out. And out of Erebos the souls gathered of the corpses of those who had died, brides and bachelors and old men who had suffered much, and tender maidens whose hearts were fresh in sorrow, and many who had been wounded by bronze-tipped spears, men slain in battle wearing gore-spattered armor, many of whom hovered round the pit on every side with a tremendous shout.... I myself drew my sharp sword from beside my thigh and stayed put, and did not let the feeble heads of the dead go near the blood till I could learn from Tiresias. First came Elpenor, for he had not yet been buried beneath the wide-traveled earth.... We sat, and on the one side I held my sword over the blood. On the other side the phantom [*eidōlon*] of my companion told me much. Then came the soul [*psuchē*] of my mother who had died, Anticleia, daughter of the great-hearted Autolycos, whom I had left alive when I went to sacred Ilion. I wept when I saw her and pitied her in my spirit [*thumō*], but though I grieved heavily, I did not let her get near the blood first till I could learn from Tiresias. Then the soul of Theban Tiresias came up, holding a gold scepter; he knew me and spoke to me: "Zeus-born son of Laertes, Odysseus of many devices, why, hapless man, have you left the light of the sun and come here to see the dead and a joyless place? But draw back from the pit and hold back your sharp sword so I may drink the blood and speak to you unerringly." So he said. I drew back and thrust the silver-studded sword into the sheath.[5]

This hero of oral epic and this other hero of literate philosophy are both questers who seek to understand their pathway to the future by interrogating their past. For one hero, to recall the past means to call back the dead; for the other, to recall is to call to mind traces of sensory experience. Odysseus journeys to the cloud-shrouded shores of Kimmeria, performs a blood-sacrifice, and invokes the shadowy visual likenesses (*eidōla*) who persist in a kind of half-life in the "house of Hades," to rise before him. Augustine goes to a place within himself, to the forecourt of a vast *thesaurus,* and summons forth his stored memories, his *imagines* that retain a semblance of their previous sensible form. But for both men, the act of recalling has a three-part structure: an invocation, an indiscriminate response, and a selection. As imaginal contents of the stored past, the wraiths both of the mansions of memory and of Hades evince a will of their own and stream unbidden into consciousness, where they threaten to overwhelm the quester if he fails to master their impetuous desire for resurrection. If he would learn from them what is needful, he must first learn how to lay, as well as to raise, these ghosts and to compel those who would hover and lunge toward this center of consciousness to form a line, a processional order. Odysseus cannot attend to more than one image at a time because those to whom he gives the blood become *verbal* images, what we might term auditory as well as visual hallucinations, and thereby bind themselves to the linearity of speech. Yet even the mute women sent by Persephone to compose a sort of ballad of dead ladies (ll. 225–329) must be linearized (*promnestinai*, l. 233) and presented in that "unflurried series" (*imperturbata series*) that Augustine associates with the rehearsal of memorized texts. As creatures now of verbal visuality, these heroines must have their stories separately, that is, serially, told.[6]

Homer's narrativized psychology poignantly reminds us that our stored past is peopled by our dead and by all the irrecoverable experiences that are destined over time to simplification and diminishment. We and they, the living as well as the dead, are obliged to sip from the waters of Lethe. Poetry, which like the other arts began as a means of opposing this encroaching darkness, a means of remembering, honoring, and evoking the powers of the beloved dead, still is a means of preserving a link, albeit attenuated, between the living and the dead, between consciousness and oblivion. If the link is maintained long enough between a particular life and those who memorialize it, especially in a process of oral transmission, its details become worn away and reshaped to conform to traditional paradigms; it eventually becomes assimilated into a heroic archetype.

Verbal poiesis causes and also preserves the traces of this memorial metamorphosis. When Achilles died, "all nine Muses in alternate verses sang [his] dirge with lovely voices" (*Odyssey* 24.60–61). The source of this information is not Odysseus or Homer-as-narrator but rather the *eidōlon* of Agamemnon in the act of consoling the *eidōlon* of Achilles. That is to say, one self-existent mental image converses with another self-existent mental image within the collective experiential memory of a community that has preserved the text that now allows us as readers to visualize these two dead men reflecting upon their own poietic afterlife. The process is circular, as is experience and recall, as is seeing with the body's eye and reseeing with the mind's eye. It is also a self-reflexive moment when characters within the text comment on their own textualization. (Similarly, Augustine's account of accessing memory comments on the process by which the entire *Confessions* came to be.) "You would not have seen any of the Argives who did not weep, so moving was the Muses' song" (24.61–62). The Daughters of Memory did their work well, so says the one image to reassure the other image: "The gods loved you dearly. Though dead, you have not lost your name; among all men you will have renown, Achilles" (ll. 92–94). The man whose name began the first epic appears for the last time in the last book of the second epic as a mere name and in the grammatical case of the addressee, the vocative—"*Achilleu.*"

Homer's invocations of the Muse had therefore been prayers to recall the dead through her agency. She was to him, in effect, what the Cumaean Sibyl was to Aeneas and what Vergil and Beatrice were to Dante. She was a divine shamaness, the power that Wallace Stevens invoked as "of the sisterhood of the living dead" ("To the One of Fictive Music"). Countless texts have celebrated this theurgic power; among the more concise statements is Walter Landor's "Past Ruined Ilion Helen Lives":

> Past ruined Ilion Helen lives,
>   Alcestis rises from the shades;
> Verse calls them forth; 'tis verse that gives
>   Immortal youth to mortal maids.
>
> Soon shall Oblivion's deepening veil
>   Hide all the peopled hills you see,
> The gay, the proud, while lovers hail
>   In distant ages you and me.
>
> The tear for fading beauty check,
>   For passing glory cease to sigh;
> One form shall rise above the wreck,
>   One name, Ianthe, shall not die.

Ilion, Helen, and Alcestis: these we have stored in the cultural code, a reservoir that may be termed a collective experiential memory. These are the schemata that verbal visuality preserves and by this memorializing act Landor has placed this name-constituted person, Ianthe, among these figures. Like "The Magi" and countless other visionary texts, this poem demonstrates how conventional contents behave within experiential formats and how poetic play induces what are essentially mere words to perform actions, mere types to come to life, albeit stiffly like archaic *korai*.

If memory storage is a kind of burial within the individual mind and within the collective mind of an entire people, it follows that retrieval must become a kind of resurrection, a process that, when introspected as an event, assumes the aspect of a visionary episode. In this light, poetics becomes a study of how poets and readers overhear the dead softly talking among themselves, reseeing their lives and resaying their names. When introspection, as a conjuring of absence into presence, is thematized in literature as visionary texts, it creates an allegory of the imaginative act itself. Yet even when a text presents no overt visionary theme, we as readers find ourselves stepping forth like Odysseus into that strange, though strangely familiar, inner landscape of images, that Kimmerian no man's land where the living and the dead perpetually come to meet.

Notes

Chapter 1: Verbal Visuality

1. Dramas written for the radio form a unique mimetic genre in which narrative bridges, voice-overs, and sound effects can prompt a high degree of mental imaging simply because perceptual visuality is eliminated. This is also the case with radio broadcasts of sports events.
2. Aristotle himself referred to the reciter's art as *diēgēmatikē mimēsis*, i.e., the imitation proper to narration (*Poetics* 1459b33, 37).
3. Roman Jakobson said of the epic genre that its dominant factor is its referential context (Sebeok, ed., 357). One practical reason why traditional epics tend to maintain a uniformity of diction despite the differences of speakers may stem from the diegetic situation: a reciter could not hold his audience's attention fixed upon the referents of his speakers' words if he insisted on portraying these speakers in too much dialectical particularity. We have only to compare the stylistic differentiation of Shakespeare's speakers with those of Milton's in *Paradise Lost*.
4. We need not accept the Whorf-Sapir hypothesis in its extreme form: lexicon and grammar of a community can be stretched to encompass altered world views. This is the task of poets.
5. See *De Doctrina Christiana*, II.1–26

Chapter 2: Science on the Nature of Imagination

1. This point had also troubled the most celebrated of English associationists, David Hartley (1705–57), who in 1749 presented a systematic study of human nature, *Observations on Man*, based entirely on the supposed laws of association. For him the most general, and therefore generative, principles were temporal succession and spatial simultaneity. His studies as a physician inspired in him a concern for what later psychologists would call "information processing" and he was quick to note the distinction between the sequential and the parallel processing of information. His willingness to apply these distinctions to the storage and representation of information anticipated twentieth-century approaches to the study both of behavior and cognition.
2. Cf. Fichte: "Die schaffende Einbildungskraft bildet nur insofern, in wiefern im Ich Gefühl vorhanden ist" (*Sämmtliche Werke* [1846] II [3] 298–299). Robert Bly, though not explicitly replying to the Coleridge quote, observes that

"powerful feeling makes the mind associate faster, and evidently the presence of swift association makes the emotions still more alive" (28). As will become apparent, I also regard association and affect as functionally related.

3. Lindauer's position is not wholly clear to me. In 1983, nine years after the statement printed above, he judged that "the empirical literature on imagery in general has little to say about the arts" because it has "lost its ecological validity" (in Sheikh, ed., 469, 471), but the next year in Natoli's *Psychological Perspectives on Literature* (251) in an article recommending an "empirical approach" he declared that "the psychological meaning of literary material is neither obvious nor easily accessible. *Literature is not data* [my emphasis]; it is fiction, written in the past, and for reasons unrelated to research." By literary empiricism he now seems to mean content analysis, an alternative that is—to my mind—of dubious merit.

4. For a critique of psychoanalytic criticism from a reader-response perspective see Iser, *Act of Reading* 38–45.

5. Jonathan Culler, "Prolegomena to a Theory of Reading," reprinted in Suleiman and Crosman, eds., 55.

Chapter 3: The Poetics of Play: Reopening Jakobson's "Closing Statement"

1. Jakobson himself had only two years earlier related metaphor and metonymy to brain function and dysfunction (Jakobson and Halle 76–83).

2. See Gregory Bateson, "A Theory of Play and Fantasy" 177–193. Among his numerous valuable insights into play behavior Bateson characterizes play as a "special combination of [Freud's] primary and secondary processes." In primary process the representation (or "map") is confounded with the reality (or "territory"), the signifier with the signified. "In secondary process, they can be discriminated. In play, they are both equated and discriminated" (185). The double set toward the poetic message, which I have been discussing, would therefore be as follows: the hermeneutical set would be the secondary process; the poetic set would be play. Primary process, in its pure state, would not enter into the reader's experience unless the text triggered a hallucination of its referents.

3. Exceptions to this would include dialogic impasses such as that between Prufrock and his interlocutrix, between Lewis Carroll's White Knight and the old man, and between countless characters in the works of Beckett and Ionesco, but in these cases one is actually faced with a collision of incompatible contexts.

4. Cf. Walter Pater, *Appreciations* 18: "For to the grave reader words too are grave; and the ornamental word, the figure, the accessory form or colour or reference, is rarely content to die to thought precisely at the right moment, but will inevitably linger awhile, stirring a long 'brainwave' behind it of perhaps quite alien associations." This "brainwave" is apparently an uncontrollable "train" of associations.

5. For an excellent study of subvocal speech in dialogue, reading, and thought see Aleksandr Sokolov's *Inner Speech and Thought*.

Chapter 4: Tactics and Timing

1. The Italian text also presents this as a single sentence.
2. See, for example, Toynbee, trans., xx–xxi.

3. Augustine understood that the act of reading (or reciting or singing) a known text was an analogue to God's reading of his own scripted *fatum*. In *De Musica* VI.29 he alludes to the old notion of the cosmic *renovatio*, the moment when the planets all line up together to commence a new cosmic age. "So earthly things, subject to celestial, join their own temporal circuits in numbered succession with, as it were, the song of the universe" (*Ita coelestibus terrena subjecta orbes temporum suorum numerosa successione quasi carmini universitatis*). He goes on to say that many of these earthly affairs seem disordered and troubled "because we have been stitched (*assuti*) into their order according to our merits, not knowing what beauty Divine Providence produces from us" (VI.30). Every *carmen*, he implies, is like a *universitas*, a totality that continually turns round to a fresh beginning but appears as this totality only to the mind that knows the text.

4. Keats, or his persona, does not present the Cortez incident as though he had actually witnessed it. It is a piece of historical (mis)information (Balboa, as all the anthology footnoters feel obliged to tell us, was the real viewer), an episode presumed to be common knowledge: some such Spaniard at least did something like this. I will discuss this kind of pseudo-retrospection in Chapter 5.

5. Edward Gibbon enunciated the new affective criteria when he remarked on the poet Claudian's deficiencies: "It would not be easy to produce a passage that deserves the epithet of sublime or pathetic; to select a verse that melts the heart or enlarges the imagination." *Decline and Fall of the Roman Empire*, ch. 30.

6. Cf. Denise Levertov: "there must be a place in the poem for rifts. . . . Great gaps between perception and perception which must be leapt across if they are to be crossed at all.

"The X factor, the magic, is when we come to those rifts and make those leaps. A religious devotion to the truth, to the splendor of the authentic, involves the writer in a process rewarding in itself; but when that devotion brings us to undreamed abysses and we find ourselves sailing slowly over them and landing on the other side—that's ecstasy" (145).

Chapter 5: Simulations of Perception

1. Cf. Derek H. Finder: The eye is a servomechanism with a complex set of feedback loops, some "completed outside the body. For example, a man who wants to pick up an object observes with his eyes the closing gap between his hand and the object: the visual sense measures the 'error' in hand position" (24).

2. For evidence that subjects with paralyzed eye muscles can shift their point of focus by the *intention* to move their eyes, see Gale and Findlay's summary of their findings in Groner et al., eds., 147. If the focal field can be to any appreciable degree directed at a cortical level, even incipient overt eye movements during imaging would seem superfluous.

3. It is interesting to note that at the medical school of the University of Pennsylvania Williams's special interest was neurology. In his *Autobiography* (52) he says he almost specialized in it.

4. This common textbook measure—that the focal field is more or less the size of our thumbnail held at arm's length—may have evolutionary as well as descriptive significance: if eye and hand are as intimately coordinated as they

seem, is it not possible that binocular focal vision developed *pari passu* with the freeing of the front legs to manipulate tools. If so, it is perhaps worth speculating that the size of the focal field and the size of the opposable thumb are roughly the same because the closing of the fist by the thumb at arm's length had to be monitored by the eyes. It is also interesting to note that species that have also evolved binocular vision, for example, raptorial birds and certain higher mammals, also possess limbs specialized for gripping and manipulating objects.

5. For a study of this process see Anne Treisman.

6. "Wie gelangen wir zu der deutlichen Vorstellung eines Dinges im Raume? Erst betrachten wir die Teile desselben einzeln, hierauf die Verbindung dieser Teile und endlich das Ganze. Unsere Sinne verrichten diese verschiedene Operationen mit einer so erstaunlichen Schnelligkeit, dass sie uns nur eine einzige zu sein bedünken" (426).

7. Paivio, with Ian Begg, restated this modality contrast in their *Psychology of Language* (1981):

The image system organizes information in a *synchronous* or spatial manner, so that different components of a complex thing or scene are available at once in memory. . . . In contrast, verbal information is organized *sequentially* into higher-order structures. This is a characteristic of the auditory and motor systems used in hearing and speaking language. Linguistic units unfold sequentially over time, and the assumption is that the cognitive system that deals most directly with speech is similarly specialized for sequential processing. (70–71)

Paivio and Begg omit from their logic the latent period between the first part-perceptions (and part-images) and their final integration, a set of cognitive operations that Roger Shepard in his chronometric experiments had already calibrated to the microsecond. (Paivio seems to have retrenched his position since the mid-seventies when he seemed somewhat more receptive to the temporal aspects of imaging. See, for example, Nicholas, ed., 63.)

8. For a useful study of Williams's debt to the visual arts, see Bram Dijkstra.

9. Some psychologists have reported "incipient motor reactions" in response to reading texts, not simply glottal and laryngeal contractions associated with subvocal speech, but evidence that subjects were enacting the situations they were imaging. See F. J. McGuigan.

10. Of course all binocularly viewed objects are processed by the eyes as double images. When we look at our hand at arm's length and cover first one, then the other eye, we notice that our hand shifts position relative to its background. Using its two eyes, our brain gathers stereoptic information from the double image but at the same time suppresses the appearance of doubleness.

11. But Pound's term "phanopoeia," that is, the making of verbal imagery, continued to be identified by spatialists with a fixed pictorial configuration, the text-as-a-totality (or holon) with an atemporal hypostasis, and the text-as-complex-signifier (or megaword) with fixity of meaning. Note, for example, the following: "The power of phanopoeia—a seen juxtaposition of visual elements, the generation of thought and meaning from that relationship within a spatial form . . . [: this] gives the reader a single, new word" (Welsh 113).

12. See my "Figure, Ground, and Open Field."

13. For other examples of pursuit eye movement in Williams's poetry see "The Yachts" and "The Well Disciplined Bargeman" (*CEP*, 104; *CLP*, 98).

14. Cf. Ted Hughes's "The Wodwo." See also Jacqueline Tyrwhitt's article "The Moving Eye."

15. The recognized authority on the vestibulo-ocular mechanism, Geoffrey Melville Jones, gives some vivid examples: "Imagine . . . the 'engineering' accomplishment of a system which allows one to 'keep one's eye on the ball' when running and weaving at top speed in a football game, or to hold the eye on successive 'stepping stones' during an exhilarating run down a mountain path" (3).

16. For a general study of Emersonian perception and the premises upon which it was based see my *Uses of Observation*. Even more drastically altered states of vision are brief, however. As has been proven by numerous experiments, notably those using prism-equipped goggles, our visual system on the cortical level of processing readily adjusts to even the most radical distortions and delivers us back within a day to our old familiar world. See Kohler.

17. For example: "it is hard to forego the impression that Williams's observations are taken from one of that painter's [John Marin's] watercolors rather than from a landscape personally seen" (Dijkstra 184).

18. Cf. Merleau-Ponty, 230–231.

Chapter 6: Transformations of Memory

1. "Episodic memory receives and stores information about temporally dated episodes and events, and temporal-spatial relations among these events. [Such information] is stored solely in terms of its perceptible properties or attributes . . . [and] in terms of its autobiographical reference to already existing contents of the episodic memory store" ("Episodic and Semantic Memory" 385–386). This, Tulving maintains, is a memory system, not merely a kind of content. It operates differently from the *semantic* memory (a term that psychologists had come to apply loosely to all forms of propositional memory.) When new bits of information are entered into this semantic memory system, they "are always referred to an existing cognitive structure, that is, they always have some cognitive reference, and the information they contain is information about the referent they signify rather than information about the input signal as such" (389).

2. See Tulving in his *Elements of Episodic Memory* 56, where he quotes A. D. Yarmey: "The hearsay rule says that the witness must testify only about matters that he has seen, heard, touched, tasted, or smelled. If a witness reports secondhand knowledge of what he has heard others say, his testimony is considered hearsay evidence" (*The Psychology of Eyewitness Testimony* [New York: The Free Press, 1979], 23)

3. The social psychologist Theodore Sarbin has observed a correlation between visual imaging skills and ability to "play roles." What we might call "vivid imagination" Sarbin calls "*hypothetical instantiation* (synonyms: suppositional instantiation, imitated perception, quasiperception, pretend instantiation, *as if* or metaphorical instantiation . . . *as if* behavior)" (340). Of further relevance to literary imaging is his finding that "ambiguity of setting . . . facilitates *as if* behavior . . ." (352). The less information the role-playing imager actually

possesses about the situation, the more actively involved he or she becomes in assuming the appropriate fictive self. It may well be that one of the functions of stylistic deviation, allusion, contextual gaps, even outright obscurity, is to encourage the self-shaping activity of imitative play.

4. Readers of literature will perhaps have less difficulty construing the meanings of that formula: they regularly confront deviations from the doxical norm. Cf. Melville's description of Ahab, "pausing vehemently."

Chapter 7: Introspection and the Visionary Imagination

1. As this illustration makes clear, a mutual reminiscence is really several different episodic accounts of what is agreed to be a single event. It is not an example of collective experiential memory, which is a single account of a single event conventionally stored and transmitted.

2. "Vehicle" is an especially unfortunate term here: the misconstrued stimulus-object is actually a vehicle that momentarily carries the projected image, which embodies the tenor, the gist of meaning latent in the mind of the beholder. Richards's terms make much more sense when applied to the standard abstract + concrete metaphor. My misconstruction theory can account for that sort of metaphor, too, but of course with no connection to optical misconstruction. Macbeth did not literally look at life and mistake it for a walking shadow.

3. The fact that the sun and the moon each present an apparent disk of approximately the same number of degrees in diameter as the human foveal field suggests a possible connection between visual meditation (on the moon directly, on the sun indirectly). This optical coincidence must certainly have enhanced the human fascination with these two groundless luminaries.

4. That Hope's "glass" ("Grongar Hill," page 144) was also monocular accounted for its delusive character. Monocular viewers would of course still have some cues as to depth, for example, relative size, the contraction of the ciliary muscle in accommodation, occlusion, and atmospheric perspective, but the lack of retinal image disparity means the absence of visual *relief.*

5. All the dead in the Homeric Underworld are *eidōla,* self-existent spectral likenesses, but not all *eidōla* are confined to this dark necropolis. Dreams (*oneiroi*) are *eidōla* that wander the night. Divine beings assume this purely imaginal presence (Herakles, now a divinized hero and installed among the Olympians, is encountered later by Odysseus as an *eidōlon* who still haunts the scene of his earlier trespass. The unburied dead, like Elpenor, are restless *eidōla* that yearn for the status of the legitimate citizens of this nether realm, the *psuchai,* the frail, disembodied life-spirits who must feed on sacrificial blood in order to communicate with the living. Odysseus is driven by *thumos,* the energic soul, as well as animated by the *psuchē,* because he is still alive.

6. I would not go so far as to suggest that Augustine consciously alludes to the Nekuia, but his allegorical figuration presents an interesting correlation. He concludes from his introspection that his life is *multimoda,* a rare expression that one lexicographer, Aegidius Forcellinus (*Totius Latinitatis Lexicon,* 1831), totally innocent of my speculations, glosses as *polytropos,* the epithet that introduces Odysseus in the first line of the epic.

For a superb development of the thesis that "underworld is the mythological style of describing a psychological cosmos" (46) see James Hillman's *The Dream and the Underworld.*

Bibliography

Addison, Joseph. *Essays in Criticism and Literary Theory.* Ed. John Loftis. Northbrook, Ill.: AHM, 1975.
Allen, Donald M., and Warren Tallman, eds. *The Poetics of the New American Poetry.* New York: Grove, 1973.
Ahsen, Akhter. "Image Psychology and the Empirical Method." *Journal of Mental Imagery* 11 (Fall/Winter 1987): 1–38.
Arnheim, Rudolf. "Visual Thinking in Education." In Sheikh and Shaffer, eds., 215–223.
Augustine of Hippo. *Confessionum libri tredecem.* Leipzig: Teubner, 1898.
Avant, Lloyd L. "Vision in the Ganzfeld." *Psychological Bulletin* 64 (1965): 4, 246–258.
Bachelard, Gaston. *On the Poetic Imagination and Reverie: Selections from the Works of Gaston Bachelard.* Trans. and ed. Colette Gaudin. Indianapolis, Ind.: Bobbs-Merrill, 1971.
Baddeley, Alan D., and Vivien J. Lewis. "Inner Active Processes in Reading: The Inner Voice, the Inner Ear, and the Inner Eye." In *Interactive Processes in Reading,* Alan M. Lesgold and Charles A. Perfetti, eds. Hillsdale, N.J.: Erlbaum, 1981.
Bailey, R. W., L. Matejka, and P. Steiner. *The Sign: Semiotics Around the World.* Ann Arbor: Michigan Slavic Publications, 1980.
Bakhtin, Mikhail. "Discourse Typology in Prose." In Matejka and Pomorska, eds., 176–198.
Barfield, Owen. *What Coleridge Thought.* Middletown, Conn.: Wesleyan University Press, 1971.
Barthes, Roland. *The Pleasure of the Text.* Trans. Richard Miller. New York: Hill and Wang, 1978.
Bartlett, F. C. *Remembering.* London: Cambridge University Press, 1932.
Bateson, Gregory. "A Theory of Play and Fantasy." In his *Steps to an Ecology of Mind.* New York: Chandler, 1972.
Berg, Stephen, and Robert Mezey, eds. *Naked Poetry: Recent American Poetry in Open Forms.* New York: Bobbs-Merrill, 1969.
Biederman, I. "Recognition-by-Components: A Theory of Human Image Understanding." *Psychological Review* 94 (1987): 115–147.
Bleich, David. *Subjective Criticism.* Baltimore: Johns Hopkins University Press, 1978.
Bliss, Eugene L., and Lincoln D. Clark. "Visual Hallucinations." In West, ed.
Block, Ned, ed. *Imagery.* Cambridge, Mass.: MIT Press, 1981.

Bibliography

Bloom, Harold. *Wallace Stevens: The Poems of Our Climate.* Ithaca, N.Y.: Cornell University Press, 1971.
Bly, Robert. *Leaping Poetry.* Boston: Beacon Press, 1975.
Boccaccio, Giovanni. *The Decamoron.* Trans. J. M. Rigg. Everyman's Library. New York: Dutton, 1930.
Brazier, M. A. B., ed. *The Central Nervous System and Behavior.* New York: Macy Foundation, 1960.
Brown, Roger. *Words and Things.* Glencoe, Ill.: Free Press, 1958.
Buckler, William, and J. McAvoy. *American College Handbook of English Fundamentals.* New York: American Book, 1960.
Bugelski, B. R. "The Definition of Image." In Segal, ed., 49–68.
Bundy, Murray Wright. *The Theory of Imagination in Classical and Medieval Thought.* N.p.: University of Illinois Press, 1927.
Burke, Kenneth. *Counter-Statement.* 2nd ed. Los Altos, Calif.: Hermes, 1953.
———. "Heaven's First Law." *The Dial* 72 (1922). Reprinted in J. Hillis Miller, ed., 47–49.
———. "William Carlos Williams, 1883–1963." *New York Review of Books* 1, no. 2 (1963). Reprinted in J. Hillis Miller, ed., 53.
Buswell, Guy Thomas. *How People Look at Pictures: A Study of the Psychology of Perception in Art.* Chicago: University of Chicago Press, 1935.
Butcher, S. H. *Aristotle's Theory of Poetry and Fine Art.* 4th ed. London: St. Martins, 1907.
Carpenter, Edmund, and Marshall McLuhan, eds. *Explorations in Communication.* Boston: Beacon Press, 1960.
Carpenter, P. A., and P. Eisenberg. "Mental Rotation and the Frame of Reference in Blind and Sighted Individuals." *Perception and Psychophysics* 23 (1978): 117–124.
Carterette, Edward C., and Morton P. Friedman, eds. *Language and Speech.* Vol. VII of *Handbook of Perception.* New York: Academic Press, 1976.
Chapman, Gerald Wester, ed. *Literary Criticism in England, 1660–1800.* New York: Knopf, 1966.
Chatman, Seymour, Umberto Eco, and Jean-Marie Klinkenberg, eds. *A Semiotic Landscape: Proceedings of the First Congress of the International Association for Semiotic Studies, Milan, June 1974.* The Hague: Mouton, 1979.
Chomsky, Noam. *Current Issues in Linguistic Theory.* The Hague: Mouton, 1966.
Coleridge, Samuel Taylor. *Biographia Literaria,* ed. J. Shawcross. 2 vols. London: Oxford University Press, 1909.
———. *Letters,* ed. E. H. Coleridge. Vol. I. Boston: Houghton-Mifflin, 1895.
———. *The Notebooks of Samuel Taylor Coleridge.* Ed. Kathleen Coburn. Vol. 1. New York: Pantheon, 1957.
Collins, Christopher. *The Uses of Observation: Correspondential Vision in the Writings of Emerson, Thoreau, and Whitman.* The Hague: Mouton, 1971.
———. "Figure, Ground, and Open Field." *New York Quarterly* 10 (Winter 1972): 118–126.
———. "Groundless Figures: Reader Response to Verbal Imagery." *The Critic* 51, no. 1 (Fall 1988): 11–29.
———. *Reading the Written Image: Interpretation, Verbal Play, and the Roots of Iconophobia.* University Park: Pennsylvania State University Press, 1991.
Conrad, Joseph. *Youth, Heart of Darkness, The End of the Tether.* Ed. Robert Kimbrough. Oxford: Oxford University Press: 1984.

Cotton, John W., and Roberta Klatzky, eds. *Semantic Factors in Cognition.* Hillsdale, N.J.: Erlbaum, 1978.
Crews, Frederick C., ed. *Psychoanalysis and Literary Process.* Cambridge, Mass.: Winthrop, 1966.
Culler, Jonathan. *Structuralist Poetics: Structuralism, Linguistics, and the Study of Literature.* Ithaca, N.Y.: Cornell University Press, 1975.
———. *The Pursuit of Signs: Semiotics, Literature, and Deconstruction.* Ithaca, N.Y.: Cornell University Press, 1981.
Davis, Robert Con, ed. *Contemporary Literary Criticism: Modernism Through Poststructuralism.* New York: Longman, 1986.
Dennett, Daniel C. *Brainstorms.* Montgomery, Vt.: Bradford, 1980.
Derrida, Jacques. "White Mythology: Metaphors in the Text of Philosophy." In *Margins of Philosophy,* 207–271. Trans. Alan Bass. Chicago: University of Chicago Press, 1982.
Di Cento, James. *Hermeneutics and the Disclosure of Truth: A Study in the Work of Heidegger, Gadamer, and Ricoeur.* Charlottesville: University Press of Virginia, 1990.
Dijkstra, Bram. *The Hieroglyphics of a New Speech: Cubism, Stieglitz, and the Early Poetry of William Carlos Williams.* Princeton, N.J.: Princeton University Press, 1969.
Downey, June E. *Creative Imagination: Studies in the Psychology of Literature.* New York: Harcourt, Brace, 1929.
Drever, James. *A Dictionary of Psychology.* Revised by Harvey Wallenstein. Baltimore: Penguin, 1964.
Donoghue, Denis. *Ferocious Alphabets.* Boston: Little, Brown, 1982.
Eagleton, Terry. *Literary Theory: An Introduction.* Minneapolis: University of Minnesota Press, 1983.
Eastman, Max. *The Literary Mind.* New York: Scribners, 1932.
Ehrlich, Stephane. "Semantic Memory: A Free-Elements System." In Puff, ed., 195–218.
Ehrmann, Jacques. *Game, Play, Literature.* Boston: Beacon Press, 1968.
Eliot, T. S. *Collected Poems, 1909–1962.* New York: Harcourt, Brace, 1964.
Emerson, Ralph Waldo. *Selections.* Ed. Stephen E. Whicher. Boston: Houghton-Mifflin, 1957.
Empson, William. *The Structure of Complex Words.* New York: New Directions, 1951.
Engell, James. *The Creative Imagination: Enlightenment to Romanticism.* Cambridge, Mass.: Harvard University Press, 1981.
Erdman, David V., ed. *The Poetry and Prose of William Blake.* Garden City, N.Y.: Doubleday, 1965.
Erlich, Victor *Russian Formalism: History—Doctrine.* The Hague: Mouton, 1965.
Eysenck, Michael W. *Human Memory: Theory, Research and Individual Differences.* Oxford: Pergamon Press, 1977.
Farah, M. J. "Is Visual Memory Really Visual? Overlooked Evidence from Neuropsychology." *Psychological Review* 95 (1988): 307–317.
Farmer, E. W., J. V. F. Berman, and Y. L. Fletcher. "Evidence for a Visuo-Spatial Sketch-Pad in Working Memory." *Quarterly Journal of Experimental Psychology* 38A (1986): 675–688.
Fenollosa, Ernest. "The Chinese Written Character as a Medium for Poetry," ed. Ezra Pound. In Allen and Tallman, eds., 13–35.

Finder, Derek H. "Control Mechanisms of the Eye." *Scientific American*, July 1964, pp. 80–92.
Finke, Ronald A. *Principles of Mental Imagery.* Cambridge, Mass.: MIT Press, 1989.
Fish, Stanley E. *Self-Consuming Artifacts: The Experience of Seventeenth-Century Literature.* Berkeley: University of California Press, 1972.
———. *Is There a Text in This Class? The Authority of Interpretive Communities.* Cambridge, Mass.: Harvard University Press, 1980.
Fodor, Jerry A. *The Modularity of Mind: An Essay on Faculty Psychology.* Cambridge, Mass.: MIT Press, 1983.
Freund, Elizabeth. *The Return of the Reader: Reader-Response Criticism.* New York: Methuen, 1987.
Friedrich, Paul. *Language, Context, and the Imagination.* Selected and introduced by Anwar S. Dil. Stanford, Calif.: Stanford University Press, 1979.
Frye, Northrop. *Anatomy of Criticism: Four Essays.* New York: Atheneum, 1970.
Gardiner, John M. *Readings in Human Memory.* London: Methuen, 1976.
Ghiselin, Brewster, ed. *The Creative Process: A Symposium.* New York: Mentor, 1955.
Gibson, James J. *The Perception of the Visual World.* Boston: Houghton-Mifflin, 1950.
———. *The Senses Considered as Perceptual Systems.* Boston: Houghton-Mifflin, 1966.
Gifford, Don. *The Farther Shore: A Natural History of Perception, 1798–1984.* New York: Vintage Books, 1990.
Ginsberg, Allen. *Howl and Other Poems.* San Francisco: City Lights, 1956.
Goffman, Erving. *The Presentation of Self in Everyday Life.* Garden City, N.Y.: Doubleday Anchor, 1959.
———. *Encounters: Two Studies in the Sociology of Interaction.* Indianapolis: Bobbs-Merrill, 1961.
Gordon, Rosemary. "A Very Private World." In Sheehan, ed., 63–80.
Groner, Rudolf, et al., eds. *Eye Movements and Psychological Processes: International Views.* Hillsdale, N.J.: Lawrence Erlbaum, 1983.
Hampson, Peter J., David Marks, and John T. E. Richardson. *Imagery: Current Developments.* London: Routledge, 1990.
Harnad, Stevan. "Metaphor and Mental Duality." In Simon and Scholes, eds., 189–211.
Hartman, Geoffrey. "Literary Criticism and Its Discontents." *Critical Inquiry* 3 (1976): 203–220.
Hartmann, R. R. K., and F. C. Stork. *Dictionary of Language and Linguistics.* New York: Wiley, 1972.
Hebb, D. O. *The Organization of Behavior.* New York: Wiley, 1958.
———. "Concerning Imagery." *Psychological Review* 75 (1968): 466–477. Rpt. in Nicholas, ed., 139–153.
Hillman, James. *The Dream and the Underworld.* New York: Harper and Row, 1979.
Hirsch, E. D., Jr. *Validity in Interpretation.* New Haven, Conn.: Yale University Press, 1967.
Hobbes, Thomas. *Leviathan.* Ed. Michael Oakeshott. Oxford: Blackwell, 1946.
Holland, Norman N. *The Dynamics of Literary Response.* New York: Oxford University Press, 1968.
———. *Poems in Persons: An Introduction to the Psychoanalysis of Literature.* New York: Norton, 1975.

---. *The Brain of Robert Frost: A Cognitive Approach to Literature.* New York: Routledge, 1988.
Holt, Robert. "Imagery: The Return of the Ostracized." *American Psychologist* 19 (1964): 154–164.
Homer. *The Odyssey,* trans. Albert Cook. New York: Norton, 1967.
Horowitz, Mardi J. *Image Formation and Cognition.* 2nd ed. New York: Appleton-Century-Crofts, 1978.
Hughes, Ted. *Wodwo.* London: Faber and Faber, 1967.
Hume, David. *An Enquiry Concerning Human Understanding.* Oxford: Clarendon Press, 1928.
Husserl, Edmund. *Cartesian Meditations: An Introduction to Phenomenology.* Trans. Dorion Cairns. The Hague: Nijhoff, 1960.
---. *Phenomenology of Internal Time-Consciousness.* Bloomington: Indiana University Press, 1964.
Ingarden, Roman. *The Cognition of the Literary Work of Art.* Trans. R. A. Crowley and K. R. Olson. Evanston, Ill.: Northwestern University Press, 1973.
Iser, Wolfgang. *The Implied Reader: Patterns in Communication in Prose Fiction from Bunyan to Beckett.* Baltimore: Johns Hopkins University Press, 1974.
---. *The Act of Reading: A Theory of Aesthetic Response.* Baltimore: Johns Hopkins University Press, 1978.
---. "The Reading Process: A Phenomenological Approach." In Tompkins, ed., 50–69.
Izard, C. E., J. Kagan, and R. B. Zajonc, eds. *Emotions, Cognition, and Behaviour.* London: Cambridge University Press, 1984.
Jakobson, Roman. "Closing Statement: Linguistics and Poetics." In Sebeok, ed., 350–377.
Jakobson, Roman, and Morris Halle. *Fundamentals of Language.* The Hague: Mouton, 1956.
James, William. *Principles of Psychology.* New York: Dover, 1950. Orig. pub. 1890.
Jones, Geoffrey Melville. "The Vestibular System for Eye Movement Control." In Monty and Senders, eds., 3–18.
Jusczyk, Peter W., and Raymond M. Klein. *The Nature of Thought: Essays in Honor of D. O. Hebb.* Hillsdale, N.J.: Lawrence Erlbaum, 1980.
Kant, Immanuel. *Kritik der reinen Vernunft.* Ed. Wilhelm Weischedel. Wiesbaden: Insel, 1956.
Katz, Albert N. "What Does It Mean to be a High Imager?" In Yuille, ed.
Kaufman, Lloyd. *Sight and the Mind: Introduction to Visual Perception.* New York: Oxford University Press, 1974.
Kennedy, Alan, and Alan Wilkes. *Studies in Long Term Memory.* London: Wiley, 1975.
Kintgen, Eugene R. *The Perception of Poetry.* Bloomington: Indiana University Press, 1983.
Klinger, Eric, ed. *Imagery: Concepts, Results, and Applications.* Vol. 2. New York: Plenum, 1981.
Kohler, Iro. *The Formation and Transformation of the Perceptual World,* trans. H. Fiss. New York: International Universities Press, 1964.
Korzybski, A. *Science and Sanity.* New York: Science Press, 1941.
Kosslyn, Stephen. *Image and Mind.* Cambridge, Mass.: Harvard University Press, 1980.
---. *Ghosts in the Mind's Machine: Creating and Using Images in the Brain.* New York: Norton, 1983.

Kosslyn, Stephen, C. B. Cave, D. A. Provost, and S. M. von Gierke. "Sequential Processes in Image Generation." *Cognitive Psychology* 20 (1988): 319–343.
Krieger, Murray. *Theory of Criticism: A Tradition and Its System*. Baltimore: Johns Hopkins University Press, 1976.
Kuhn, Thomas. *The Copernican Revolution*. Cambridge, Mass.: Harvard University Press, 1957.
Lachman, Janet L., and Roy Lachman. "Theories of Memory Organization and Human Evolution." In Puff, ed., 133–193.
Langacker, Ronald W. *Language and Structure*. 2nd ed. New York: Harcourt, Brace, Jovanovich, 1973.
Langer, Susanne K. *Philosophy in a New Key: A Study of the Symbolism of Reason, Rite, and Art*. New York: Mentor, 1948.
———. *Feeling and Form*. New York: Scribners, 1953.
Lawall, Sarah. *Critics of Consciousness: Existential Structures of Literature*. Cambridge, Mass.: Harvard University Press, 1968.
Lee, Philip, and Robert E. Ornstein, eds. *Symposium on Consciousness*. (Presented at the annual meeting of the American Association for the Advancement of Science, Feb. 1974.) New York: Viking, 1976.
Lentricchia, Frank. *After the New Criticism*. Chicago: University of Chicago Press, 1980.
Lessing, G. E. *Laokoon oder Ueber die Grenzen der Malerei und Poesie*. In *Gotthold Ephraim Lessing Werke*. Ed. Uwe Lassen. Hamburg: Hoffmann und Campe, 1963.
Levertov, Denise. "Some Notes on Organic Forms." In Berg and Mezey, eds., 141–145.
Levich, Martin, ed. *Aesthetics and the Philosophy of Criticism*. New York: Random House, 1963.
Lewin, Bertram. *The Image and the Past*. New York: International Universities Press, 1968.
Lindauer, Martin S. *The Psychological Study of Literature: Limitations, Possibilities, and Accomplishments*. Chicago: Nelson Hall, 1974.
———. "Imagery and the Arts." In Sheikh, ed., 468–506.
———. "An Empirical Approach to the Psychology of Literature." In Natoli, ed.
Locke, John. *An Essay Concerning Human Understanding*. London: Dent, 1961.
Logie, R. H. "Visuo-Spatial Processing in Working Memory." *Quarterly Journal of Experimental Psychology* 38A (1986): 229–247.
Longus. *Daphnis and Chloe*. Trans. Christopher Collins. Barre, Mass.: Imprint Society, 1972.
Lucas, F. L. *Literature and Psychology*. London: Cassell, 1951.
Luria, A. R. *The Mind of a Mnemonist*. New York: Basic Books, 1968.
Mac Cormac, Earl R. *A Cognitive Theory of Metaphor*. Cambridge, Mass.: MIT Press, 1985.
Martinez-Bonati, Felix. *Fictive Discourse and the Structures of Literature*. Trans. Philip W. Silver. Ithaca, N.Y.: Cornell University Press, 1981.
Matejka, Ladislav, and Krystyna Pomorska, eds. *Readings in Russian Poetics: Formalist and Structuralist Views*. Ann Arbor: Michigan Slavic Publications, 1978.
Matejka, Ladislav, and Irwin R. Titunik, eds., *Semiotics of Art: Prague School Contributions*. Cambridge, Mass.: MIT Press, 1976.
McDaniel, M. A., and M. Pressley, eds. *Imagery and Related Mnemonic Processes: Theories, Individual Differences, and Application*. New York: Springer, 1987.

McGuigan, F. J. "Imagery and Thinking: Covert Functioning of the Motor System." In Schwartz and Shapiro, eds., 2: 37–100.
Merleau-Ponty, Maurice. *Phenomenology of Perception*. New York: Humanities Press, 1962.
Miller, George A. "Closing Statement." In Sebeok, ed., 386–395.
Miller, George A., and Philip N. Johnson-Laird. *Language and Perception*. Cambridge, Mass.: Belknap Press of Harvard University Press, 1976.
Miller, George A., and Elizabeth Lenneberg, eds. *Psychology and Biology of Language and Thought: Essays in Honor of Eric Lenneberg*. New York: Academic Press, 1978.
Miller, J. Hillis. *Poets of Reality: Six Twentieth-Century Writers*. New York: Atheneum, 1969.
———, ed. *William Carlos Williams: A Collection of Critical Essays*. Englewood Cliffs, N.J.: Prentice-Hall, 1966.
———. "Stevens' Rock and Criticism as Cure, II." In Davis, ed., 416–427.
———. "Heart of Darkness Revisited." In *Heart of Darkness: A Case Study in Contemporary Criticism*. Ed. Ross C. Murfin. New York: St. Martin's Press, 1989.
Mitchell, W. J. T., ed. *The Language of Images*. Chicago: University of Chicago Press, 1980.
———. *Iconology: Image, Text, and Ideology*. Chicago: University of Chicago Press, 1986.
Monty, Richard A., and John W. Senders, eds. *Eye Movements and Psychological Processes*. Hillsdale, N.J.: Lawrence Erlbaum, 1979.
Morris, Peter E., and Peter J. Hampson. *Imagery and Consciousness*. New York: Academic Press, 1983.
Natoli, Joseph, ed. *Psychological Perspectives on Literature: Freudian Dissidents and Non-Freudians*. Hamden, Conn.: Shoe String Press, 1984.
Neisser, Ulric. *Cognitive Psychology*. Englewood Cliffs, N.J.: Prentice-Hall, 1967.
Nelson, Benjamin, ed. *Sigmund Freud: On Creativity and the Unconscious*. New York: Harper and Row, 1958.
Neumann, Erich. *Art and the Creative Unconscious*. Trans. Ralph Manheim. Bollingen Series LXI. New York: Pantheon, 1959.
Nicholas, John M., ed. *Images, Perception, and Knowledge*. (Papers deriving from and related to the Philosophy of Science Workshop held in Ontario, Canada, May 1974.) Boston: Reidel, 1977.
Paivio, Allan. *Imagery and Verbal Processes*. New York: Holt, Rinehart, and Winston, 1971.
———. "Images, Propositions, and Knowledge." In Nicholas, ed., 47–71.
Paivio, Allan, and Ian Begg. *Psychology of Language*. Englewood Cliffs, N.J.: Prentice-Hall, 1981.
Pater, Walter. *Appreciations*. London: Macmillan, 1922.
Peirce, Charles S. *Collected Papers*. Ed. Charles Hartshorne and Paul Weiss. Cambridge, Mass.: Harvard University Press, 1931.
Pick, Herbert L., Jr., and Linda P. Acredolo, eds. *Spatial Orientation: Theory, Research, and Application*. New York: Plenum Press, 1983.
Polanyi, Michael. *Personal Knowledge: Towards a Post-Critical Philosophy*. Chicago: University of Chicago Press, 1962.
Polletta, Gregory T., ed. *Issues in Contemporary Literary Criticism*. Boston: Little, Brown, 1973.
Pope, Keneth S., and Jerome L. Singer, eds. *The Stream of Consciousness: Scien-*

tific Investigations into the Flow of Human Consciousness. New York: Plenum Press, 1978.

Posner, Roland. "Poetic Communication versus Literary Language, or The Linguistic Fallacy in Poetics." In Chatman, Eco, and Klinkenberg, eds., 689–697.

Poulet, Georges. "Criticism and the Experience of Interiority." In Tompkins, ed., 41–49.

Pound, Ezra. *ABC of Reading.* New York: New Directions, 1960.

———. *Personae.* New York: New Directions, 1926.

Puff, C. Richard, ed. *Memory Organization and Structure.* New York: Academic Press, 1979.

Pylyshyn, Zenon W. "What the Mind's Eye Tells the Mind's Brain: A Critique of Mental Imagery." *Psychological Bulletin* 80 (1973): 1–24.

Richards, I. A. *Principles of Literary Criticism.* London: Kegan Paul, 1924. Reprint, New York: Harcourt, Brace, 1959.

Richardson, Alan. *Mental Imagery.* London: Routledge and Kegan Paul, 1969.

———. "Voluntary Control of the Memory Image." In Sheehan, ed., 109–131.

Riffaterre, Michael. *Semiotics of Poetry.* Bloomington: Indiana University Press, 1978.

———. "Describing Poetic Structures: Two Approaches to Baudelaire's 'Les Chats.'" In Tompkins, ed., 26–40.

Rubin, D. C., ed. *Autobiographical Memory.* London: Cambridge University Press, 1986.

Sarbin, Theodore R. "Imagining as Muted Role-Taking: A Historical-Linguistic Analysis." In Sheehan, ed., 333–354.

Sartre, Jean-Paul. *The Psychology of Imagination.* New York: Philosophical Library, 1948.

———. *Being and Nothingness.* Trans. Hazel E. Barnes. New York: Philosophical Library, 1956.

———. *What Is Literature?* Trans. Bernard Frechtman. New York: Washington Square Press, 1966.

Saussure, Ferdinand de. *Cours de linguistique générale.* Paris: Payot, 1916.

Scholes, Robert. *Structuralism in Literature: An Introduction.* New Haven, Conn.: Yale University Press, 1974.

Schwartz, Gary E., and David Shapiro, eds. *Consciousness and Self-Regulation: Advances in Research.* Vol. I. New York: Plenum, 1976. Vol. II, New York: Plenum Press, 1978.

Sebeok, Thomas A., ed. *Style in Language.* (Papers presented at the Conference on Style held at Indiana University, 1958.) New York: Wiley, 1960.

Segal, Sydney J. ed. *Imagery: Current Cognitive Approaches.* New York: Academic Press, 1971.

Sheehan, Peter W. "Visual Imagery and the Organizational Properties of Perceived Stimuli." *British Journal of Psychology* 58 (1967): 247–252.

———, ed. *The Function and Nature of Imagery.* New York: Academic Press, 1972.

Sheikh, Anees A., ed. *Imagery: Current Theory, Research, and Application.* New York: Wiley, 1983.

Sheikh, Anees A., and John T. Shaffer, eds. *The Potential of Fantasy and Imagination.* New York: Brandon House, 1979.

Shepard, Roger, and L. A. Cooper. *Mental Images and Their Transformations.* Cambridge, Mass.: MIT Press, 1982.

Simon, Thomas W., and Robert J. Scholes, eds. *Language, Mind, and Brain.* Hillsdale, N.J.: Lawrence Erlbaum, 1982.
Smirnov, A. A. *Problems of the Psychology of Memory.* Trans. Samuel A. Corson. New York: Plenum Press, 1973.
Smith, Barbara Herrnstein. *Poetic Closure: A Study of How Poems End.* Chicago: University of Chicago Press, 1968.
Sokolov, Aleksandr Nikolaevich. *Inner Speech and Thought.* Trans. Donald B. Lindsley. New York: Plenum Press, 1972.
Solomon, Philip, and Jack Mendelson. "Hallucinations in Sensory Deprivation." In West, ed.
Stafford, William. *Things That Happen Where There Aren't Any People.* Brockport, N.Y.: Boa, 1980.
Stewart, Dugald. *Elements of the Philosophy of the Human Mind,* vol. I. London: n.p., 1792.
Suleiman, Susan R., and Inge Crosman, eds. *The Reader in the Text: Essays on Audience and Interpretation.* Princeton, N.J.: Princeton University Press, 1980.
Talmy, Leonard. "How Language Structures Space." In Pick and Acredolo, eds., 225–282.
Tompkins, Jane P., ed. *Reader-Response Criticism: From Formalism to Post-Structuralism.* Baltimore: Johns Hopkins University Press, 1980.
Toynbee, Arnold, trans. *Greek Historical Thought.* New York: Mentor, 1952.
Treisman, Anne. "Features and Objects in Visual Processing." *Scientific American,* Nov. 1986, 1114B–125.
Tulving, Endel. "Episodic and Semantic Memory." In *The Organization of Memory.* Ed. Endel Tulving and Wayne Donaldson, 381–403. New York: Academic Press, 1972.
———. *Elements of Episodic Memory.* Oxford Psychology Series, no. 2. New York: Oxford University Press, 1983.
Tyler, Stephen A. *The Said and the Unsaid: Mind, Meaning, and Culture.* New York: Academic Press, 1978.
Tyrwhitt, Jacqueline. "The Moving Eye." In Carpenter and McLuhan, eds., 90–95.
Urbantschitsch, Victor. *Ueber Subjektive Optische Anschauungsbilder.* Vienna: Franz Deuticke, 1907.
Vernon, J. *Inside the Black Room: Studies in Sensory Deprivation.* London: Souvenir Press, 1963.
Vygotsky, L. S. *The Psychology of Art.* Trans. Scripta Technica. Cambridge, Mass.: MIT Press, 1971.
———. *Thought and Language.* Ed. and trans. Eugenia Hanfmann and Gertrude Vakar. Cambridge, Mass.: MIT Press, 1978.
Wallas, Graham. *The Art of Thought.* London: Cape, 1926.
Watson, John Broadus. "Psychology as the Behaviorist Sees It." *Psychological Review* 20 (1913): 158–177.
———. *The Ways of Behaviorism.* New York: Harper, 1928.
Weingartner, Herbert, and Elizabeth S. Parker. *Memory Consolidation: Psychobiology of Cognition.* Hillsdale, N.J.: Erlbaum, 1984.
Wellek, René. "Closing Statement." In Sebeok, ed., 408–419.
Wellek, René, and Austin Warren. *A Theory of Literature.* 3rd ed. New York: Harcourt, Brace, and World, 1956.
Welsh, Andrew. *Roots of Lyric: Primitive Poetry and Modern Poetics.* Princeton, N.J.: Princeton University Press, 1978.

West, Louis Jolyon, ed. *Hallucination.* New York: Grune and Stratton, 1962.
Williams, William Carlos. *The Collected Earlier Poems of William Carlos Williams.* New York: New Directions, 1938.
———. *Collected Later Poems of William Carlos Williams.* New York: New Directions, 1950.
Wilner, Eleanor. *Gathering the Winds: Visionary Imagination and Radical Transformation of Self and Society.* Baltimore: Johns Hopkins University Press, 1975.
Wilson, Richard Albert. *The Miraculous Birth of Language.* New York: Philosophical Library, 1948.
Wimsatt, W. K. *The Verbal Icon: Studies in the Meaning of Poetry.* New York: Noonday, 1960.
———. "Battering the Object." In *Day of the Leopards: Essays in Defense of Poems.* New Haven, Conn.: Yale University Press, 1976.
Winnicott, D. W. *Playing and Reality.* London: Tavistock, 1971.
Yeats, W. B. *The Collected Poems of W. B. Yeats.* New York: Macmillan, 1933.
Yuille, John C., ed. *Imagery, Memory, and Cognition: Essays in Honor of Allan Paivio.* Hillsdale, N.J.: Erlbaum, 1983.

Index

Addison, Joseph, 27–28, 31
Addressee (Jakobson), 56–58
Addresser (Jakobson), 55–56
Adjectives, 116
Affect: and cognition, 85–88; and emotive addresser, 55–56; in literary theory and psychology, 30–38. *See also* "Psychologism"
Akenside, Mark (*The Pleasures of Imagination*), 31
Ambiguity, 51–53
Anderson, Sherwood, 70
Aquinas, Thomas, 27
Aristotle, xx, 10, 25, 27, 30, 33, 80–81
Assertion (cognitive mode), 80–82, 86, 135, 137–41. *See also* Gnome; Memory, experiential and conventional
Associationism, 25–31, 47, 64, 85
Auden, W. H., 82
Augustine of Hippo: memory retrieval, 163–66; temporality, 78–79; types of *visio*, 17–18

Babbitt, Irving, 37
Bachelard, Gaston, 150
Bacon, Francis, 26, 30
Bakhtin, Mikhail, 49, 62–63, 139
Barthes, Roland, xvii–xviii, 149–50
Bateson, Gregory, xxiii–xxiv
Baudelaire, Charles-Pierre, 31
Beardsley, Monroe C., 34
Behaviorist psychology, 43–45, 47
Belief, simulated, 155–56
Bible, 17–18, 80
Bion, 12
Blackmur, R. P., 38

Blake, William, 61, 136, 140, 152–53
Bleich, David, xiv
Bloom, Harold, 85, 88
Boccaccio, Giovanni, 69
Brecht, Bertolt, 6
Brooke, Henry, 34–35
Brooks, Cleanth, 41
Brown, Roger, 43–44, 48
Brown, Thomas, 29
Browning, Robert, 134–36, 155
Bruno, Giordano, 23
Bugelski, B. R., 115
Burke, Edmund, 31
Burke, Kenneth, 95–96, 112
Burns, Robert, 145

Campbell, Joseph, 13
Camus, Albert, 72
Carnap, Rudolf, 35
Carroll, Lewis, 120
Chapman, George, 83
Chatman, Seymour, 48
Chomsky, Noam, 141
Cicero, 16
Closure, poetic, 75–76
Code, analogic, 64–66; 144
Cognitive modes, 58–60; shifts of, 64, 79–88. *See also* Assertion; Expectation; Introspection; Judgment; Perception; Retrospection
Cognitive psychology, 41–43, 45–46
Coleridge, Samuel Taylor: associationism and affect, 30–31, 85–86; imagination, theory of, 94, 132–34; visual illusions, 110, 158–59; willing suspension of disbelief, xxiii–xxiv, 156

186 Index

Collins, Jesse Blake, 116
Co-locational order (Talmy), 114–15
Conrad, Joseph, 8–9
Contact, dialogic, 61–64, 86
Context, monologic, 60–61
Convention. *See* Memory, experiential and conventional
Conversant, 63–64, 86
Copernicus, 23
Correspondences, doctrine of, 21
Crews, Frederick, 45–46
Cromwell, Oliver, 23
Crosman, Inge, xix, xx
Crosman, Robert, xix
Culler, Jonathan, 54, 85, 88

Dante, 73
De Man, Paul, 60
Depth perception, 102–5
Derrida, Jacques, xvi, xviii, 19, 99
Descartes, René, 29
Dialogue, internal. *See* Bakhtin; Conversant; Contact, dialogic
Dilthey, Wilhelm, ix
Dominant, 48, 50–51, 60
Donne, John, 23–24
Donoghue, Denis, xviii
Dryden, John, 31
Dyer, John ("Grongar Hill"), 144–45

Eastman, Max, 45
Eliot, T. S., 37, 72, 87, 134, 161
Emerson, Ralph Waldo, 74, 109
Emotion. *See* Affect
Empson, William, 36, 52
Erdman, David, 140
Expectation (cognitive mode), 82, 87, 90
Experience. *See* Memory, experiential and conventional

Factors and functions (Jakobson), 50–66
Feelings. *See* Affect
Fenollosa, Ernest, 117
Figure-ground perception: in imaging, 153–63; in motion parallax, 109–10
Fish, Stanley, xiii, xviii, xx, xxi, 75, 99
Fixation, visual. *See* Nouns; Saccade
Formalism, Russian, 47–50
Fontanier, Pierre, 19
Frank, Joseph, 48

Freud, Sigmund, xxiv, 38–40, 44–45, 66. *See also* Psychoanalysis, as hermeneutic
Frost, Robert, 86, 110, 155
Frye, Northrup, 40

Gadamer, Hans-Georg, ix
Galton, Francis, 36
Gnome: genre, 128–29, 136–37; paradox, 138–41; wit and anomaly, 140–41
Goffman, Erving, 141

Habermas, Jürgen, ix
Hartman, Geoffrey, xvi
Heidegger, Martin, ix
Hermeneutics. *See* Poetics and hermeneutics; Psychoanalysis, as hermeneutic
Hirsch, E. D., xiv
Holland, Norman, xix, 40–43
Holt, Robert, 43, 45
Homer, 9–10, 71, 164–67
Horace, 13, 31, 55
Husserl, Edmund, 74
Hypotaxis: and cognitive modes, 83–84, 102; in grammar, 68–72

Imagination: Coleridge on, 132–34; empiricist theories of, 24, 26–30; Kant on, 133–34; mechanistic models of, 34–36; "pleasures of," 31; psychopathologies of, 32–33; William Carlos Williams on, 94
Imaginal field, 91. *See also* Visual field
Ingarden, Roman, xviii, 49, 73–74, 87, 150
Interference (of verbal and visual processes), 2–4, 73, 156
Interpretation, x–xxi
Introspection (cognitive mode), 81–84, 142–67. *See also* Tropes, metaphor
Iser, Wolfgang: on gaps, xii–xiii, 150; on "response," xviii–xix; on temporality, 73–74; on the two-fold reader, 56–57

Jakobson, Roman: on poetics and linguistics, 48–66; on redundancy, 98–99; on tropology, 143–44
James, Henry, 106
James, William, 73–74, 77
Jauss, Hans Robert, xix
Judgment (cognitive mode), 82, 86, 90

Kant, Immanuel, 33, 133, 160
Kairos: as play, 76–79; as ritual, 95
Keats, John, xv, 54, 61, 83–85
Kosslyn, Stephen, 91, 93, 100
Krieger, Murray, xviii
Kuhn, Thomas, 25, 28

Lacan, Jacques, xiv
Lander, Walter Savage, 166–67
Langer, Susanne, 35, 37, 99
Lawall, Sarah, 45
Lessing, Gotthold Ephraim (*Laokoon*), 72–73, 98, 106
Lévi-Strauss, Claude, 49–54
Levich, Martin, 38
Linguistics and poetics, 46–66
Literacy, its impact on imagination, 9–20, 79–80
Locke, John, 24–25, 32
Longus (*Daphnis and Chloe*), 12–14

Mallarmé, Stéphane, 94
Martinez-Bonati, Felix, 62
Memory, 119–41; episodic and semantic, 123–24; experiential and conventional, 124–32, 135–41, 151–55, 161–62, 167; procedural and propositional, 122–23. *See also* Assertion; Retrospection
Message (Jakobson), 54–55, 65; sets toward, 51–53, 66
Mental rotation, 91–92
Mental walk (Simonides), 92
Metaphor. *See* Tropes
Metonymy. *See* Tropes
Miller, George, 48, 50
Miller, J. Hillis, xvi–xvii, 9, 96
Mood. *See* Affect
More, Paul Elmer, 37
Moschus, 12
Moving images, 106–13
Mukařovský, Jan, 49
Muybridge, Eadweard, 108

Narrative: genre, 128–29; parable, 138; story and myth, 137
Neisser, Ulric, 45, 97
Nerval, Gérard de, 32
New Criticism, xiv, 47–50
Newton, Isaac, 25

Nouns, 114–17, 134–37, 150–56; pluralized, 101, 104–5

Orality, 2–9, 67; contrasted with literacy, 9–20; oral diegesis, 4–9; oral mimesis, 2–4

Paivio, Allan, 92, 99
Parable. *See* Narrative
Paradox. *See* Gnome
Parataxis, 68, 72–76, 102
Part-perception (Hebb), 93
Pastoral, 12–14
Peirce, Charles Sanders, xi, 4, 17
Perception (cognitive mode): compared with introspection, 142–44, 161; in reading writing, 81–82, 148–49; simulated, 86, 90–118, 132, 145–47
Play and play theory: Bateson and Coleridge, on, xxiii–xxv; and cognitive modes, 57–60, 67, 143, 146–49; and hypothesis, 15; and metalanguage, 65–66
Plato, 40, 106, 137
Poe, Edgar Allen, 32
Poetics and hermeneutics, ix–xxi, 43, 52–53, 65–66
Poulet, Georges, xviii, 45, 56
Pound, Ezra, 72, 74, 87, 106, 163
Prepositions, 114–16
Pronouns, 116
Psychoanalysis as hermeneutic, 38–43, 46, 143
"Psychologism," 36–38, 41, 49–50
Pursuit (eye movement), 106–8
Pylyshyn, Zenon, 115

Quintillian, 16

Ransom, John Crowe, 37
Reader-response criticism, xviii–xxi
"Real 'me'" and "alien 'me'" (Iser), 57–60, 67, 81, 87, 89–90, 129, 145
Retrospection (cognitive mode), 80, 82, 83–84, 86, 90–91, 129–35, 145, 149. *See also* Narrative; Memory, experiential and conventional
Rhyme, 65–66
Richards, I. A., xx, 37, 45, 144
Ricoeur, Paul, ix

Riffaterre, Michael: "heuristic and retrospective readings," xiv; on linguistic analysis, 54–56; on phatic contact, 62; "ungrammaticality," 138
Rosenblatt, Louise, xviii
Ryle, Gilbert, 44

Saccade (eye movement): in verbal imaging, 98–105, 111, 114–17; in visual perception, 91, 97–98
Sampson, John, 140
Saporta, Sol, 48
Sartre, Jean-Paul, 45
Saussure, Ferdinand de, 56, 151
Schema, or schematic image: in conventional memory, 81, 96, 114, 125–27, 141, 158; in introspective mode, 148, 158; in visionary poetics, 160–63, 167
Scholes, Robert, 46
Segal, Sydney Joelson, 122
Semiotics, 4–5, 16–18
Shakespeare, William, 3–8, 22–23, 28, 126, 157–58
Shelley, Mary, 31
Shepard, Roger, 91–92, 100
Simile. *See* Tropes: metaphor
Simonides of Ceos, 25, 92, 106
Smith, Barbara Herrnstein, xiii, 75
Spatial information, verbally mediated, 114–18
Stafford, William, 153–55
Stein, Gertrude, 72
Stewart, Dugald, 29
Structuralism, 47–48
Suleiman, Susan, xix, xx
Successive order, 163–65
Synecdoche. *See* Tropes: metonymy

Talmy, Leonard, 114–16
Text, as stored and reused language, xii, xiv–xv, 9, 11, 67–68, 75–76, 89, 98–99

Thoreau, Henry David, 138–39
Time and timing, 67–68, 73–88. *See also* Kairos
Titchener, E. B., 36, 44
Tompkins, Jane, xix–xx
Toscanini, Arturo, 150
Tropes: metaphor, 16–20, 66, 74–75, 83–84, 113, 143–48, 158–59; metonymy, 16, 19–20, 66, 134, 143–45
Tulving, Endel, 123–24
Two-dimensionality, 162–63

Verbs, 116–17
Vergence (eye movement), 103–5, 111
Vergil, 12
Vestibulo-ocular mechanism, 108–9, 112
Visions, 17, 81, 157; simulated, 155
Visual deficiency, conditions of: ganzfeld phenomenon (homogeneous visual fields), 156, 159; visual deprivation, 156
Visual field: focal field (foveal and macular), 96, 155–56; peripheral field, 97–98, 132, 150, 155–56
Vygotsky, L. S., 45, 63

Wagner, Richard, 110
Warren, Austin, xiv, 38, 48, 50
Watson, John Broadus, 43–44
Wellek, René, xiv, 36, 48, 50
Whiter, Walter, 28
Whitman, Walt, 59–60
Williams, Raymond, 12
Williams, William Carlos, 91, 93–96, 100–113, 158
Wimsatt, W. K., xiv, 34, 41, 48, 65–66
Winnicott, D. W., 124
Wordsworth, William, 28, 144–48
Wundt, Wilhelm, 36, 44

Yeats, William Butler, 159–63, 167

This book was set in Baskerville and Eras typefaces. Baskerville was designed by John Baskerville at his private press in Birmingham, England, in the eighteenth century. The first typeface to depart from oldstyle typeface design, Baskerville has more variation between thick and thin strokes. In an effort to insure that the thick and thin strokes of his typeface reproduced well on paper, John Baskerville developed the first wove paper, the surface of which was much smoother than the laid paper of the time. The development of wove paper was partly responsible for the introduction of typefaces classified as modern, which have even more contrast between thick and thin strokes.

Eras was designed in 1969 by Studio Hollenstein in Paris for the Wagner Typefoundry. A contemporary script-like version of a sans-serif typeface, the letters of Eras have a monotone stroke and are slightly inclined.

Printed on acid-free paper.